Georgia's Land of the Golden Isles

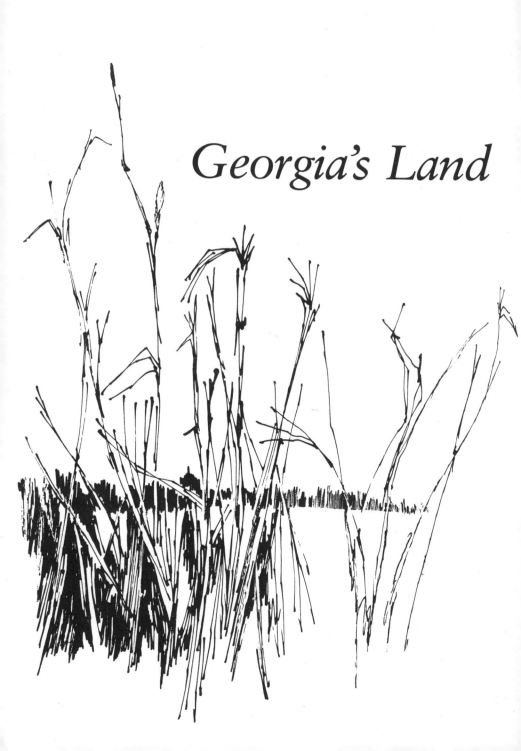

Georgia's Land

of the Golden Isles

NEW EDITION

BURNETTE VANSTORY
Foreword by Eugenia Price

BROWN THRASHER BOOKS
The University of Georgia Press · Athens and London

Set in VIP Sabon
Printed in the United States of America
Design by Design for Publishing

97 98 99 00 01   5 6 7 8 9

Library of Congress Cataloging in Publication Data

Vanstory, Burnette Lightle.
Georgia's land of the Golden Isles.

Bibliography: p.
Includes index.
I. Golden Isles.   I. Title.
F292.G58V36   1980   975.8'7   80-28565
ISBN 0-8203-0557-X
ISBN 0-8203-0558-8 (pbk.)

Contents

Foreword

"I would not have so much mail to answer if everyone who reads the novels in my St. Simons trilogy would also read *Georgia's Land of the Golden Isles*."

I wrote those lines when the first revision of this amazing book was made some years ago. I repeat my statement now—with emphasis—because this new, silver anniversary edition of Burnette Vanstory's amazing book is better than ever. "Amazing" is an over-used word, but when a book is still being read after a quarter of a century in numbers large enough to warrant still another revision, "amazing" is the word anyone connected with publishing will inevitably choose. These days books stay in print only as long as lots and lots of readers buy them.

Naturally, I am pleased that people of all ages are still sufficiently involved in my St. Simons novels to send me their often provocative questions pertaining to the history surrounding my stories. Normally, I cannot answer them because only certain facts directly relevant to the story can be woven into fiction. I admit there are times when my own research drags on so long that I feel as though I am being forced to learn it all. I am not. A novelist's primary purpose is simply to tell a good story. But because I try for historical accuracy, often during the writing of each novel set along the southeastern coast, I call upon my friend Burnette Vanstory: either by telephone or by reaching for

Georgia's Land of the Golden Isles, which is never more than
two feet from my desk. In my opinion, she is the only living person knowledgeable enough to tie together the entire historical
picture of the Georgia coast from Ossabaw to St. Marys.

I doubt that anyone has bought more published books on this
region than I during the twenty years I have lived and worked
here. *Georgia's Land of the Golden Isles* stands tall—unique
among them all. First, because it is comprehensive; not only invaluable to any student of coastal history, but to the interested
visitor, who can broaden his or her knowledge of our fascinating
history by reading and then hunting up the places about which
Mrs. Vanstory writes with such expertise. Tourist books are
sometimes accurate, sometimes not. This book is. But unlike
others—and this adds to its unique quality—*Georgia's Land of
the Golden Isles* is colorfully and humanly written. It is factual
history and it is also an experience in reliving. It is as well, the
Golden Isles *today*. In this new twenty-fifth anniversary edition,
the reader will find not only the latest historical discoveries
made since the book was first published twenty-five years ago,
but the *feel* of the Golden Isles now. And Mrs. Vanstory, exact-
ing in her research, does not stop there. In every line, you will see
for yourself that she has not forgotten to delineate the often elu-
sive *personality* of the region. Not once, in her intensive quest
for validity, does she forget that *people* will be reading her book.

My heart-deep thanks to the University of Georgia Press for
this new revised edition of *Georgia's Land of the Golden Isles*.
Hurrah for them—hurrah for Burnette Vanstory—and hurray
for you who read.

EUGENIA PRICE
St. Simons Island, 1981

Preface

When I first visited St. Simons Island, years ago, I had an inexplicable feeling of coming home—a feeling that has never changed. Later, with a beach cottage for vacations and future retirement, my family became part-time residents of the beautiful island.

Living, even part of the time, surrounded by so much beauty, romance, and history soon started me dreaming of finding out all about all of the Golden Isles and about the river plantations and the coastal towns near the islands. Perhaps some day I could even write a book about this fascinating part of the country.

I read and reread Margaret Davis Cate's *Our Todays and Yesterdays*, Caroline Couper Lovell's *Golden Isles of Georgia*, Lydia (Mrs. Maxfield) Parrish's *Slave Songs of the Georgia Sea Islands*, and E. Merton Coulter's *Thomas Spalding of Sapelo*. When I met Dr. Coulter later, in the History Department of the University of Georgia, and told him of my ambition to write a book about the Georgia coast, he was encouraging and helpful. Ralph Stephens, then director of the University of Georgia Press, was receptive to the idea and offered advice and encouragement.

My first research was guided by Lilla M. Hawes, director of the Georgia Historical Society in Savannah. I also received valuable help from Mary Givens Bryan of the Georgia Department of Archives and History in Atlanta. At the University of Georgia

Library in Athens I was assisted by John Bonner and Carroll Hart. Additional material was found in the St. Simons Public Library and in libraries in North and South Carolina.

At first I must have seemed to concentrate more on the places than on the people concerned, for one librarian remarked, "The places are your characters and the people are merely incidental." But when I met descendants of the coastal planters and twentieth-century owners of the islands and old plantations, all generous with their help and with their friendship, I knew the librarian was only half right. Even if the places were my characters, their people could never be "merely incidental."

It was my good fortune, in those early days, to talk to some of the older residents whose parents had grown up on their family plantations; in a short while their reminiscences would have been lost. Among those who contributed much to my work but did not live to see the book in print were Buford King Aiken of St. Simons, Miss Miriam Dent of Hofwyl Plantation, Mr. Harry du Bignon and Colonel John Couper Stiles, both of Brunswick. Other Couper descendants who were generous with family information were Mary Traylor Thiesen of Atlanta and Margaret Couper Sanger of Marietta.

Others who provided valuable information were Miss Ophelia Dent of Hofwyl Plantation, Mr. L. J. Leavy of Brunswick, Miss Bessie Lewis of McIntosh County, Mrs. Vara A. Majette of St. Simons, Mr. I. F. Arnow of St. Marys, Mrs. Beatrice F. Lang of Camden County, and Mrs. Donald Fraser Martin of Liberty County.

There was a memorable visit to Ossabaw Island at the invitation of the owner, Mrs. H. N. Torrey; a day on Cumberland Island through the courtesy of Captain O. J. Olsen, and a helpful correspondence with Mrs. Robert W. Ferguson, a descendant of Cumberland's Thomas Carnegie. A day's visit to Sapelo was arranged by Richard Orme Flinn, Jr., with Sapelo information contributed by his sister-in-law, Elizabeth Blackshear Flinn, and her parents, the Perry Blackshears.

With a day spent on Jekyll earlier and a visit to St. Catherines later, I had met all of my island "characters" and was impressed with their similarities and their differences. To me they were like brothers and sisters who share a family resemblance but have different personalities.

In my five years of research and writing *Georgia's Land of the Golden Isles* there were so many tempting bypaths that I could easily have spent twice as long. But the time had come to share all that I had learned about the historic Georgia coast. Perhaps more could be added another time.

That other time came when I met Eugenia Price, who was researching and writing her trilogy of historical novels with a St. Simons setting, *Beloved Invader, New Moon Rising,* and *Lighthouse.* It was at her suggestion that a partial revision of *Georgia's Land of the Golden Isles* appeared in 1970. As a result of Miss Price's generosity in sharing her extensive research into the history of the Gould family, the revision contained much information not included in the original edition.

Also included in the revision was W. Harry Parker's history of the Frewin-Stevens family of Frederica; additional information about the Wylly-Cater-Postell families was supplied by Frances Postell Burns of the German Village, St. Simons. The story of the Johnston-McNish family of Long View, first published in the 1970 edition, was contributed by Elizabeth Taylor Houseman of Brunswick. A separate chapter for Brunswick was added, as well as new material for Christ Church, Frederica, with assistance from Junius J. Martin, rector for twenty-five years of the historic church.

The partial revision allowed for no alteration in the first half of the book, but even as early as 1970 the islands described in earlier chapters were beginning to sense the changes that would take place over the next decade. In 1969 the upper half of Sapelo Island had been sold to the State of Georgia, and there were rumors about the future of other coastal islands.

Eventually the whole history of the Georgia coast needed to be brought up to date, and *Georgia's Land of the Golden Isles* must be completely revised or be hopelessly outdated. Which brings me to my debts of gratitude for the 1981 edition.

For information on the present status of Ossabaw Island I am grateful to Eleanor Torrey West, whose parents bought Ossabaw more than fifty years ago.

My appreciation to Mr. John Lukas of the New York Zoological Society for an account of the changes that have taken place on St. Catherines and for supplying illustrations.

My gratitude to Mr. Alfred W. Jones of Sea Island for his help with information on Sapelo Island today. Mr. Jones was also helpful with chapters on Altama Plantation and Sea Island. My special thanks to Rachel Kelly, Mr. Jones's secretary, for expert assistance in collecting illustrations.

For additional Sapelo information I am indebted to Mr. L. S. Staples, formerly of Sapelo, now of Brunswick; and to Mrs. Mary Lou Waters of the Department of Natural Resources, Sapelo Island.

My thanks to my friend Jan McKeithen of St. Marys for the latest news of her town.

For her proficiency in locating needed material and in answering a writer's many questions, I am grateful to Miss Marcia Hodges, reference librarian at the Brunswick–Glynn County Regional Library.

My special appreciation to Karen Orchard, managing editor of the University of Georgia Press, for her patience, understanding, and expertise in the task of preparing a revised book for publication.

When I think of all those who have helped me through three editions of *Georgia's Land of the Golden Isles*, I feel humble and everlastingly grateful for everyone's generosity and unselfishness.

BURNETTE VANSTORY
St. Simons Island, 1981

Georgia's Land of the Golden Isles

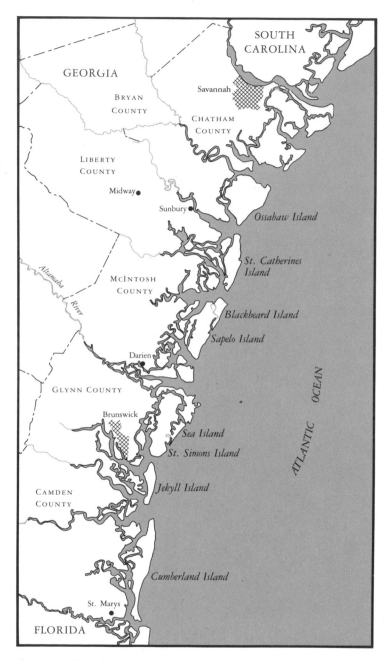

Georgia's Land of the Golden Isles

I   Land of the Golden Isles

The Golden Isles of Georgia, fabulous, beautiful, romantic! From prehistoric time until the present the saga of these coastal islands is peopled by Indian brave and Spanish don, by priest and pirate, Puritan and Scottish Highlander, by planter, plunderer, soldier, statesman, by slave and millionaire, recluse and vacationer, by seaman, fisherman, and flyer. Their forests have echoed to war whoop and mission bell, to the ax of colonists, the skirl of bagpipes, and the boom of cannon, to the chantey of slave and the rattle of musket, to the roar of the airliner, the clatter of the blimp, and the swift passing of the jet. The islands have known the urgency of war, the gracious life of plantation days, the chaos of destruction, the loneliness of ruin and desolation, the gaiety of year-round vacationers. Their waters have seen Indian canoe and Spanish galleon, black-sailed pirate ship and English gunboat, slave ship and dugout, tramp freighter and shrimper's craft, mahogany yacht and fisherman's bateau; have heard the shrill chatter of the racing boat and the secret whine of the submarine.

The mainland of the state of Georgia is separated from the Atlantic Ocean by a chain of barrier islands scattered along nearly one hundred and fifty miles of coastline. Of these, Ossabaw, St. Catherines, Sapelo, St. Simons, Jekyll, and Cumberland are best known as the Golden Isles. Historians say they were given the name by adventurers in search of gold, but more imaginative folk believe the word *golden* refers to less tangible treasure. Serene, verdant, beautiful, the islands are high and heavily wooded; almost to the water's edge grow longleaf pine and moss-hung oak, magnolia, palm, and palmetto, cypress and cedar, fragrant sea myrtle and red-berried cassina. Between islands and mainland lie great stretches of sea marsh threaded with a network of creeks and rivers.

Ancient burial mounds found on the Golden Isles have been of interest to archaeologists in the study of prehistoric inhabitants of the coastland. It is said that the natives, the Lower Creeks of history, were not mound builders, and that they knew nothing of the burial mounds when questioned by some of the earliest travelers into the region. The Creeks, one of the so-called Five Civilized Nations of Indians, were a nomadic people. They moved from one village to another with the seasons, fishing and hunting, bathing and feasting upon the islands, following the migratory wild fowl, fishing the inland streams, hunting alligators in the coastal rivers and buffalo and deer on the mainland.

Among the first traders believed to have come to the coast were tribes from north Georgia who followed the Old Indian Path from the mountains to the sea. They came bringing weapons, tools, and arrowheads of stone and flint to trade for dried fish and fowl, for fruits and herbs, and especially for the dried leaf of the cassina, which grows in profusion along the coast and from which a potent ceremonial drink was brewed. Untold numbers of arrowheads found upon the islands are in public and private collections—arrowheads made from stone that is not native to the coast.

In addition to their domestic trade, the coastal Indians established foreign trade relations in the sixteenth century when they supplied French sailing ships with cargoes of sassafras, skins, wax, rosin, and wild turkeys. It has been said that people in France were enjoying turkey from the southern coast long before the first Thanksgiving feast of the Pilgrims.

When Jean Ribaut sailed up the coast in 1562 he gave French

names to rivers, sounds, and inlets; and he reported that the region was the "fairest, fruitfullest, and pleasantest" he had ever seen. Ribaut with his band of Huguenots and Pedro Menéndez de Avillés with his Spanish fleet both coveted the Golden Isles and both laid claim to the coastland. The French placenames of Jean Ribaut were short-lived, for within a year after the founding of St. Augustine in 1565 Menendez made a trip of exploration, gave Spanish names to the coastal territory, and selected locations for settlements upon islands and mainland. Although some of the natives resented the newcomers, many were inclined to be friendly toward the Jesuit friars who came to live among them.

Since the Spaniard sought to conquer "with crossbow and cross," it was the custom for missionary and soldier to go side by side into new territories. Missions were established where the farmer-priests could plant their gardens and orchards and teach and convert the natives. Presidios, or forts, were built to protect the missions, and the larger and more successful of the mission-presidios grew into villages where the Spanish settlements were surrounded by the huts and gardens of loyal converts.

In spite of the friendly attitude of many of the natives, the coastal missions had few peaceful years. Some of the Indians remained hostile to the Spaniards and were encouraged by the French to make depredations upon the presidios, and in a succession of attacks missions were destroyed and the Jesuit friars were driven out. They were succeeded by Franciscans, who established more amicable relations with the savages; here on the beautiful islands, their chapels lighted by candles made from the waxen berries of surrounding shrubs, their gardens a profusion of tropical vegetables, fruits, and flowers, the forests and waters an unending source of game and fish, the kindly friars with their "poor and scanty use of earthly goods" must have found nature most bountiful. Their missions endured for more than a century as the Franciscans cultivated the soil of the golden islands and the soul of the red man.

But throughout the years there were many times of trouble

and unrest, filled with threats from every side. Sir Francis Drake made raids along the coast after his attack upon St. Augustine; and the freedom-loving Indians sometimes rebelled against the regulations of mission life. In 1597 a group of unconverted natives incited some of the converts to join them in open rebellion, with widespread destruction of missions and massacre of the friars; but the presidios were rebuilt and new converts were made, and in 1606 the Bishop of Cuba visited the coastal missions and baptized more than a thousand Indians.

As the American colonies were settled and the English pushed farther and farther south, they set up trading posts near the region occupied by the Spaniards. The valuable skins which the native hunters brought to these posts were in great demand for export, and there was a lively trade between English and Indian. Though the medium of exchange with the French traders of earlier days is not known, records of barter with the English disclose that a gun could be bought for ten buckskins, and ammunition at the rate of sixty bullets for one buckskin and two measures of powder for another. A falling ax brought two buckskins, while hatchets were priced at one buckskin for the small size and three doeskins for the large. Brass kettles were one buckskin per pound and looking glasses two doeskins each. Three yards of gartering cost one doeskin, and blankets brought three to five buckskins depending upon size and color.

The proximity of the English colonists added to the troubles of the mission priests. English and Spanish settlers eyed each other with the well-founded mistrust of traditional enemies. The English traders stirred up friction between Indian and Spaniard. The Carolinas feared attack by Spanish forces in Florida, and the Spaniards resented England's intrusion into the vicinity of their settlements. To add to the vicissitudes of the friars, their missions were plundered by pirates sailing the coastal waters. In 1686 the Spaniards finally gave up their efforts to settle the sea islands; the mission-presidios were abandoned, and for nearly half a century the Golden Isles were again hunting and fishing grounds for the Indians.

The coastal islands may have been termed "golden" by early explorers in search of treasure, but they came to be known throughout the world as the Golden Islands in 1717 when Sir Robert Montgomery planned his "Margravate of Azilia," the margravate to include Ossabaw, St. Catherines, Sapelo, and St. Simons. With an idealistic dream of establishing a settlement that would be an earthly paradise, the Scottish nobleman formed a syndicate of wealthy Londoners and wrote a *Discourse Concerning the Design'd Establishment of a New Colony*, extolling the beauties and opportunities of the region, to which he gave the "well deserved Denomination of the Golden Islands." The prospect of life in a wilderness, however beautiful and idyllic, perhaps appeared a bit too rugged for the margrave class; at any rate the dream of Azilia proved to be only a dream.

It remained for James Edward Oglethorpe, less than a score of years later, to make a more practical approach toward developing this thirteenth colony—the three-fold plan of defense against the Spaniards in Florida; a haven for oppressed persons; and a new source of revenue for the Crown. The territory between the Savannah and Altamaha rivers was designated by George II as the colony of Georgia, the charter to be for twenty-one years under the control of a board of trustees composed of twenty-one prominent Englishmen represented by "the trusty and well beloved James Oglethorpe." The land upon which the new colony was founded had originally belonged to the vast province of Carolina, which had included coastal territory as far south as Spanish-held Florida; but when the colony of Georgia was formed, England and Spain agreed to leave the region below the Altamaha as a sort of no-man's-land known as the Debatable Land.

When General Oglethorpe arrived in 1733 with his first colonists he won the friendship of the Indian mico, or chief, Tomochichi, who persuaded the Creeks to give peaceable possession of the territory to Great Britain. And so the colony of Georgia was founded, and settlements were started and fortifications built upon islands and mainland. The town of Savannah was es-

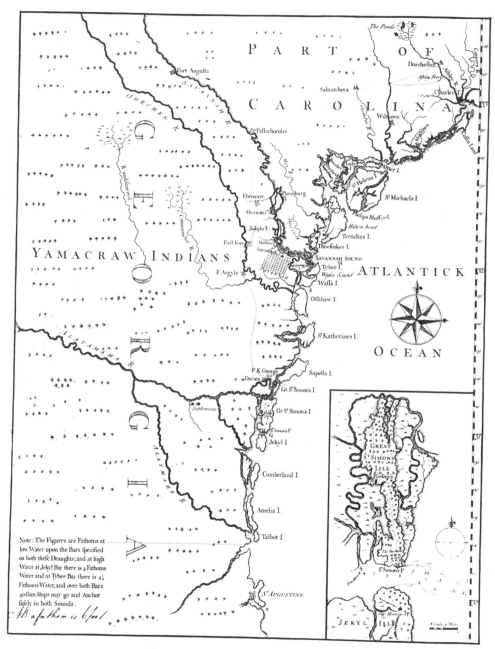

An eighteenth-century map of the Georgia coast

tablished; and a fort was built and a settlement made upon the island of St. Simons. All along the coast the colonists found the fruit groves of the friars still bearing—those groves of oranges, lemons, pomegranates, olives, and figs introduced into the New World by the Spaniards—heritage to the Georgia coast from her first white inhabitants. Oglethorpe's dealings with the natives were, from the first, remarkably successful. He was always just and fair, and in the settling of his colony there were none of the atrocities experienced by some of the earlier colonists nor the tragedies that had occurred in the ill-fated missions of the martyr priests.

There was a mutual friendship and admiration between 37-year-old Oglethorpe and 90-year-old Tomochichi that lasted until the old mico's death. They hunted and fished together, and the friendly chieftain was always the mediator between the English and the Indians. Just as Sir Alexander Cumming had taken some of the Cherokees on a visit to England when he returned from "Charles Town" in 1730, so General Oglethorpe persuaded a group of Creek Indians to accompany him to London in 1734; most important among them were his friend Tomochichi with his wife and their adopted son and heir, a nephew Toonahowie. Their arrival was announced by the London *Gentleman's Magazine and Monthly Intelligencer* of June 1734: "James Oglethorpe Esq. being arrived from Georgia, waited on their Majesties at St. James's, and Afterwards on the Trustees . . . and brought with him several Indian Chiefs."

In London society, sated with the artificiality of Court life, the native Americans created a sensation. They were presented at Court, where, says the *Gentleman's Magazine*: "His Majesty received them seated on his Throne. The War Captain Hillispilli and other Attendants of Tomochichi were very importunate to appear in the manner they go in their own Country, which is only with a proper Covering around their Waste, the rest of their Body being naked, but were dissuaded from it by Mr. O. But their Faces were variously painted after their Country manner. Tomochichi and Senauki his Wife were dressed in Scarlet trimmed with Gold."

In the August 1734 *Intelligencer*: "Tomochichi and the rest of the Indians din'd with Lady Dutry at Putney; and then waited on the A.Bp. of Canterbury who received them with the utmost Kindness and Tenderness." In this same month the death notices list: "One of the Indian Chiefs, Attendant to King Tomochichi of the Small-Pox." It is added that he was buried "according to Indian Custom with clothes and glass beads thrown into the Grave."

While they were in England Tomochichi and Toonahowie sat for the portrait so familiar to every school child in Georgia. The Indian lad, holding a captive eagle in his arms, is seated beside the old mico whose strong intelligent face, direct piercing gaze, and proud erect bearing belie his ninety years and proclaim the blood of the chieftain. In October 1734 the "Indian King, Queen, and Prince etc. set out from the Georgia office in the King's Coaches for Gravesend to embark on their Return home. During their Stay, which has been about 4 months they have been entertained in the most agreeable manner possible. . . . Nothing has been wanting among all Degrees of Men to contribute to their Diversion and Amusement."

General Oglethorpe's friendly relations with the natives stood him in good stead when his army came into hand-to-hand conflict with the Spaniards. With their knowledge of the forests and waterways, and of scouting and tracking, the Indian allies were invaluable. After the Spanish forces were conquered in 1742 the colony settled down over the years into an agricultural community. Much was expected from this thirteenth colony—this New Georgia. It had proved its right to be born as a buffer between the Spaniards and the Carolinas, and now it must prove itself a source of revenue to the mother country as well.

The early planters were encouraged to cultivate indigo, mulberry trees, and vineyards, as the soil and climate were believed suitable for the production of dyestuffs, silk, and wines. "Silk throwsters" from Italy and dyemakers from Jamaica were brought into the colony. Experienced vintners and the finest varieties of grape vines were brought from France. The vines of muscadines, the wild grape of the South, which festooned every bush and shrub along the coast, gave promise of successful vineyards; but the imported grapes did not thrive, and wine made from the hardy and prolific muscadine was not fine enough for export. The mulberry trees grew well, and perfect silk was made in the province, but never in a large enough quantity to prove a profitable enterprise. The production of dyes was more successful, and indigo remained for years one of the chief exports. Other products, according to an account of New Georgia in the *Gentleman's Magazine* in 1756, were rice, pitch, tar, hemp, flax, vegetable wax, and beeswax, while lumbering and cattle raising were becoming profitable in the colony.

During succeeding years prosperous planters came into the land of the Golden Isles and began development of the great island empires of Georgia. The fertile acres were extensively cultivated and the islands prospered for more than a decade before they were almost deserted when their forests and beaches echoed to the boom of cannons from British gunboats during the Revolutionary War. At the end of hostilities the fields were replanted and more were prepared as their owners sold timbers to the government for shipbuilding, and cleared thousands of acres for the plow.

The coast was once more subjected to enemy raids in the latter part of the War of 1812, but during the peaceful years of the next half-century the Golden Isles flourished in the high noon of the plantation era. When the clouds of war again gathered in the 1860s, the "twilight of the halcyon days was at hand," and war's end saw the end of an epoch. Five flags had flown over the islands in the more than three centuries since white men had discovered them—French, Spanish, English, the Stars and Stripes, and the Stars and Bars of the Confederacy. And each flag was raised and each torn down to the dread accompaniment of the drums of war.

Devastated and deserted and weary with war the islands dozed in the sun; and time healed their wounds, and nature covered their scars with the lush green of vine and fern and the profligate beauty of tropical flower. Before the turn of the century seekers of relaxation and pleasure and lovers of beauty were finding their way to the Georgia coast, and the Golden Isles entered a new period of prosperity. Just as the late seventeen and early eighteen hundreds had seen the extensive development of Georgia's coastal region, so the late eighteen and early nineteen hundreds saw the restoration of some of the great plantations. Five of the six Golden Isles became the property of leading financiers of the nation and were restored to their status of island empires. Up and down the inland waterway steam yachts carried the owners back and forth between the islands just as sailing boats and dugouts had carried earlier owners. Once again the "great of the nation" enjoyed the lavish hospitality of coastal Georgia.

Lightly touched by World War I, the islands played their part in World War II. Patrolled by Coast Guard, airplane, and blimp, their waters were protected from enemy submarines that preyed upon shipping along the seaboard. Sentry and lookout stations, shipyards, air bases, and training schools were located upon the coast, and the region was alive with youth being readied for the grim business of war. When peace came again many of those who had discovered the land of the Golden Isles in the war years found themselves drawn back to the enchanted region. They came in ever-increasing numbers, some to visit, others to stay. And the patriarchal oaks spread their gray-bearded branches over the newcomers with the same serene welcome always extended to older residents.

Still standing upon the Golden Isles and along the coastal mainland are numerous picturesque old ruins in a fair state of preservation, as lasting as the many legends that cling about them. It is difficult to determine the age of their concrete-like construction, a mixture of oyster shell, sand, lime from burned shell, and water, known as "tabby," a favorite building material of the region from time immemorial. As to the origin of the word *tabby*, there are various theories: one says it derives from the Spanish *tapia*; another suggests that it comes from the African *tabax*. Some of the early writers call it *tappy* and say that the method of tapping the forms to make the mixture settle gave the material the name which became *tabby* in the soft-spoken speech of the South.

Although study of old Spanish records shows mission-presidios at the approximate locations of some of the ruins that exist today, it is hard to pinpoint these sites; perhaps because of the constant shifting of coastlines and channels caused by centuries of erosion which can wash away landmarks as though they had never existed. Many of the ruins have been the subject of interested speculation for years. Some say they were built by nineteenth-century planters for sugarhouses and mills, while others believe that the deserted structures found in the forests when the fields were cleared for cultivation were repaired and put to use as storehouses or as mills for sugar and rice. Historians search old records; archaeologists dig; dreamers dream; and the old vine-covered ruins remain inscrutable, enigmatic, beautiful.

2 Ossabaw Island

Ossabaw, northernmost of the Golden Isles, lies off the coast twenty miles below Savannah in the County of Chatham. Privately owned, it is one of the largest of the barrier islands, with an area more than three times that of Bermuda. Like all of the coastal islands Ossabaw is rich with history and tradition, with ruins and memories and beauty. In the vast evergreen forest there are pines, palms, magnolias, giant holly trees, and ancient live oaks; there are dogwood and wild azalea and climbing yellow jasmine. There are saltwater creeks, inlets, a tidal river, and freshwater ponds formed by the overflow from deep, cold artesian wells. There are wide sweeps of salt marsh where the tall reedy grass is new green in spring and summer, old gold in fall and winter.

Mounds on the island have yielded their secrets to interested excavators. Some have told of the burial customs of prehistoric tribes, while others have been found to be merely kitchen middens, or great piles of oyster shells, testifying no doubt to many a feast and pow-wow when Ossabaw was a favorite hunting and fishing ground of the Indians. Early colonists, too, enjoyed the abundant game on the wooded island; an old South Carolina journal records that parties of hunters shot deer on Ossabaw as early as 1687.

A wide and interesting variety in the spelling of the name of the island appears on old records and deeds—Ossebah, Ussuy-baw, Hussaper, and Hussaba have the sound of words originating in the Indian tongue, but the occasional Obispa makes the student of history wonder if the island was named by the Spaniards in honor of one of their favorite bishops. Ossabaw was also known at one time as Ogeche and at another time was called Montgomery, this last when Sir Robert was planning his Margravate of Azilia. The grant made in 1717 included the "Golden Islands of St. Symon, Sapella, St. Catarina, and Ogeche," and a report on the Margravate in 1720 says that the name of Ogeche had been changed to Montgomery.

Always privately owned, Ossabaw can trace its title back to the first property transfer in Georgia. When General Oglethorpe landed on Yamacraw Bluff and struck up his famous friendship with old Chief Tomochichi, it was agreed that the Creeks should retain Ossabaw along with neighboring St. Catherines and Sapelo as their Hunting Islands. Oglethorpe's interpreter in his dealings with the Indians was Mary Musgrove, a half-breed woman who operated a trading post near Yamacraw. Widow of a Car-

General Oglethorpe with Mary Musgrove and Tomochichi

olina trader, Mary Musgrove was later married to Thomas Bosomworth, who had been "commissioned to perform ecclesiastic duties" in Georgia. Niece of one of the Indian chiefs, Mary was acknowledged as a princess of the tribe, and in a private treaty between the Bosomworths and the Indians it was agreed that the Hunting Islands be granted to Princess Mary. The recorded "consideration" paid to the Creeks was "ten pieces stroud, twelve pieces duffle, two hundredweight powder, two hundredweight lead, twenty guns, two pair pistols, one hundredweight vermillion." Dated the fourth day of the windy moon the grant was made for "as long as the sun shall shine or the waters run in the rivers, forever."

The original charter of the Province of Georgia had prohibited the slave labor necessary for profitable operation of large plantations, but when the ban upon slaves was lifted in 1749 the uncleared areas along the coast were in demand as farmlands. The Bosomworths took possession of the three valuable islands, which they planned to develop into great plantations; but their grant was protested by the trustees, and Thomas Bosomworth carried the case into court. He made claims at the same time for sums of money said to be owed his wife for services as interpreter as well as for goods furnished the colonists by her trading post. The case, which remained in the courts for more than a decade, created bitter controversy at the time and discussion among historians for years afterward.

While their case was pending the Bosomworths had cleared and planted fields and built a house upon St. Catherines and were using the island of Ossabaw as range for cattle. The coastal islands with their open range and year-round grazing were recognized even in those early days as "well situated for raising horned cattle." When the Bosomworth case was finally settled in 1760 it was agreed that they be granted St. Catherines, and that the other two Hunting Islands, Ossabaw and Sapelo, be purchased by the governor of the province "for use of the crown," the proceeds presumably paid to the Bosomworths.

Soon after this, Ossabaw was advertised at public outcry,

forty thousand acres of virgin timber, fertile soil, and marsh-lands, with the "privilege of hunting, hawking, and fowling;" and for the sum of £1,300 the island was granted to Grey Elliott, a prominent resident of the colony before the Revolutionary War. Records in the Georgia Historical Society show that Elliott deeded Ossabaw for the same amount to Henri Bourquin, who in turn sold it to his son-in-law John Morel, the first owner to clear and cultivate the property. Within a few years the Morels had built a residence on the north end of the island and had set out an avenue of live oaks. At this time lumber was one of the chief exports of the colony, and quantities of white pine and oak were cut and shipped from the forests of Ossabaw.

As the land was cleared, fields were planted with indigo—a valuable crop in the days before synthetic dyes were developed. In the fertile soil of the island, fields prepared in March and sown in April yielded two crops during the long hot summer; one in June, another in August. The cultivation and processing of indigo made it necessary to settle hundreds of slaves upon the island—field hands to cut the green plants at dawn before the sun could dry the leaves, workers at the vats in which the leaves were immersed to draw out the dye, more workers at the "beat-ing vats" where the extract was stirred with paddles until well aerated, and skilled men to handle the actual preparation of the dye, when the sediment must be boiled with water, drained, and pressed into molds. After the molds had been thoroughly dried in the sun, the indigo was ready to be loaded upon barges and taken to Savannah to be shipped to foreign markets. And so with its plantation house and workers' quarters, its docks and wharves, its lumber crews, field hands, dye workers, boat and loading crews, Ossabaw became one of the first of the great is-land empires of the Georgia coast.

The master of Ossabaw was an experienced planter who owned several rice and cotton plantations upon the mainland. The Morels, who had come to the colonies in the 1730s and had settled upon the Ashley River in South Carolina, were among the first of the Carolina planters to develop property on the Georgia coast. Always prominently identified with the early growth of the colony, from the time of the original General Assembly the name of Morel is found in old records of Georgia. Ardent patriots, the Morels were among the group who voted to send five hundred barrels of rice to Massachusetts upon the occasion of the Boston Tea Party; they were on the Council of Safety, in the Provincial Congress, and among the officers of the Revolutionary Army.

Agriculture and lumbering were at a standstill during the American Revolution. In October 1776 there was a "small detachment of troops under Summers upon Ausabaw," but in that same month it was recommended that the sea islands be evacuated immediately. Shelled by British gunboats sailing the coastal waters, Ossabaw was the scene of at least one engagement in 1778 when two patriot galleys are recorded to have been run aground upon the island and burned by their crews to escape capture by the enemy. And in 1781 American privateers off Ossabaw seized a British ship bound for the West Indies with a cargo of rice. During the years while Georgia was in the hands of the enemy, Ossabaw was a place of refuge for some of those whose sympathies lay with the colonists; and stories are told of trees felled in the forests for small boats that were secretly built upon the island for the use of the patriots.

After the end of the war, the Ossabaw forests supplied timber to the government for shipbuilding, the fields were enlarged and improved, and the island became a self-contained community which produced everything necessary for the great plantation. The property was divided into three sections: North End Place, where the family residence was located; Middle Place, and South End. During the life of John Morel these sections were merely settlements of houses built for the hands who worked those parts of the island. At the death of their father three of the Morel sons inherited the Ossabaw plantation; North End Place became the property of Bryan Morel; Middle Place of Peter Henry; and South End of John the second.

About this time it was decided that the fertile semitropical sea islands were ideally suited to the cultivation of a species of cotton that had been found growing on the little island of Anguilla in the West Indies by colonists who had refugeed there during the American Revolution. Seed plants brought to the coastal islands were developed into the most superior cotton ever grown. The Ossabaw indigo fields were given over to that aristocrat of agriculture, the temperamental long-staple sea island cotton that could demand twice the price of ordinary cotton in the markets of the world.

In the War of 1812 many island inhabitants sought the safety of the mainland; when the British attacked the coast of Georgia some of the islands were invaded, but there is no record of enemy landings upon Ossabaw. The war years were followed by a long period of peace and prosperity. These were the vintage years for the coastal planters. In 1823 the Liverpool market reported nearly three quarters of a million bales of cotton imported into Great Britain, much of it from Georgia and South Carolina. Ossabaw fields were white with cotton, her wharves busy with barges, schooners, and boats of happy groups for houseparties and hunting parties as the Morels pursued their business and social affairs.

Life on the island empires has been described as having a sort of primitive elegance—semi-luxurious and semi-barbarous. There were all the luxuries of furnishings and clothing, of books and ornaments, and of delicacies imported from the Old World. There was the luxury of privacy and seclusion. But tutors and governesses must be provided for children too young to be sent away to school, worship must be in family chapels, and sudden illness must be treated by home remedies. All communication was dependent upon travel by boat, and when rough weather made the water impassable and the islands were cut off from the outside world, their inhabitants must depend upon their own resourcefulness and ingenuity in emergencies. However, the planters usually had other residences upon the mainland where they spent a part of their time; and nearby Savannah was an important seaport with a busy social, political, and cultural life, together with ample opportunity for shopping. Advertisements in newspapers of the day offered "compleat assortments of European and East India Goods proper for the place and season."

The planters organized agricultural societies, hunt clubs, and boating clubs. There were hunt breakfasts, horse races, and regattas; there were packs of deer hounds, stables of hunters and barouches with crested doors and high-stepping horses. There were sailboats, longboats and dugouts, and flatboats to carry horses and carriages between island and mainland. Some fine hunters and racers were bred along the coast. Horses brought into the region by the Spaniards had originated the small, hardy "tackies" that were found roaming the marshes; and descended as they were from excellent stock they produced well-formed fleetfooted colts when cross-bred with blooded horses imported from England, colts with the speed and stamina necessary for racing or hunting.

Each generation of Morels cherishes favorite legends of their ancestors, tales of valor when the men of the family went to war or made secret plans with the patriots; tales of hilarious meetings of the Hunt Club when wagers of astronomical figures were made on the fleetest horse. And one night when the revelers raced on the shell road in the moonlight, a steed bred on Ossabaw and a thoroughbred imported from England easily outstripped the others. But alas, the race ended with the English horse's neck broken in a headlong collision with a tree, and with the two owners weeping convivially, arm in arm.

The present-day generation of one branch of the family smile fondly over the courtship of great-grandpere and great-grandmere. They like to tell how he, just turned twenty, sailed all the way down the inland passage to Jekyll Island to pay his court to the eighteen-year-old visitor from France. Met at the wharf by the master of the Jekyll plantation, ushered ceremoniously into the drawing room of the French mansion, the young suitor sat sedately upon one side of the room, the demoiselle demurely upon the other, as they listened respectfully to the conversation of their elders. In due time there was a wedding and the young couple went to live upon Ossabaw. Both were opposed to the institution of slavery, and as soon as they came into their inheritance they freed every slave on their plantation and paid them wages to do the work.

In those days when the coastal planters had "company for breakfast, dinner, tea, and supper, and drawing rooms were lighted by whole dozens of spermaceti candles high blazing from glass chandeliers," a beautiful custom in the Morel family was the molding of the candles of Ossabaw. Once a year a twelve-month supply of hand-dipped candles was made of wax from the island apiaries, the deep honey color of the beeswax bleached to the rich creamy whiteness of magnolia buds by a method passed down from one generation to the next. Made in varying sizes the tapers were used in the family chapel and in the plantation houses as well. On festive occasions they burned in chandeliers, in wall sconces, candlesticks, and candelabra; and approaching visitors were welcomed by the gleaming light from "whole dozens" of the candles of Ossabaw.

After the death of Peter Henry Morel ownership of Middle Place passed to David Johnston, to Sir Patrick Houstoun, and to Alexander McDonald. The south end of the island was divided in 1852 into two plantations; one, called Buckhead, was retained by the Morel family; and the other, which kept the old name of South End Place, was sold to George Jones Kollock. The Kollocks never lived upon the island, but George Kollock made frequent trips from his plantation in Habersham County to supervise the coastal property, and the family enjoyed South End Place as a vacation home.

Ossabaw was evacuated by the owners during the War Between the States, the sound was blockaded, and there was a federal battery upon the north end of the island where a number of troops were stationed in the summer of 1863. In the following years the fields were left uncultivated and the property was sold. When North End Place was sold it had been in the Morel family for more than a hundred years. When Buckhead was sold it had belonged to Morels and their descendants for nearly a century and a half. Visitors to the island during these years after the war found the property greatly damaged, and only a portion of the old North End House remained. Other buildings were in bad repair and the only inhabitants were a few of the former slaves, among them old Prince who lived at Middle Place. Prince, who had been born on the island and had lived there all his life, loved to tell stories of the days when "there was always company, and gentlemen came from all over—from London and Philadelphia, Charleston and Savannah and New Orleans, to shoot ducks and deer with the master."

Around the turn of the century the island was owned almost entirely by the Wanamakers of Philadelphia, and Ossabaw dropped back into her old role of a hunting island. Some of the plantation buildings were repaired and put back into use, and a clubhouse was erected at the North End—one of the earliest of the prefabricated houses, which was brought from Philadelphia, where it is said to have been on exhibit at the Centennial Exposition of 1876. In the 1890s Ossabaw's ancient mounds were examined by archaeologists, and some of the artifacts such as mortuary urns, pottery bowls, and pottery discs are in the collection of prehistoric relics in the Smithsonian Institution.

In the first quarter of the twentieth century Ossabaw passed through various hands, and in 1924 when it became the property of Dr. H. N. Torrey of Grosse Pointe, Michigan, the island had been uninhabited for so long that it was over-run by wild cattle and hogs. Conditioned though it was over the centuries to twang of Indian bow and toll of mission bell, to stealthy rattle of oar-lock and boom of hostile cannon, the old island was shaken out of its serenity during the succeeding twelve months. Now the ancient forests, beaches, and marshlands echoed to the "yippee" of the cowboy and the zing of his lariat as a group of Texas cowpokes rode herd on two thousand head of wild tick-infested cattle until the last dogie was rounded up. Attempts to eliminate the thousands of wild hogs proved an even more exciting task, as the boars are savage beasts ready to turn with hoof and tusk upon dog and hunter. More welcome inhabitants of the island were wild turkey, pheasant, quail, marsh hen, and heron, blue

and white. Migratory duck by the thousands visited the freshwater lakes, and in April rare white egret came to the summer
rookery at Egret Pond in such numbers that their sudden flights
literally filled the air with the flutter of their wings.

Little of the history of Ossabaw had been published before it
became the property of the Torreys, and the romance and charm
of the island so captured the interest of Dr. Torrey that he determined to trace its history for himself. The original royal grant
and some maps and deeds dated as early as 1760 were included
with the title papers, and after exhaustive research through state
records and in the famous DeRenne collection the owner of the
island compiled and had printed *The Story of Ossabaw*, an interesting and informative little book about the "dear old place."

When the Torreys started making plans for a winter residence,
they found, even in the twentieth century, that the difficulties of
building upon a coastal island were almost as great as those that
confronted mission builder, colonist, and planter in the centuries
before. As it was estimated that the house would be two years in
the building, a boarding house was built to supplement the clubhouse as quarters for the small army of workers employed in the
construction, while the owners lived aboard their yacht when
they were in residence.

Located at the north end of the island in view of Ossabaw
Sound, the completed house was surrounded by the beautiful
gardens described in the 1933 *Garden History of Georgia*. With
its walls of Bermuda pink and roof of Castilian tile, its iron grill-
work, balconies, and walled patio, the spreading two-storied
house was reminiscent of Spanish ambitions for the Golden Isles.
Colonial days were recalled by the central feature of the great
beamed living room, a massive fireplace with a romance and history of its own. Fireplace, mantel, and chimney were made of
stones brought to the coast in sailing ships. There is no stone
native to the barrier islands; all rocks and stones came as ship
ballast to be replaced by cargoes of peltries, indigo, rice, cotton,
and lumber.

After the family settled into their island home Ossabaw again
dispensed the hospitality of plantation days. The huge leather-

The House at Ossabaw

bound guest book, signed first by the Henry Fords, held many a well-known name, even more perhaps than in the days remembered by old Prince when "company came from all over." Once more the historic island was the center of houseparties and gatherings of sportsmen for hunting and fishing. A popular and engaging member of the household was Lulu Belle, a French damsel who might once have been the pride of some master-craftsman's waxworks display. Amazingly lifelike and as beautiful as any mademoiselle who ever visited Ossabaw in earlier days, Lulu Belle lent herself charmingly to many a prank on unsuspecting house-party guests.

As Torrey ownership of Ossabaw entered its fourth decade, the island became once more a family partnership as in the time of the Morels a century and a half before. When there was a revival of interest in the cattle raising that had proved profitable on the coast in the 1700s, Ossabaw was stocked with a herd of beef cattle and the island became an open range as it was in the days of Mary, princess of the Creeks. Sharing the natural range with the cattle were deer so tame they must be kept from the gardens by inconspicuous wire fences in the shrubbery. And on almost a hundred miles of unpaved island roads, pedestrian, motorist, and equestrian were accepted with equanimity by white-faced calf or dappled fawn.

In addition to cattle boats at the Ossabaw wharf, there were lumber barges, for in order to enlarge grazing areas another of the earlier industries, lumbering, was revived. To preserve the beauty of the woodlands, the trees to be felled were as carefully selected as those of colonial days when trees in the coastal forests were "marked with the arrow of the King."

Ossabaw's trees have always been the pride and pleasure of her owners, and each generation has had its favorites. The avenue of oaks set out by the Morels still stood when Dr. and Mrs. Torrey and their young son and daughter came to the island, but some of the old trees, badly damaged by storm, required the services of tree surgeons. Necessary pruning gave one gnarled oak the appearance of a grotesque figure that led the children to call it the "gnome tree." A favorite from other days was the "breakfast tree" with its twisted, tablelike trunk that held the food packets of many an early morning hunter.

Ossabaw was inherited by Eleanor Torrey West and the sons and daughter of her late brother, William; and for years the island was enjoyed by three generations of the family. But times change, and eventually only Mrs. West chose to devote most of her time to Ossabaw. Owning an island, however beloved, is no small responsibility; and in an effort to protect the "dear old place," to preserve its natural wildness, and to make it available for serious work, the Ossabaw Foundation was incorporated in 1961 by Clifford and Eleanor Torrey West.

Administered by the foundation, the Ossabaw Island Project was established, a unique program in which qualified creative persons were offered the opportunity for concentrated work in pleasant surroundings far removed from the interruptions of daily life.

As unique in its way was the program known as Genesis, established in 1970. Located at the site of old Middle Place Plantation, with few amenities, Genesis is a community in which participants share responsibilities while working on individual projects.

Included in the Ossabaw Foundation's four programs is Professional Research, in which qualified scientists and graduate students have a rare opportunity for research and study in an unspoiled "outdoor laboratory" of wilderness and uncontaminated saltwater and freshwater marshes.

The fourth program administered by the Ossabaw Foundation is Public Use and Education, in which small groups of school and college students, Scouts, teachers, and others are offered camp sites where they may experience Ossabaw in natural surroundings. Also under this program, such organizations as the Audubon Society and the Sierra Club arrange day visits for observation and hiking.

Even though the foundation's programs have proved highly successful, attracting participants from all over the world, the problem of the future of Ossabaw, as a whole, remained unsolved.

In 1978 the decision was made to sell the island to the State of Georgia through the Heritage Trust Program, with Mrs. West retaining her home and thirty acres of land. By agreement with the Department of Natural Resources, the foundation's programs will continue.

Under state ownership Ossabaw will be used solely for research, study, and education while the ecosystem of the island will be preserved. There are no plans for public recreation with the exception of a program of limited hunts introduced in 1979 to control the increasing deer population.

In spite of all the changes that have taken place, Ossabaw still retains its natural beauty and charm, its atmosphere of timelessness and relaxation. The people who have come and gone have left little impression on most of the island—fragments of Indian pottery in the forests, crumbling foundations of tabby, rusting cannon balls in the marshes, contours of old plantation fields . . . a venerable live oak at the South End estimated to have stood for half a dozen centuries.

There is an old saying that coastal live oaks spend three hundred years growing, three hundred years living, and three hundred years dying. If this is true, the moss-hung branches of the ancient tree may for centuries yet to come spread their shade over Ossabaw's inhabitants and visitors as in bygone days they sheltered mound builder and Indian brave, priest, patriot and planter.

3   St. Catherines Island

The island of St. Catherines, next below Ossabaw in the chain of Golden Isles, lies between St. Catherines Sound and Sapelo Sound in Liberty County. Heavily wooded, as are all of the barrier islands, St. Catherines' distinguishing feature is a high, beautiful promontory on the eastern side overlooking beach and ocean. Perhaps it was this vantage point that made the island a favorite with the Creek Indians. One of their largest villages, headquarters for the mico or chieftain of the tribe, was located here, and numerous smaller settlements were situated upon the 25,000-acre island.

When Menéndez made his trip up the coast after founding St. Augustine he was received with friendly courtesy by the Indian chief, and it was here that the first of the island missions was established in 1566. Called Santa Catalina, it became the most important mission of the region with outposts upon other parts of the island and upon Ossabaw. The name Guale, or Gualé, (pronounced Wallie), which was used for both island and chieftain, and which came to designate all of the coastal Creeks as well as their territory, has been a puzzle to scholars. Neither a Spanish nor a Creek word, its meaning is unknown, although it has been suggested by Dr. John R. Swanton in his *Indian Tribes of North America* (1950) that it may have been the Spanish interpretation of the Indian word *wahali*, "the south."

Santa Catalina de Guale and its sister mission established at the same time farther up the coast, in South Carolina, are believed to have been the first settlements north of Mexico for regular Spanish mission work. In reports made by missionaries we learn that one of the earliest Santa Catalina friars, Domingo Augustin, wrote a grammar for use in teaching the Indians. It is a pity that this manuscript did not survive the mission, and is not in existence today, for it was the first book written in our country.

In spite of their friendly reception and encouraging beginning, the Jesuit missionaries were harassed by hostile natives, and the mission of Santa Catalina was soon abandoned. Reorganized under the Franciscans in 1573, the mission work was zealously carried on for more than a score of years until the Indian revolt of 1597, when the friars were murdered and their churches despoiled. Punitive forces sent from St. Augustine burned villages and destroyed crops until the pagans were subdued.

Once the Indians were under submission Santa Catalina was again restored to its early importance, and for most of the seventeenth century the dark-robed friars traveled the coastal waters in their piraguas ministering to the spiritual needs of the natives. Although they made many converts their lives were so beset by troubles and dangers that the Franciscans, like the Jesuits, were finally forced to give up their work. Captain Dunlop, a Carolinian who visited the island in 1687, saw the ruins of the great settlement which he was "informed the Spanish had deserted about 3 years agoe." And so for another half-century the Indian once more roamed the forests and fished the waters of this favored island, even clinging to it after the white man came again to the coast.

During the first years of the colony of Georgia, St. Catherines was the setting for a romantic interlude in the early life of one of the most distinguished of the colonists. It was upon the shores of St. Catherines that John Wesley and Sophie Hopkey tarried when that engaging young woman sought to win the affections of the youthful preacher, and when Oglethorpe, stepping from the role of general into that of matchmaker, tried to aid Miss Sophie's cause. The story goes that Miss Sophie, who had been visiting at Frederica on St. Simons Island, was encouraged to take passage in the same boat in which Wesley was returning to Savannah. Northeast winds forced the party to land on the south end of St. Catherines, but in spite of the romance of a campfire in the shelter of the beautiful island the earnest young man spent the hours quoting chapter and verse of the Holy Writ to a discouraged and thwarted Miss Sophie.

Turbulent days, too, were in store for the island in those early years when it was a bone of contention in the notorious Bosomworth case. Home of Princess Mary and her "consort" while they were trying to prove their title to the Hunting Islands, St. Catherines was the scene of plotting, machination, and intrigue in 1747 when the Bosomworths and their Indian cohorts planned their fabulous march upon Savannah to demand their rights. Led by the princess in her royal trappings and Thomas Bosomworth in his canonical robes, two hundred Indian braves marched into the seaport city, where they remained for a fortnight threatening the authorities and intimidating the residents.

Partially appeased with the presents and promises of the royal governor, the Bosomworths and their followers finally withdrew from Savannah, and the couple returned to their island home. During the following years the Bosomworths journeyed to South Carolina and to England as they continued to press their claims until they were given their royal grant in 1760. Within a few years after they were granted possession of St. Catherines, Mary Musgrove Bosomworth died and Thomas married again; and in September 1765 the following newspaper notice appeared: "To be leased for a number of years—the valuable Island of St. Catherine with the Stock and Cattle and the use of the Timber. For particulars enquire of the Rev. Mr. Bosomworth on the said island." But instead of being leased, St. Catherines was sold, and the purchaser was Button Gwinnett.

Written indelibly in St. Catherines' history are the stirring years preceding the American Revolution when the island was the plantation home of Button Gwinnett, planter, patriot, states-man, signer of the Declaration of Independence, man of mystery. Gwinnett's name first appears in the *Georgia Gazette* in 1765. As proprietor of a mercantile business in Savannah he offered a variety of goods: "Dr. James's powders for fever; mustard; tin-ware; plain, silver and gold-laced hats; silk and thread hose; jewelry, pickles, earthen and delftware, fine beer, Irish linen, cheese, butter, nails, bed-furniture and other items too tedious to mention." Gwinnett must have disposed shortly of his mercan-tile business, as his purchase of St. Catherines is recorded within the year. Before the end of 1765 he had settled on the island with his wife and young daughter, Elizabeth Ann (Betsy), to enjoy the life of a gentleman planter.

Button Gwinnett, Esquire, was soon playing a prominent role in the political affairs of the colony. He was a member of the Commission of the Peace of the Province and was elected to the Commons House of Assembly in Savannah; he was appointed to committees, was making addresses. He served St. Johns Parish as layman justice of the Inferior Court, a position introduced by Georgia's English Trustees in order that the colony might be "happy and flourishing . . . free of the pest and scourge of man-kind called lawyers."

When the colonies rebelled against English rule, Gwinnett took a leading part in the cause of the patriots. He was sent from St. Johns Parish as a delegate to the Continental Congress, where John Adams wrote of him as "intelligent and spirited." He was appointed to the Committee of Ways and Means, to the Com-mittee of Articles of Confederation, to a special five-member committee that included Thomas Jefferson, and to the important Marine Committee.

One of Georgia's three signers of the Declaration of Independ-ence, Gwinnett returned home to help write the first constitu-tion of the state. In 1777, when Georgia's president, Archibald Bulloch, died suddenly, Button Gwinnett was appointed to suc-ceed him. Soon a bitter dispute with General Lachlan McIntosh led to the duel in which Gwinnett was injured in the left leg.

The duel between Button Gwinnett and Lachlan McIntosh

Gangrene set in and three days later he was dead. He was forty-two.

His will left half of his estate to his wife and daughter, half to Thomas Bosomworth, to whom he was under heavy financial obligations. After her father's death, Betsy Gwinnett went to school in Charleston and later married a South Carolinian according to a 1779 marriage record which lists "Peter Belin, Santee—Eliz. Gwinnet, Georgia." Mrs. Button Gwinnett died soon after the marriage, and it is believed that her daughter did not long survive her. Eventually all trace of the family must have been lost, as a notice signed by a New York insurance company appeared later in Georgia newspapers requesting information of heirs of "Ann Gwinnett . . . who was the daughter of Button or Britton Gwinnett and married Mr. Peter Belin or Beline."

The signer apparently left no descendants and little is known of his private life. A brief glimpse of an engaging personality appears in the whimsical name of his schooner, *Beggar's Benison*, for able statesman though he was, fragmentary records of debts and financial difficulties indicate that Gwinnett was singularly unsuccessful in managing his personal affairs.

Today, his name on any papers connected with his precarious financial state would be worth many times the amount involved, as collectors of signatures of the signers have found that of Button Gwinnett one of the rarest in existence. Only fifty-one were listed in a 1960 count, with only one in possession of the State of Georgia. One of the coveted signatures sold for $51,000.

For years little was known of the man with the intriguing name of "Button," a name viewed with suspicion by more than one early writer. Some students of the signatures of the Signers expressed the opinion that the name Button Gwinnett was a pseudonym "assumed for some unknown purpose." It remained for biographer Charles Francis Jenkins of Philadelphia to dispel some of the mystery a century and a half after the signing, in his *Button Gwinnett* published in 1926.

The signature suspected of being spurious was found to be merely that of a clergyman's son named for a prominent relative, the Arctic explorer Sir Thomas Button. Born in Gloucestershire, England, Gwinnett worked as a young man for a tea merchant in Wolverhampton, where he married his employer's daughter.

For almost two centuries the man who for a decade played such a leading role in Georgia history lay buried in an unknown grave. After many attempts to locate his burial place on St. Catherines Island, a grave was found in Savannah's Colonial Cemetery with an ancient, broken marker bearing letters and numerals that could have been part of Gwinnett's inscription. When the remains were exhumed and examined, the left leg bone showed signs of an injury; and the age pronounced by anatomists agreed with Gwinnett's age at the time of his death. A committee was appointed to make the final decision and, when exhaustive research disclosed no conclusive proof, it was agreed that the grave was, in all probability, that of Button Gwinnett. In 1964 a monument was unveiled on the site with appropriate ceremonies honoring the Georgia signer.

Button Gwinnett flashed across the pages of history, then passed into oblivion, his signature alone giving him immortal fame. Of a man so spectacular, so mysterious, it is not surprising that tales and legends about him have been handed down through the generations. On a dark night, when waters of the sound are whipped high by the wind and small craft stay prudently in dock, they say that *Beggar's Benison* may be seen through the mist riding the waves, her bold master in the bow. And sometimes at ebbtide, just after nightfall, the tired clop-clop of hooves may be heard on the shell road as Button Gwinnett's saddle horse again nears the end of that month-long journey from Philadelphia, where "one of the greatest questions ever to be debated among men" was decided.

After Gwinnett's death, St. Catherines again became the home of Thomas Bosomworth. Bosomworth and his second wife, Sarah, lived on the island for the rest of their lives. According to tradition Thomas, Sarah, and Mary are buried under a common mound, and it is said that their house stood for almost a century before being destroyed by fire. Another residence called the Old House was known through the years as the home of Button Gwinnett.

In 1800 St. Catherines became the property of Jacob Waldburg, who developed two large plantations on the island, one at the north end and one at the south. During the War Between the States St. Catherines was evacuated, and after the war it was claimed by a black man, Tunis Campbell, who styled himself "Governor of St. Catherines." After Campbell's removal by Federal troops, the island returned to the possession of Jacob Waldburg, who in 1872 sold it to Anna M. Rodriguiz. Bought in 1876 by John J. Rauers of Savannah, St. Catherines became one of the finest country homes and private game preserves in the nation. The Big House, built at the north end of the island near the old Gwinnett house, was a great, rambling place known the country over for its hospitality.

When in 1927 St. Catherines was bought by Howard Coffin of Sapelo and his friends C. M. Keys and James Willson of New York, the Old House was still standing, a simple, gabled, dilapidated cottage, its only claim to distinction the tradition that it had been the home of Button Gwinnett. With a deep appreciation of its historic associations the owners had the old place remodeled and enlarged, preserving many of its original features such as mantel and stair rail and wide-board hand-pegged floors. The Rauers house was razed; and a wing was added at the rear of the Old House making it large enough for a vacation residence, while restored slave cabins nearby made picturesque

Button Gwinnett's home on St. Catherines Island

guest cottages. In 1929 C. M. Keys became sole owner of St. Catherines, and local residents of the mainland recall with pleasure when the island was a part-time home for the Keys family.

In 1943 St. Catherines was purchased by Edward J. Noble of New York, and the island proved, like other parts of the coast, to be ideal for cattle raising; not the "horned cattle" of the early colonists, but great herds of purebred Black Angus. Mr. Noble died in 1958, and in 1969 St. Catherines Island was transferred from the Noble estate to the Edward J. Noble Foundation, which has made substantial contributions to science, education, and the arts.

In 1974 St. Catherines entered what must be the most unusual period in her varied history when the island became one of the New York Zoological Society's Rare Animal Survival Centers. The acres that were once fields of sea island cotton, then pastures for herds of Black Angus cattle, became grazing areas for exotic animals from such far-flung places as Uganda, the Sudan, Kenya, the Sahara, Arabia, and South America. Included in the Georgia island's rare and endangered species of antelopes is the only herd of hartebeests in North America.

In recognition of the worldwide decrease in wild animal populations, the center on St. Catherines supports a scientific pro-

Sable Antelope family, St. Catherines Island

Grevy Zebra, St. Catherines Island

gram conducive to the natural reproduction that will preserve many species threatened with extinction. As the populations increase, rare specimens can be supplied to zoos and animal centers; and it is hoped that small herds may form the nucleus for repopulating countries where certain species have totally disappeared.

In addition to the work of the survival center, a number of archaeological explorations have been undertaken on St. Catherines, first by the University of Georgia, then under the auspices of the American Museum of Natural History. Relics of sixteenth-century Spanish occupation have been discovered; and examination of prehistoric mounds has revealed artifacts dating from 2000 B.C.

4 Midway and Old Sunbury

S ections of the mainland along the coast are so closely related
to the Golden Isles by location and history as to be almost a
part of them. The island of St. Catherines was in St. Johns Parish, and across the sound from Gwinnett's home on the island
was Sunbury, seaport and principal town of the parish. Located
upon a bluff near the mouth of the Midway River, Sunbury was
founded upon historic ground. It was here that the Old Indian
Path ended—the one the Indian traders traveled, that led all the
way from the mountains to the sea. And, according to tradition,
it was under a great oak tree on this bluff that General Oglethorpe organized the first Masonic Lodge in Georgia in 1734.

A few miles inland along the Old Indian Path from the site of
Sunbury stands Midway Church, a white-steepled meetinghouse
as typically New England as any of Grandma Moses's own
paintings. This part of the coastal region of Georgia gives visiting New Englanders a vague sense of kinship; and well it may,
for it was here that a whole community of Puritan-Congrega-
tionalists settled in the 1750s. Their ancestors had migrated
originally from Dorchester, England, and had established a village of the same name in Massachusetts about 1630. In the late
1600s a congregation of the New Englanders had come with
their minister to South Carolina, where they built a community
of prosperous farms and plantations around another Dorchester.

When the rules against owning slaves were relaxed in Georgia and immigration began from the other colonies, some three-score of these families petitioned for land in the new territory. In recommending the petition the secretary of the colony stated that an extraordinary character of the group came from all quarters, and prophetically remarked that he considered the coming of these people to be one of the most providential circumstances that could befall the colony. The earliest of the settlers came in 1752, additional families joined the first group, and soon a community of nearly three hundred people with twice that many slaves were living along the Midway and Newport rivers where the land was "considered proper for rice." Here on a royal grant of thirty thousand acres they cleared fields for their plantations and laid out their village of Dorchester.

Within two years after the community was started the citizens organized themselves into the Midway and Newport Society, whose original Articles and Rules of Incorporation have been preserved. Dated August 28, 1754, the rules of the society begin: "We the Subscribers settled on Midway and Newport in Georgia . . . being Willing to lay a Foundation by the Blessing of God, of Peace and Harmony among ourselves and inoffensiveness to all our Neighbors . . ." Subscribers whose signatures are still legible include those well-known names of Osgood, Bacon, and Baker; Way, Maxwell, Andrew, and Winn; Quarterman, Stacy, Stevens, Graves, Goulding, and Lambert.

Selectmen were chosen as in a New England community, but the real leader of the group was their pastor, the Reverend John Osgood, and the center of community life was the church or meetinghouse—in those early days a temporary log building on Midway Neck. Although the Midway settlers were prosperous planters and successful businessmen, their town and plantation buildings reflected the simple conservative tastes of the Puritan. Most of the residences were gabled cottages with dormer bedrooms and open porches, while the larger dwellings were usually plain and square with an open veranda around the lower floor. In spite of their unpretentious architecture the interiors of the houses were often beautifully finished with hand-carved mantels and paneling.

The people of the Midway Society were an exclusive group. Not only were they "inoffensive to their neighbors" but they "kept themselves to themselves." They had strict moral and religious views and an education superior to that of many of the other settlers of the region. They formed a Library Society and they engaged well-qualified teachers for their children. It was the custom for four or five families within a few miles of each other to support a school where the curriculum included Latin, Greek, algebra, and geometry, as well as the three R's.

Midway and Medway seem to have been used almost interchangeably in early records. Perhaps the river was originally called Medway for the river of that name in England, but both river and community later became known as Midway, located as they were about halfway between the Savannah and the Altamaha rivers. But every student of old records and histories knows that early scribes, however erudite, were individualists in the art of spelling.

The plantations along the Midway and Newport prospered from the start, and in records of a meeting in September 1756 the community was beginning to "raise a Meeting House at the cross paths." * The minister's salary was to be paid by rental of pews, and the question was discussed whether a child under six years should be "Intitled to a whole seat or half seat." A half seat was voted. In January 1757 the first sermon was preached in the new meetinghouse—the first Congregational Church in Georgia.

---

* Land for the meetinghouse erected in 1756 was deeded by John Stevens and his wife, Mary, to the following subscribers: Benjamin Andrew; Samuel and Joseph Bacon; William, Benjamin, Richard, and Samuel Baker; Nathaniel Clark, William Dunham, John Elliott, Isaac Girardeau, William and John Graves, James Harley, Isaac Lines, John Lupton, Joseph Massey, Audley Maxwell, John Mitchell, John and Josiah Osgood, Thomas Peacock, John Quarterman, John Shaves, Richard Spencer, Samuel Stevens, John Stewart, Edward Sumner, Nathaniel Taylor, John and Joseph Winn; Parmenas, Edward, Moses, Thomas, Nathaniel, Andrew, and Samuel Way. (From *History and Records of Midway Church* by Baker and Quarterman, 1951, p. 284.)

Overland transportation was difficult to the nearest shipping point at Savannah, and need for a convenient outlet for products of the surrounding countryside led to building the port town of Sunbury. The land upon which the town was built was part of an extensive tract originally owned by Captain Mark Carr, an early settler of the colony who had received large grants in the coastal region. The tract on the bluff was laid off in lots, streets, and commons and deeded by Captain Carr in 1758 to a board of trustees composed of prominent citizens of the community. Called Sunbury for Sunbury-on-Thames, or according to some historians "because it was truly the residence of the sun," the town became a thriving shipping port second only to Savannah in importance. One of Midway's selectmen, John Martin, was Naval Officer of the Port, and many of the Midway people built summer places or permanent homes in the new town whose location near the sea was "considered most salubrious."

Dr. Lyman Hall, physician, statesman, planter, owned a plantation, Hall's Knoll, in the parish and lived in Sunbury. Born in Wallingford, Connecticut, young Dr. Hall had moved to Dorchester, South Carolina, a few years after his graduation from Yale; but after practicing there for a short while he had joined the group in Georgia. Physicians were the first professional men to come to the colony, and many of them were prosperous planters as well as prominent and influential men in their communities.

The cause and cure of malaria had yet to be discovered, and it was the custom throughout the low country for entire households to move from the rice plantations during the warmer months to escape the "country fever." Planters of the Midway community who did not have houses in Sunbury had summer retreats in the "resinous pinelands" near their homes. Here the families lived from May to November while the men rode back and forth daily to attend to plantation affairs.

On Sundays everybody from miles around gathered at the meetinghouse. Early travel was by horseback and wagon; then the two-wheeled one-horse gig came into use. With increasing prosperity equipages became more pretentious as well as more colorful; we find mention of a four-wheeled conveyance painted light blue, and feminine riders using neat blue-fringed sidesaddles; and later, at the height of the prosperous plantation era, the ladies were driven to church in the family coach while the gentlemen rode alongside on horseback.

When Sunbury was recommended as a port of entry in the early 1760s, it was described as a town of eighty dwellings and "considerable merchant stores." A customhouse and naval office were located in the new port; ships from the northern colonies, from the West Indies, from Great Britain, and other countries came here for cargoes of rice, indigo, skins, lumber, tar, and rosin. William Bartram, who visited Sunbury on his journey along the Georgia coast, described it as a town of two-story houses "with pleasant piazzas around them where the genteel, wealthy planters resorted to partake of the sea breeze, bathing, and sporting on the Sea Islands."

In 1764 another physician came to Midway—Dr. Nathan Brownson. Like Lyman Hall, Dr. Brownson was a native of Connecticut and a graduate of Yale, and like Dr. Hall he took an active interest in the community. When the dynamic Button Gwinnett moved into the parish the three men became a power in the political life of the country.

It was in this prosperous period before the American Revolution that still another important property owner came into the community. John Eatton LeConte, of the well-known Huguenot family of scientists, came from New York State and developed the plantation Woodmanston, where he and his family spent the fall and winter months. The LeConte children loved the country life, and the surrounding swamps and woodlands were an unlimited source of interest to those embryo scientists, John Eatton, Jr., and Louis.

The first murmurings of dissatisfaction against British rule were scarcely heard in Georgia, and even when some of the colonies took the first steps toward independence Georgia was slow to join the patriots. The colony as a whole was satisfied, their royal governor was well liked, and many of the people had so lately come from England that they still identified themselves more with the mother country than with their sister colonies. But the residents of the Midway community with their New England heritage were quick to resent the injustices felt by the older colonies.

Impatient with the rest of the province, St. Johns Parish called their own meeting of patriots and selected a delegate to represent them at the Continental Congress. Lyman Hall, one of the staunchest supporters of the cause of liberty, was chairman of this first meeting and was chosen to go to Philadelphia. When Georgia finally joined the other colonies, two more delegates were sent from St. Johns Parish—Button Gwinnett and Nathan Brownson. When Hall and Gwinnett signed the Declaration of Independence, Dr. Brownson was not present at the Congress and so did not become one of the immortal fifty-six.

The years of unrest directly preceding the Revolutionary War found Midway Church without a pastor. The beloved minister Dr. John Osgood had died, and his nearly two-score years of leadership seemed for awhile an irreplaceable loss. The pulpit was filled by supply preachers and visitors until after the beginning of the war when a young New Englander, Moses Allen, accepted a call to the pastorate.

Many citizens of the province remained loyal to England. The war of independence has truthfully been called a civil war in Georgia. The question of joining the revolution had been fiercely debated and the people found themselves divided into warring factions—neighbor against neighbor, friend against friend. But there was no division of loyalty in St. Johns Parish. The sons of Midway threw themselves into the cause of liberty with all the righteous courage of their Puritan forebears.

James Screven, who had represented the parish at the Provincial Congress, was a brigadier general in the Continental Army; Colonel John Baker was leading the volunteer St. Johns Riflemen in attacks against Tories to the south; Major John Jones was an aide to General McIntosh. Fifteen-year-old Daniel Stewart was fighting a man's fight in the swamps of Carolina. The Reverend

Moses Allen was a commissioned chaplain. Lyman Hall, Nathan Brownson, and Richard Howley were serving as delegates to the Continental Congress, while Dr. Brownson for a time acted as surgeon in a Georgia brigade as well. The port of Sunbury was protected by Fort Morris, the coastal fort that achieved its place in Georgia history when its commander, Colonel John McIntosh, made his defiant answer "Come and Take It!" to the British demand for surrender.

Georgia was once more keeping an anxious eye on her southern outposts. By the Treaty of Paris in 1763 England had ceded Havana to Spain in return for possession of "the Floridas," which now gave the British forces a base for attack from the south. When Prevost led his army up the coast in 1778 he met with stubborn resistance in the Midway district. A mile from the meetinghouse there was a bloody battle in which General Screven was killed. At the same time enemy warships attacked the coast, and sturdy old Fort Morris held out to the last before it was captured and renamed Fort George.

The patriots suffered defeat after defeat. Major John Jones was killed; young Daniel Stewart was captured, but made a daring escape from the ship where he was held prisoner. The Reverend Moses Allen was confined to a prison ship from which he too escaped; but he was drowned trying to swim to safety. A prison camp was located at Sunbury, and legend has it that some of the original members of the Masonic Lodge, while prisoners of war here, received permission from Masons among the British officers to hold a meeting under the tree where the lodge had been organized by General Oglethorpe.

Many residents of the coast had refugeed to Augusta, and when Savannah was captured and Augusta became patriot capital, Richard Howley of the Midway community was elected governor of the demoralized state, and at the same time served as a delegate to the Continental Congress. When Augusta, too, fell to the British the people refugeed across the river into South Carolina; but the city was recaptured in 1781, Midway's Dr. Nathan Brownson was elected governor, and under his leadership the patriot government began to be efficiently reorganized. Throughout the years while Georgia was held by the enemy the coastal region suffered "the harshest of reprisals," for England had expected loyalty from this youngest colony in which she had placed such high hopes and which was little more than a generation removed from the mother country.

When the tide of war turned and Georgia was freed in 1782 from nearly four years of British occupation, the residents of Midway returned to find their community devastated. The church had been burned, crops destroyed; Lyman Hall's plantation was laid waste; the Woodmanston house of the LeContes was burned, as were many other buildings in the district. Tranquil Plantation, the home of young Daniel Stewart's family, had been used as headquarters for Colonel Prevost's staff, and it is said that the returning owners proudly preserved a wall upon which the British had burned the words, "This house was the home of a nest of rebels." St. Johns Parish was included in Liberty County, and Sunbury was made the county seat; in an address at the first superior court held here in 1783, Chief Justice George Walton said that Georgia had suffered more than any other state in the Revolution and that the citizens of Liberty County had drunk deep in the stream of distress.

The Midway community began to work at the slow and painful task of postwar recovery. Houses were rebuilt, fields replanted, timbers cut for shipbuilding, and as soon as there were once more products for export commerce was resumed. In a report on South Atlantic seaports a few years after the war, Sunbury and Savannah are listed as the only harbors in Georgia open to vessels from the Cape of Good Hope or beyond it. The community had indeed drunk deep in the stream of distress; but Liberty was one of the most important counties in the state, and Midway's sons continued to make history. Lyman Hall, who had served in the Continental Congress throughout the war, was elected governor in 1783, and it was under his farsighted leadership that Georgia began to lay the foundations for its educational system.

Church services were held in the homes of the impoverished congregation until the society voted in 1784 to build a temporary or "coarse Meeting House near the Spot where the former stood." A new minister was called, a native of New England and a graduate of Yale as were so many of Midway's leaders—Abiel Holmes, father of Oliver Wendell Holmes. The six years of Dr. Holmes's pastorate were spent in helping to rebuild the foundations of the community. The Library Society was revived, schools reopened, plans begun for a permanent church. In 1787 Dr. Holmes's health made a temporary change of climate necessary, and the Midway pulpit was supplied for a year by Jedidiah Morse, author of the *American Universal Geography* and father of S. F. B. Morse, inventor of the telegraph. What an experience his year in Georgia must have been for the young New Englander, for we find the community suffering Indian depredations in 1787 and 1788. Men carried firearms everywhere, even to church, and the plantation owners built stockades near their houses where family and slaves could barricade themselves in case of attack. But by 1791 troubles with the Indians had been settled, the community had recovered some of its prewar prosperity, and plans were going forward for the permanent meetinghouse.

The Reverend Cyrus Gildersleeve was pastor when the new church was built in 1792. A two-storied structure of hand-hewn timbers, white-painted, simple, unadorned, it stood in a grove of live oaks. There were hitching-rails where saddle and carriage horses from surrounding plantations could stand in the shade of the trees; and each family had its own "arbor," a sort of shelter or hut where babies and their nurses could stay during church and where lunch was spread between services of spend-the-day preaching.

As the community returned to normal, interest increased in cultural and educational affairs. The Library Society grew to be such an important organization that in 1799 the Savannah newspaper records an act passed by the General Assembly incorporating the Midway and Newport Library Society of Liberty

Midway Church

County. It was in this last decade of the 1700s that an academy was established at Sunbury with the Reverend Dr. William Mc-Whir as headmaster—a man who was to be one of the town's longest lived and best loved citizens. Born in Ireland, William McWhir prepared for the Presbyterian ministry and came to the United States when he was only twenty-four years old. The young minister first settled in Virginia as a teacher in the Alexandria Academy of which George Washington was a trustee and in which his nephews George Steptoe and Lawrence Washington were students. In Washington's diaries "McQuerr" is mentioned several times as visiting and dining at Mount Vernon, and some original letters from the teacher to Washington are in the Library of Congress. One of the outstanding Greek and Latin scholars of his day, Dr. McWhir made Sunbury Academy one of the best known schools in the South. It is said that a young man graduated from Dr. McWhir's academy was prepared to enter the junior class at Yale, Princeton, or Harvard.

By the turn of the century the plantations were flourishing again and Liberty County like other sections of the coast became one of the most prosperous agricultural regions in the world. But although the county was thriving, Sunbury was losing its importance as a seaport. A bridge built at the town of Riceboro made transportation easy to the port of Darien to the south, and improvement of roads made the larger port of Savannah more accessible. Commerce began to move away from Sunbury, the population dwindled, and the county seat was moved to Riceboro. Although decreased in commercial importance and in permanent population Sunbury remained for years a favorite resort of plantation families, and the academy continued to be one of the leading schools in the state.

When British gunboats came down the coast in the War of 1812 Liberty County fortified itself against invasion. A body of students took over old Fort Morris and renamed it Fort Defense; but no attack was made at this point. In the following years the Midway community continued to prosper, and although Sunbury had lost its importance as a town, Dr. McWhir remained one of the most distinguished educators in the state. He served well over a quarter-century as headmaster of the academy, and even after he retired to his plantation, Springfield, near Sunbury, students came to him to be privately tutored. In addition to his duties as a teacher, Dr. McWhir served through the years as supply minister in various churches along the coast, and he was sent as the first Presbyterian minister into Florida, where he was instrumental in organizing churches at St. Augustine and at Mandarin.

Other men of the Midway community made their mark upon the pages of history in the nineteenth century. In 1810 the church records the birth of Francis Goulding, one of Georgia's favorite sons. A Presbyterian minister, he was pastor in Sumter County, South Carolina, and in various towns in Georgia. Francis Goulding was also an inventor and an author. While he lived in Eatonton, Georgia, he is said to have invented a sewing machine before the first one was patented, but he never sought a patent for his invention. Best known among Goulding's writings was his book *The Young Marooners*, a sort of youthful Robinson Crusoe story with the coastal islands as its location. Said to have been based on an actual experience in the author's own family, it was one of the most popular young people's books of its day, published in many editions in the United States, six editions in Great Britain, and translated into French.

John E. Ward, born in 1814, was a Liberty County man who had his place in world history and whose father was a native son of the community. In his eventful life John E. Ward served as United States district attorney, as mayor of Savannah, as speaker of the house in the state legislature, as president of the state senate, and as the first United States minister to China.

Midway's Daniel Stewart, who had fought in the Revolutionary War as a lad in his teens, distinguished himself in the Indian wars, and was made a brigadier general. His daughter married the grandson of Archibald Bulloch, and their daughter Martha Bulloch, "Miss Mittie," was the mother of President Theodore Roosevelt.

Charles C. Jones, Jr., a descendant of Major John Jones, became one of the best known of Georgia's early historians; young John Elliott, grandson of the original settler John Elliott, was elected to the United States Senate; and another of the community's native sons, Robert Quarterman, became pastor of Midway Church. During the latter years of his long pastorate he had as his assistant I. S. K. Axson, who was elected to the pulpit at Dr. Quarterman's death in 1849. Thirty-six years later, when Dr. Axson was pastor of the Independent Presbyterian Church in Savannah, he officiated at the marriage of his granddaughter, Ellen Louise Axson, to the young lawyer Thomas Woodrow Wilson.

In 1818 and 1823 two of Georgia's most illustrious sons were born in Midway, those eminent scientists and educators, John and Joseph LeConte. Their father, Louis, had come to live on the family plantation, Woodmanston, and had married Ann Quarterman, daughter of one of the first Midway families. Louis LeConte had studied medicine, but his great interest, next to the management of the large plantation, was science, especially chemistry and botany. The boys were allowed to watch their father's experiments in his laboratory, and they grew up in a house surrounded by one of the most beautiful gardens in the world. Joseph LeConte describes as one of his fondest recollections his father, cup of coffee in hand, enjoying an early morning walk among the flowers. Botanists from all over the United States and from Europe came to see the LeConte gardens and to go with Louis LeConte on excursions into the forests and swamps in search of rare plants and shrubs. It was on Woodmanston Plantation that the LeConte pear was developed, and many an orchard was started from cuttings of the original tree, which is said to have borne prolifically for well over half a century.

John and Joseph LeConte received their early education in a neighborhood school where one of their first teachers was Alexander H. Stephens, "Little Alec," vice-president of the Confederacy. The brothers later attended the University of Georgia, and after graduation both continued their education at the College of Physicians and Surgeons in New York, where they received degrees in medicine. But although John practiced in Savannah for four years and Joseph was a physician in Macon, Georgia, for five years, neither was to make the practice of medicine his life's work. The elder brother joined the faculty of the University of Georgia in 1846 while the younger went to Harvard in 1850 to study geology and zoology under the world-renowned Swiss scientist Louis Agassiz. And what a year of experience it was for young Joseph LeConte, still in his twenties. He was on intimate terms with such distinguished men as Longfellow, Lowell, and Holmes; and he was chosen to accompany Professor Agassiz on his exploration of the Florida reefs for the government coast survey.

Upon his return to Georgia, Dr. Joseph LeConte taught for one year at Oglethorpe University, which was then near Milledgeville; and in 1852 he joined his brother on the faculty of the University of Georgia. From this time the two were never separated. In 1856 both accepted positions at the University of South Carolina, where they remained until that university was closed in the 1860s. The LeContes offered their services to the Southern states and both were appointed as chemists in a factory operated by the Confederate government in Columbia. When the university was reopened after the war, the brothers resumed their places on the faculty; but the struggling institution had little to offer men of their stature. Their opportunities limited for service to the world of science, their fortunes irrevocably lost in the war, it would seem that life itself had little to offer the two middle-aged professors. But John and Joseph LeConte turned with youthful enthusiasm toward the opportunities of the West.

In 1868 they were appointed to the first faculty of the newly chartered University of California, John as professor of physics, Joseph of geology, botany, and natural history. After the university was moved from Oakland to the village of Berkeley in 1872, both LeContes were active in forming the early government of the growing city; and the brothers devoted the rest of their lives to the building of the great California institution of learning. In

1875 Dr. John LeConte was elected president of the university; and Dr. Joseph LeConte was, until his death in 1901, one of its most distinguished and best loved professors.

By the late 1850s the once busy seaport of Sunbury had become almost a "deserted village." Yellow fever had taken its toll of the inhabitants, and it is said that the houses of some of the victims had been burned in an effort to stop the epidemic. Other buildings had been damaged by hurricanes and had never been rebuilt. Dr. McWhir had died in 1851, and the academy had not long survived its headmaster. The town did not survive the sixties. After the War Between the States the few remaining houses of any value were moved to the neighboring village of Dorchester. One of the few relics of the old seaport still in use is the bell from the market, now in the Dorchester Presbyterian Church. Except for its graveyard, Sunbury has completely disappeared—truly one of the "dead towns" of Georgia. And here where the shouts of his boys echoed for two generations sleeps Dr. McWhir under a marble slab "Sacred to the memory of Rev. William Mc-Whir D.D. . . . . His long and eventful life was devoted to the cause of Christianity and Education, and his labors to promote these objects were eminently successful. . . ."

Not far from the cemetery and near the site of old Fort Morris is the Sunbury Historic Site visitors' center opened in November 1978 by the Georgia Department of Natural Resources.

Devastated in the 1860s the community of Midway never recovered its former prosperity. Lacking even means of transportation, the citizens who returned to their property found themselves unable to continue the custom of gathering at the old meetinghouse. They formed small communities of their own where they followed the traditions of their forefathers in cultural and religious interests and in love of their homes and flower gardens.

And the Midway people who went out into the world picked up the threads of their lives and continued the pattern set by their ancestors. Perhaps the steel of the Puritan character, forged on the rugged shores of New England, tempered in the warmth of the southern sun, held those ingredients that produced individuals with an inherent gift for leadership, men and women to whom the obstacles of life were only challenges.

Wherever they went, sons and daughters of Midway made their imprint upon their communities, had their share in guiding the destiny of the nation—they were statesmen, judges, military men, scientists, doctors, historians, authors, teachers, editors. Nearly a hundred ministers went out from Midway, many of them foreign missionaries who carried into all parts of the world the influence of the little Georgia church.

But for the old meetinghouse itself the sands of the hour glass were running out. The surrounding plantations a thing of the past, the port of Sunbury gone without a trace, the bustling town of Dorchester dwindled to a tiny village, old Midway's last lesson had been taught, its last hymn sung, its last sermon preached. The last line had been traced upon the pages of history. The chapter was finished. The book was closed.

The double entrance doors open upon the empty silence of the historic old church; empty, but not with a feeling of bereavement; rather with a feeling of dignified pride and quiet meditation, filled with the strangely articulate silence of the past, peopled with the spirits of the men and women who once worshiped here. The sunlight slants through uncurtained windows upon white enclosed pews, upon the graceful white curve of balcony and columns, upon the dark contrast of old organ and raised pulpit. Walking softly upon the worn boards where walked those great souls of other years, one can sense their presence, can almost hear faint echoes of their footsteps, of the hymns they sang, of the prayers they prayed.

Pausing reverently by the silent pews, wandering in the stillness of the old burying ground, the visitor is somehow grateful that the old church is allowed to sit in the sun and dream of the greatness that was hers; thankful that she is no longer the meetinghouse for the few who would come now; glad that she is not humbled by being a burden to a handful of devout people with their mundane problems of new roof and windowpane, of new paint and preacher's pay. Midway Church stands empty of everything but dreams, except on that one day of the year, the Sunday in April nearest Confederate Memorial Day, when her children's children gather to do her honor. For the Midway Society still lives. Governed, as always, by a Board of Selectmen, the society is composed of descendants of the original settlers; and it is the privilege of members of the society and of the Congregational Church of America and of friends of old Midway to keep the church in repair and to carry out plans for making it the center of an historic shrine worthy of its proud past.

In April 1954 the bicentennial anniversary of the founding of the Midway Church and Society was celebrated. People gathered from far and near to hear the address by Georgia's Senator Richard B. Russell, himself a descendant of the Midway colony, and to see the beautiful pageant which told the complete story of the famous old community.

Across the highway from the church is the old burying ground, surrounded by a wall of English bricks. A tall shaft erected by the government in honor of Midway's two generals, James Screven and Daniel Stewart, is the only monument that is not hoary with age. Most of the tombstones and markers are so old that time has all but obliterated many of their inscriptions. Vines clamber over family burial vaults; the moss-covered bricks of raised tombs sag tiredly; an age-old live oak spreads its shade over a quarter-acre of graves.

Although directly on the heavily traveled coastal highway with its constant hum of tires as cars speed by to the north, to the south, there is a deep sense of peace and serenity in the ancient graveyard of old Midway, and as the visitor closes the rusting iron gate behind him he understands how Edmund Burke "would rather sleep in the southern corner of a little country churchyard than in the tomb of the Capulets."

Midway Museum, Incorporated, organized by the St. Johns Parish Chapter, Daughters of the American Colonists and the Liberty County Chapter, United Daughters of the Confederacy, was chartered in 1946. Through the efforts of members of this organization, funds were raised for the purchase of a seven-acre tract adjoining Midway Church, as the site of the proposed museum.

The land was later deeded to the State of Georgia, and under the auspices of the Georgia Historical Commission a replica of an eighteenth-century inn was erected on the site. The Midway Colonial Museum was officially dedicated on November 29, 1959. With its early American furnishings, its rare books, and its historical and genealogical records, the museum presents a picture of life in the Midway area in colonial and antebellum days and at the same time offers valuable material for research.

Midway Colonial Museum

In March 1979 the Georgia Department of Natural Resources relinquished administration of the museum. In the same month Midway Museum, Incorporated, was reactivated, and volunteers from the organization assumed the responsibility of supplying hostesses for Midway Colonial Museum.

5 Sapelo and Blackbeard Islands

A few miles south of St. Catherines lies the third Golden Isle, the island kingdom of Sapelo—the "Zapala" of the Spaniard and the "Sapeloe" of the colonist. Endowed with all the beauty that a generous nature has lavished upon the isles, Sapelo has been further enriched and beautified over the years by three owners, each a leader in the business and financial world of his day.

Exciting evidence of prehistoric habitation is the ancient shell ring or "arena" discovered upon the island. Examination of the twelve-foot wall of shell which encloses a circular space some sixty yards in diameter has revealed artifacts that lead archaeologists to believe that it was built more than two thousand years ago. According to legend, the ring was formed by shells tossed aside by a giant chieftain who, day after day, year after year, sat cross-legged upon the ground and feasted upon his favorite food of oysters brought to him by runners, directly from the sea.

The earliest recorded history of Sapelo, like that of the other islands, is of missions, massacres, intrigue, and war. Crumbling ruins mark the supposed site of the sixteenth-century mission of San Jose de Zapala. In Captain Dunlop's *Voyage to the Southward* in April 1687, there is described a large plantation on Sapelo where "we see the ruins of houses burned by the Spaniards themselves. We see the vestiges of a fort and many great orange trees cut down by the Spaniards September last. There was great plenty of figs, peaches, artechocks, onions, etc. growing in the priest's gardens. His house had been of brick and his small chappell." As one of the hunting islands known to have been frequented by the archers and anglers of Indian days, Sapelo has been through the years the traditional sportsman's paradise.

Like Ossabaw Island, Sapelo was sold at "public vendue" in 1760 to satisfy the claims of the Bosomworths and it, too, was granted to Grey Elliott. The original grant, lost for years, was recently found, in true storybook fashion, among other Sapelo papers, deeds, and letters in the secret drawer of an old desk. It is of special interest to the historian as one of the last land grants made in the name of George II. Dated in the month of his death, October 1760, it records the purchase price of Sapelo as £725.

Two of the early owners of Sapelo were Patrick Mackay and John McQueen. The island was partly under cultivation before the Revolution, and the Lachlan McIntosh letters (published in the Georgia Historical Quarterly in 1954) report in 1776 that a British schooner carried off "a number of slaves and other valuables from Sapelo while the men of one of our guard boats were pleasuring and Idling their time."

In the following years came a period when the island belonged to a group of Frenchmen. An indenture dated "in the year of our Lord 1789 and in the thirteenth year of the Independence of the United States of America" shows that John McQueen of the County of Chatham deeded to Francis Marie Loys (?) Dumoussay Delavauxe "in consideration of £10,000 sterling the absolute purchase and inheritance of those Islands called Sapelo, Blackbeard, Caberreta, and Little Sapelo." Little Sapelo lies between the larger island and the mainland, while Blackbeard to the northeast and little Caberretta just below it are almost a part of Sapelo, separated only by narrow creeks and inlets.

By an "agreement bearing date at St. Malo in the Kingdom of France the 8th day of November 1790 made between Delavauxe,

Christopher Poullain Dubignon, Julien Joseph Hiacinta de Chappedelaine, Grand Clos Mesle, and Picot De Boisfeullet," each became owner of an "undivided fifth" of the islands. An indenture dated 1792 shows that one of these fifths was sold to another citizen of the Kingdom of France, one who signs himself Nicolas francois—Magon de la Ville Huchet. Few of these French owners made their homes upon their island property; most of them eventually sold their shares and settled in other parts of the coast.

But Monsieur and Madame de Boisfeuillet remained for some years upon Sapelo, where they had a delightful place called Bourbon. Another French aristocrat who came to live on the island was the Marquis de Montalet, who had been a planter in Santo Domingo before coming to the Georgia coast. He was for a time owner of that famous Savannah River plantation, the Hermitage, where he lived until the death of his charming eighteen-year-old marquise; then, soon after 1800, accompanied by his friend the Chevalier de la Horne, the marquis moved to his estate on Sapelo, that part of the island which had belonged to "Grand Clos Maley" (Mesle).

Here the two French gentlemen lived for the rest of their lives in the house called *Le Chatelet*, but which was called "Chocolate" by the negroes. Monsieur de Montalet had a peaceful existence in his retreat where he entertained a few friends, cultivated his gardens, trained Cupidon, his *chef de cuisine*, and searched the island hopefully for the truffles of his native land. Friends enjoyed his hospitality; tropical flowers, fruits, and vegetables flourished in his gardens; Cupidon attained such perfection in the preparation of his master's favorite dishes that the marquis placed the *cordon bleu* over the kitchen door. But the search for truffles was never successful although legend has it that de Montalet and his companion spent many hours leading a pig on a leash in the hope that it would root out the coveted delicacy. Toward the north end of the island the ruins of "Chocolate" may still be seen.

The south end of Sapelo was bought in the early 1800s by Thomas Spalding, son of the prosperous Scottish trader and

Ruins of the slave cottages at "Chocolate"

planter James Spalding of St. Simons Island. Sometimes called
the Laird of Sapelo, Thomas Spalding eventually owned nearly
all of the island; he cut timbers for shipbuilding, cleared hundreds of acres, and developed his property into one of the finest
plantations in the South. He and his wife, the former Sarah
Leake, both born on the Georgia coast, had spent several years
of their early married life traveling in the British Isles and upon
the European continent, where they were lavishly entertained
and were presented at the Court of Napoleon; but now they settled down on the island of Sapelo, where they were to spend the
rest of their lives.

Their plantation mansion, South End House, designed by the
owner himself, was noted for the perfection of its gardens, for
the luxury of its Old World furnishings, for its library, and for
the unusual beauty of its architecture. Among the old Sapelo papers fragments of a drawing of marble columns with capital and
base may be a part of Thomas Spalding's original specifications

for South End House. It was not the typical Southern colonial house with tall and graceful columns, but a house built low to the ground to withstand the fury of the wind, with columns recessed, sturdy. Not the house of brick or of white-painted clapboards like most inland mansions, but rather of square-hewn timbers and tabby walls three feet thick.

In the beautiful South End plantation home with their large family of children the Spaldings lived a life that was the perpetual houseparty of tradition. The island of Sapelo, writes Francis Goulding, was famous throughout the country for the "princely hospitality of its chief proprietor." Always ready for the unexpected guest, it was the custom for never less than a score of places to be set at the Spalding table; stables of the finest horses, a fleet of boats, and a retinue of servants were all placed at the disposal of the visitor.

Architect's drawing of the Old South-End House on Sapelo built by Thomas Spalding circa 1800

Thomas Spalding was a statesman, a businessman, and a writer, as well as one of the leading agriculturists of his day. He was an authority on the history of the coastland's long-staple cotton, and was presented with a trophy in Great Britain for his essay *The Introduction of the Sea Island or Black Seed Cotton in the United States.* In spite of his interest in cotton, Spalding had the wisdom and foresight to see the danger of concentrating on one crop to the exclusion of all others. One of the earliest advocates of diversified farming, he made speeches and wrote articles urging farmers to rotate their crops. He was a leader in the promotion of the sugarcane industry in the state, and with true Scottish thrift and ingenuity was one of the first planters to construct a mill that was operated by the power of the tide.

Thomas Spalding's opinion of the perfection of his beloved coastland is expressed in the opening sentences of his speech as first president of the Union Agricultural Society: "Gentlemen, we are in the climate of Chaldea and of Egypt, of Greece, of Tyre, and of Carthage. We are in a land where rice, wheat, and cane, indigo, cotton, and silk, where the olive and the vine not only grow but will find their favorite home if man will only lend his aid." A man of vision, Spalding "preached the gospel of grass," and he predicted that Georgia would one day be a grazing country. He believed that "syrup from cane is the most nutritious feed for cattle known in the world." What a satisfaction it would be to him today to see the herds of cattle fattening upon the rich grasslands of islands and mainland, and to see experiments being made in feeding cattle molasses and syrup.

Enthusiastic agriculturist though he was, Spalding was vitally interested in business and political affairs. One of the leaders of his day in matters concerning the welfare of the coastal section and of the state, he took an active part in organizing agricultural, social, cultural, and charitable societies. He helped to establish schools in his region, and in 1818 he was instrumental in founding the Bank of Darien, of which he was the first president. He helped to write the state constitution, was a member of the state legislature, and served two terms in the United States Congress. In 1820 a government lighthouse was built at the south end of Sapelo Island at the entrance to Doboy Sound; and Thomas Spalding tried to have the harbor developed for naval vessels. But his efforts were never successful; and the old lighthouse now stands abandoned overlooking the sound that Spalding proposed as a base for the United States Navy.

Like most of the coastal planters with their English and Scottish background, the master of Sapelo had a patriarchal attitude toward his slaves. No slave was ever sold from the plantation during Spalding's lifetime. In their settlements or villages located on different parts of the island each family had its house and plot of ground. They planted their gardens, raised their pigs and chickens, and worked in the surrounding fields much as tenant farmers do today.

Headman upon the Spalding plantation was that famous slave of the Old South, Bu Allah or Ben-Ali the Mohammedan. Believed to have been born in the French Sudan, Bul-ali, as his descendants call him, had been sold into slavery when he was a young boy. He and his family spoke a dialect strange to most of the other slaves, but they spoke English and French as well. Bul-ali enjoyed the complete confidence and respect of his master and of the men who worked under his supervision. His descendants boast that he helped win the War of 1812. They refer to those last months of the war when the British invaded the Georgia coast, and Thomas Spalding received permission from the state government to equip all the men on his plantation with arms and ammunition. Under the leadership of the Mohammedan overseer the island of Sapelo was protected from the enemy.

Father of a score of children, Bul-ali has numerous descendants living today in the coastal region, many of whom inherited his copper-toned skin and aquiline features, his height and erect carriage. Proud of their ancestry, each generation hands down tales of the Old Man. They say that his most treasured possessions were his Koran and his prayer rug, and that he always wore a black cap made like a Moslem fez. He was wise in the ways of nature; and his children and children's children knew the secrets of the moon and the tides, of the waters and the forests. When one of the family fell sick the old ones knew which roots and herbs to gather in the woodlands and how to make them into a medicinal brew or *tisan*.

Joel Chandler Harris's *Story of Aaron* mentions a book written in Arabic by Ben-Ali, a book thought to be a record or diary. This was a little leather-bound volume which Bul-ali had given to Francis Goulding, and which Dr. Goulding's son later presented to the Georgia State Library. The "diary," as it was called, created interest among scholars and historians, and it was hoped that its translation would disclose some of the mysteries of the life of the old Mohammedan. But upon examination by students of Arabic dialects, the book proved to be passages from a legal work, no doubt learned in Bul-ali's youth and set down from memory. Believed to be the only existing example of African-American writing, the volume is prized among rare books at the Georgia State Library in Atlanta.

For nearly half a century the Thomas Spaldings lived on their island plantation. Their children grew up, married, established homes on the mainland; and after his wife's death in 1843 the aging Laird lived in the South End mansion for his remaining years, alone except for his servants. He continued to take an active interest in agriculture and in political affairs, and his home still offered its famous hospitality to family and friends. At the master's death in 1851 the plantation passed by will to his young grandson Thomas Spalding II.

Sapelo was a part-time home for members of the family for a decade; and in 1861 Confederate troops were for a time stationed upon the island. It was later evacuated, and except for a number of slaves who refused to leave their homes, the plantation was left unoccupied during the war. In the following years the island was taken over by the "rag-tag-and-bob-tail" with which the South was infested in Reconstruction days; and when the Spaldings finally managed to regain possession of their property the splendid old South End mansion was uninhabitable.

Smaller houses were made livable, and young Thomas Spalding with a brother, a sister, and their families lived for some years on the beautiful island for which they had the same deep affection as had their grandparents. Among the former slaves still living on the old place was the Spaldings' nurse Betsy Beagle, who was happy to have "her children" back home. At her death in 1890, at the age of ninety-four, a stone was erected "in memory of Betsy Beagle, she was the faithful loving nurse of the Spalding children for two generations. 'My Baba,' may she rest as peacefully as the little heads she pillowed to sleep on her bosom."

Life on the island proved impractical for the young Spalding families, and although they wondered if any people would ever live on Sapelo who would love it as they did, parts of the property were sold over the years to various owners who allowed the fields to become overgrown to provide cover for birds and game. The wheel had turned full circle, and like Ossabaw and St. Catherines, Sapelo was again a hunting island; and as in the days before Thomas Spalding bought it, the island was once more divided into fifths, each belonging to a different owner.

In 1911, when the celebrated Vanderbilt Cup and Grand Prix Races attracted notables of the motoring world to Savannah, the visitors included Detroit's Howard Coffin, automobile pioneer of Hudson Motors fame. Captivated by the beauty of the coastal country the Coffins came back to Georgia on a vacation trip, and in 1912 they bought the historic island of Sapelo. The dilapidated old Spalding mansion, which had been partially restored as a clubhouse for a group of sportsmen, was renovated and used by the Coffins as a vacation home for years.

Sapelo Island, with its interesting history and its possibilities for various enterprises, offered a challenge to its owner. Like Thomas Spalding, Howard Coffin was a man of wide interests, of imagination and vision; a dreamer with the ability and resources to make dreams come true. He was fortunate in having as his associate a young cousin, Alfred W. Jones, to see to the practical details; and whenever Howard Coffin's numerous interests called him away from Sapelo the younger man was in charge of the "island empire." Between the two the wilderness was made into a plantation as complete and as varied in activities as it had been in the days of the Laird of Sapelo. Miles of shell roads were built through the woodlands, creeks were bridged, artesian wells drilled for electric and water power. Old fields were once more cultivated and great tracts of grassland were range for some two thousand head of cattle. A seafood canning enterprise provided work for the island families.

In 1925 Mr. Coffin had the Spalding house rebuilt and enlarged. One of the plantation buildings was remodeled into a dwelling known as "Long Tabby," where the family lived while the old house was transformed into a residence even more lux-

South End House, Sapelo, as rebuilt by Howard Coffin

The indoor pool at South End House

urious than it had been a century before. Set in its landscaped gardens, with a flower-bordered vista of the Atlantic, the place had a beauty and dignity unsurpassed by any other on the coast, and the Sapelo "kingdom-by-the-sea" came back into its own as one of the most magnificent properties in the country. When the house was completed the Coffins found themselves spending more and more time on the island until they eventually made it their permanent home. With a deep feeling for the romantic history of the coastland, the owners of Sapelo kept the old name South End House; they used the English spelling for the island; and their yacht was the *Zapala*.

The forests and ponds, the creeks and surf offered as wide a variety of game and fish as ever attracted those archers and anglers of Indian days; and Sapelo Plantation was again noted for the "princely hospitality" of its owner. There were boats and stables of horses once more placed at the disposal of visitors; there were long sunny days of riding and hunting and fishing; long delightful evenings of pleasant conversation, of popping corn and shelling nuts and munching apples around the big fireplace— that easy, gracious "southern" hospitality that is inherent rather than regional.

As in Thomas Spalding's time South End House again offered its hospitality to distinguished persons of the nation. An interesting early visitor was Charles Lindbergh, who spent a few days on Sapelo soon after his flight across the Atlantic. Prominent guests were the Coffins' friends the Herbert Hoovers and the Calvin Coolidges; and Georgia newspapers were agog with the rumor that President Coolidge had been offered South End as a summer White House. If he had accepted he would no doubt have found his coastal neighbors congenial, as many of them, descendants as they are of Scottish and Puritan colonists, remain today as taciturn and laconic as any down-Easter.

Charles Lindbergh on the Georgia coast

Mr. and Mrs. Howard Coffin and President and Mrs. Calvin Coolidge at Sapelo, Christmas 1928

Mrs. Coffin died in 1932, and in 1933 Sapelo Island was sold to Richard J. Reynolds of North Carolina. Following the pattern of former owners, Mr. Reynolds continued large-scale farming, cattle breeding, experimenting in various industries; and the magnificent South End House was the delight of visitors. The

Employees' houses were constructed on different parts of the island, and additional accommodations were built into the "South End Complex," a picturesque village of apartments, post office, and small shops grouped around a central green. The

Calvin Coolidge posing for a portrait by Frank Salisbury, a prominent English artist, while on the Georgia coast in 1928

principal building of the complex, a huge structure designed for a variety of uses, included an auditorium where movies were shown twice a week for employees.

Although the island was never opened for sightseeing, its "princely hospitality" was for a few years extended to visitors when Sapelo Plantation was for a time an exclusive resort.

The year 1950 marked the beginning of a new era for Sapelo. Through the generosity of Richard J. Reynolds and under the direction of Richard Orme Flinn, Jr., pastor of the First Presbyterian Church of Carrollton, Georgia, an educational program was inaugurated with the establishment of a camp for a selected group of school boys. The old Long Tabby house was remodeled for recreation rooms and library, additional buildings were constructed, and the boys, aged seven to fourteen, arrived aboard the *Kit Jones* for a summer of work, play, and study. With the cooperation of the Harvard Graduate School of Education, Mr. Flinn outlined a program so skillfully carried out that the youngsters scarcely realized they were learning.

No youth would find early American history a chore when he himself, in authentic Indian regalia, joined the war dance around the campfire or paddled his canoe in the narrow island streams. The days of the Spanish settlers came to life in exploration of the ruins of San Jose de Zapala. The science of conchology became a game when the embryo scientists visited the beach to picnic and gather shells for their collections; and archaeology was an exciting adventure when the students were permitted to watch experts at work upon the prehistoric shell ring.

Sapelo's only permanent residents, the people of the Hog Hammock community, had their part in the educational plans of the owner of Sapelo. A modern, well-equipped schoolhouse was built and teachers from the mainland were provided. The Hog Hammock families are descendants of Sapelo slaves who were deeded their property by the Spaldings after emancipation. These people whose families have lived for generations on the island are, the visitor feels, the real owners of Sapelo, with their church, their ancestral land, their homes and gardens. The Golden Isle of Sapelo is home to them as it was to their forefathers.

In 1953, as the next step in his educational program, Mr. Reynolds established and endowed the Sapelo Island Research Foundation to administer the south end of the island as a marine biological research laboratory of the University of Georgia. In 1954 a group of young scientists from the university set up the first laboratories in the South End Complex. Also in 1954 one of Sapelo's older industries was revived when lumber was cut at the north end of the island to be shipped to Cuba and Haiti.

Richard J. Reynolds died in 1964, and in 1969 the north half of Sapelo was purchased from his widow by the State of Georgia, the property to be administered by the State Game and Fish Commission. In 1975 a program of controlled deer hunting was introduced, a program that has continued to be popular over the years.

In 1976 the State of Georgia acquired the remainder of Sapelo by the purchase of the south half of the island from the Research Foundation. The announced objectives of state ownership are protection of the productive marsh nurseries for a variety of marine life, preservation of the unspoiled ecosystem, and "preservation of the scenic and natural values of the island for the education and enjoyment of Georgia citizens."

An important feature of the state-owned island is the Duplin River National Estuarine Sanctuary established under the Coastal Zone Management Act and administered by the University of Georgia Marine Institute as a "representative, undisturbed area for use as a natural field laboratory." The unique six-mile tidal river which rises and ends on Sapelo Island is ensured against contamination by the 2,800-acre sanctuary that protects it.

Sapelo was opened to public tours in 1977 with access to the island by state-operated boats. A well-planned program offers displays in the Marine Institute, guided tours of the island, visits to the beach, hikes on nature trails, and observation of marsh life from boardwalks over the marshes.

South End House serves as headquarters for Marine Institute seminars and for special groups of environmentalists, scientists, and historians. It also serves as a "second governor's mansion" where the Georgia governor hosts important officials such as the Secretary of the Interior. And during Jimmy Carter's years in the White House the presidential family enjoyed South End House occasionally as a vacation retreat.

As change has come to Sapelo, so change has come to the residents of Hog Hammock, the only privately owned land on the island. The schoolhouse built by Mr. Reynolds is now the Community Center, as the young people attend school on the mainland, going in daily by boat. In 1978 the Richard J. Reynolds

Scholarship Program was established by the Sapelo Island Research Foundation to enable worthy high-school students to complete undergraduate work at a regionally accredited college, university, or vocational and technical school.

The activity that has come with the workers, students, scientists, residents, and visitors is no new experience for the old island. There have always been visitors to Sapelo, and it has long been a place for experiment and accomplishment. There is work to be done; there are lessons to be learned, secrets to be revealed, miracles and magic to be performed.

To workers, students, and scientists, Sapelo offers the gift of time. Tension and urgency are left on the mainland; they have no place on the island. There is time to do the work; time to learn the lessons; time to reveal the secrets. There is time, too, to walk in the shadows of the centuries-old live oaks, to sit in the sun on the beach. There is time to watch the miracle of sunset, the magic of moonrise; to see the flight of the waterfowl, and to listen to the metronome of the sea as it measures out the years of measureless content.

Blackbeard Island

Blackbeard Island appears on the map as a part of Sapelo, but it is a separate small island, a part of the refuge system of the United States Fish and Wildlife Service. Its more than four thousand acres of woodlands, lakes, and marshlands provide sanctuary for migratory fowl, for deer and turkey and quail, just as its virgin forests and devious waterways provided sanctuary in former centuries for pirates who robbed Spain's treasure galleons of their hoards of gold and silver.

As the pirates roamed the sea lanes of the Atlantic between the Indies and New England, the thickly islanded coast of Georgia furnished hideaways for the buccaneers and for receivers of their ill-gotten goods. The labyrinth of rivers, creeks, and inlets offered harbor for ships flying the black flag with outline of a skeleton, murderous gully and bottle of rum in its bony hands, or with the more familiar skull and crossbones. Most of the coastal islands were haunts of the infamous brotherhood, and legend has it that many a cache of bloodstained booty still lies buried in the forests. But the island which bears the name of Blackbeard is especially rich in pirate lore and the inevitable tales of buried treasure.

It was in the early 1700s that the coast was frequented by that *bete noire* of the sea, Edward Teach or Blackbeard, who preyed upon shipping all the way from New England to his stronghold in the Virgin Islands. A legendary member of his savage crew was Israel Hands, who later sailed on the *Walrus* with Long John Silver and Captain Flint—Stevenson's Captain Flint who "died in Savannah singing and shouting for rum."

With his long black hair and beard in braids incongruously tied with ribbons, swashbuckling Blackbeard assumed all the stage effects of piracy—in fact he is said to have invented them—pistols and knives in sash, cutlass in hand, dagger in teeth. After the forty guns of his *Queen Anne's Revenge* had pounded a vessel into submission, Blackbeard would come storming aboard, slow-burning pieces of hempen rope looped in his plaits, pistols blazing, knives finding their mark with awful accuracy. He claimed to be a brother of the Devil; and to the poor wretches whom he victimized he must have seemed indeed to be breathing fire and brimstone. He boasted that nobody but he and the Devil knew where he had buried his treasure and the one that lived the longest could have it.

If his Satanic Majesty has not retrieved the loot of his bearded brother it may still lie undiscovered, for Blackbeard was killed off the coast of North Carolina in 1718 in hand-to-hand combat with Lieutenant Robert Maynard of His Majesty's *Pearl*. Decapitated by the sword of his victorious adversary, the flamboyant blackguard fell to the deck pierced with "five and twenty wounds." His head was displayed as a warning to other evildoers, and later his skull, ornamented with silver, was made into a macabre punch cup that is said to be still in existence. Early records speak of the island as a "favorite spot much dug" called locally Money-Old-Fields; but if any gold was ever discovered it was not reported. Legend says that many a treasure chest still lies buried in the forests with none to stand guard but a headless ghost, pistols and knives in sash, cutlass in hand. . . .

In a copy of the *Georgia Gazette* dated March 1800 Blackbeard Island was advertised at a marshall's sale, and from records in the Georgia State Library we find that in this same year the United States acquired the island for the purpose of cutting timber for shipbuilding. In 1808 full jurisdiction was ceded to the government by the State of Georgia, and during the yellow-fever epidemic in the middle of the nineteenth century when Savannah became a closed port, Blackbeard served as the South Atlantic Quarantine Station where ships were stopped and turned back.

In 1914 an executive order by President Woodrow Wilson made Blackbeard a wildlife preserve, and a year later jurisdiction was given to the State of Georgia. In 1924 the U.S. Department of Agriculture reassumed jurisdiction, and Blackbeard was permanently established as a wildlife refuge. Although newspapers of 1931 refer to a proposal to transfer the island to the State of Georgia under custody of McIntosh County, the change was not made.

So persistent were rumors over the years of pirate loot on Blackbeard that in 1934 a group of explorers received permission to dig for treasure trove. Newspapers reported great excitement over the venture, but, although picks and shovels were busily plied for the ten days allowed, no discovery of pieces-of-eight, of guineas or doubloons or louis d'or was ever reported.

The beaches of Blackbeard are nesting places for the huge turtles that come out of the sea at night and go above the waterline to lay their eggs. They cover their nests with sand and go back into the ocean, leaving the eggs to be hatched by the warmth of the sun. The tracks of the turtles' feet may easily be seen on the beach, and if one were to dig at the end of the trail he would uncover dozens of round white eggs the size and shape of ping pong balls; but the sport of turtle egg hunting, formerly a popular diversion for vacationers, is now prohibited by law.

Blackbeard today lies in a sort of brooding serenity, secure in its protection from the hiders and seekers of gold. The forests and beaches that once heard the curses of the buccaneer and the rattle of his cutlass now hear the cries of the sea birds, the rustle of the palm trees, and the beat of the waves upon the shore.

6 Darien

The town of Darien on the mainland near Sapelo has, like Midway, a history so closely interwoven with that of the Golden Isles as to make them inseparable. Located about thirty miles south of Midway on the Darien River, the north branch of the Altamaha, Darien today is a quiet little place scarcely noticed by travelers along the coastal highway that runs through the center of the town. The modest buildings along the shady streets on either side of the thoroughfare give no indication that Darien was once a bustling river port, leading lumber town of Georgia, and one of the important shipping and commercial centers of the state.

One of the historic spots along the coast, the bluff where Darien stands was a stratetic point for Indians, Spaniards, and colonists. It was the site of one of the larger Creek villages and is believed also to have been the location of an important mission-presidio of the sixteenth and seventeenth centuries.

In 1721 Fort King George was built upon the bluff as a frontier outpost where His Majesty's Independent Company was stationed for the protection of England's southernmost colony of Carolina. In use for only a few years, the old earthenwork fortress was already beginning to fall into ruins when the settlement of Darien was laid out—"the lots to run out to old King George's Fort."

The first settlers of Georgia had proved inadequate in both number and ability to combat the difficulties of founding a colony in the uncleared wilderness and at the same time to help protect it from its enemies; so, with the assistance of Lieutenant Hugh Mackay, a group of Scotch Highlanders had been persuaded to cast their lot with the new colony, both as homesteaders and as fighting men. Since many of them had lost their property in wars in their native land, the Scotsmen looked forward to new land and fortunes as well as to the adventure of pioneer life.

The first of the Highlanders arrived in 1736 and established the Scottish settlement on the bluff. They chose the name of Darien as a gesture of defiance toward the Spaniards, in memory of those other Scotsmen who had attempted to establish a colony in that older Darien in Panama. Although for a brief period in its history the town was called New Inverness, this name soon disappeared from colonial records.

As military leader of Darien, General Oglethorpe appointed John McIntosh Mohr, who recruited a company of Scotsmen, "all in Highland Dress." Historians say that the word *Mohr* (or *Mor*) was a suffix to distinguish John McIntosh from others of the same name. (It is interesting to note that the Gaelic word *Mor* is defined as "great or large.")

Darien was protected by ten cannon; a road was constructed to Savannah, the first highway built in Georgia; and the Highlanders set about building dwellings and stores. There were a kirk and a school, both in charge of the Reverend John McLeod, who had come to Georgia with the Scottish colonists. Other clansmen soon followed; they settled into family groups as was the custom in Scotland, and "the people of the Darien lived happy and contented."

In this colorful settlement of the New World the colonists played their bagpipes, sang their Scottish songs, and wore their plaids and bonnets; even Oglethorpe himself wore "Highland habit" when he visited Darien. Legends handed down in the region tell of a mutual admiration and respect between the Scotsmen and their Indian neighbors; tell how they worked and fought side by side and tried their skill and strength against each other in games and contests. What a sight it must have been to see the Highlander with bare knee and kilt, and the Indian in breechclout and eagle feather, competing in footraces and shooting contests, and throwing and wrestling matches! And how the forests must have resounded with the war whoops and Highland yells as the assembled tribe and clan cheered the victor.

But life was hard in the pioneer colony; not only must the wilderness be conquered, but the Spanish threat was ever present. In an expedition against the stronghold of the Spaniards at St. Augustine in 1739 a number of the courageous Highlanders lost their lives, and Captain McIntosh himself was captured and held prisoner for many months before he was exchanged and allowed to return to Darien. After the final defeat of the Spaniards in 1742, the Scotsmen hunted deer and buffalo, which were plentiful on the mainland, and sold hides to the traders; they cut timber, raised stock, and planted crops; and their settlement began to thrive. The Georgia colonists soon found indentured servants inadequate for the heavy labor required for clearing land and working farms. Many of the planters felt they should be allowed to own slaves as planters in neighboring colonies were. When the province petitioned for this right, the Scottish settlers of Darien signed a counter petition in what has been called the first recorded protest against slavery in history. A counter petition in which the Scottish second sight is reflected in the prophetic words, "Introduce slaves and we cannot but believe they will one day return to be a scourge and a curse upon our children or our children's children." But when the right to own slaves was granted the colony in 1749, the Scotsmen followed the custom of the land and worked their plantations with slave labor.

As prosperity increased, the district was given the protection of Fort Barrington, which was built in 1751 as a western outpost. The town on the bluff was listed as a city in the report on "New Georgia" published by the *Gentleman's Magazine* in 1756, but it was actually little more than a village until after the

Revolutionary War. With the development of the great river plantations along the Altamaha and of the inland farmlands, Darien's situation made it a natural center for commerce. The river, cleared and made navigable in the late 1700s, was an outlet for rich products of forests and farms of the interior, and Darien became the largest lumber town in the state as well as one of its most important shipping and commercial centers. Cotton brought down the Oconee River into the Altamaha in the famous flat-bottomed, high-sided "Oconee boxes," and rice from the neighboring plantations were loaded at the busy port for shipment all over the world. Down the Altamaha came tall straight pines for ship masts and great logs of cypress, oak, and white pine to be sawed into lumber for shipbuilding and for foreign trade.

Darien was originally in St. Andrews Parish, which was included with St. Johns Parish in the great county of Liberty after the Revolutionary War; but the district along the Altamaha formed its own county in 1793 and named it in honor of the distinguished McIntosh clan, which was so prominently identified with the early days of the colony. Although the population of the town of Darien was never large, it was the business and educational center for the surrounding region of rich plantations and farms. In 1818 it was made the county seat of McIntosh, and in this same year the first newspaper was started and the Bank of Darien with its million-dollar capital was organized.

Darien had the misfortune to suffer a number of disastrous fires over the years and few official town records remain; in the absence of such records stories handed down through the generations, old family letters and journals, and copies of early newspapers are invaluable. The rare copies of *Gazettes* and *Telegraphs* still in existence give a picture of the Darien of the 1800s. We find that there were sawmills and lumber yards, and rows of docks and shipping wharves along the river in those prosperous days of the first half of the nineteenth century. There was a customs house; there were warehouses and stores, and business houses that were branches of Liverpool mercantile establishments. Each issue of the newspaper carried a regular column of *Marine News* which listed the arrival and departure of vessels— schooners, sloops, and brigs—sometimes as many as twenty-eight or thirty arrived and cleared in a day.

Darien had a hospital, churches, a public school, and several private schools and academies. There were the Darien Hotel and the Eagle Hotel; and in 1820 the opening of a new hotel was announced—the Mansion House, whose "table was always well supplied and bedding comfortable and cleanly. Stable always well supplied with good corn, fodder, hay, etc., and every attention paid to horses as there is an attentive ostler and farrier for the purpose." Other large buildings in the port town were the Masonic Hall and that "spacious and substantial edifice," the Exchange.

There were "Merchant Taylors," a clock and watch maker, a boot and shoe manufactory. A saddler and harness maker advertised, "Carriages and Giggs repaired and lined anew." The Darien Dispensary, at the sign of the Golden Mortar, announced itself an "elegant establishment with every requisite for cure of disease and a specific for almost every malady that flesh is heir to." Mercantile stores offered an unbelievable variety of goods.

One store advertised "bags of green coffee, cologne water, Bologne sausages, English mustard, basket and blown salt, candles and bar soap, loaf and brown sugar, shot, powder, and lead in bars, American and Holland gin, Jamaica and N. E. Rum, Cognac and Spanish brandy, Madeira wines in demijohns and bottles, and London porter in hogsheads or bottles."

Another merchant offered "silk parasols, segars, almonds, riding whips, molasses, men's pantaloons and dancing pumps, fresh shoes, figured and plain Denmark Sattin, dressed and undressed Morocco." And still another store advertised "black and changeable silk, Light and deep blue Nankeen Crapes, Elegant white silk scarves, thread lace, Ladies white and black silk hose, Irish Linen, Elegant Tea China, Elegant cut glass Decanters, firkins of butter for family use, and horehound candy, as well as Millenary and Ladies Fashionable Dress Making."

Booksellers announced the arrival of shipments of books, listing some four or five hundred titles which included Homer, Milton, Shakespeare, histories, dictionaries; books on medicine, surgery, and religion; biography, philosophy, science, geography, husbandry, gardening, and political economy; *Pilgrim's Progress*, Plutarch's *Lives*, Scott's essays, and French and Latin grammars.

A surgeon-dentist informed his friends through the newspaper columns that he had arrived and taken room at the Mansion House. He suggested that those who required his professional services would find it much to their comfort and convenience to apply to his room. A builder advertised that he was equipped to install complete indoor water-works in Darien and vicinity.

Darien was a town of shady streets and comfortable houses with yards enclosed by picket fences and beautified by flowers, shrubs, and orange trees. Two of these houses were considered showplaces. One was Ashantilly, a mile or so east of town, built by Thomas Spalding for his mother, used after her death as a winter home for the family, and later the property of the Spaldings' son Charles. The other was the beautiful Troup house upon the promontory known as Cathead, a serene tree-shaded point overlooking the river and marshes on the west side of Darien.

Built in the early 1800s, the Spalding house was named for the Barony of Ashantilly to which Thomas Spalding's father had been heir in Scotland. Designed by the Laird of Sapelo himself, Ashantilly was unique and charming. A two-storied house with one-storied wings, built wide and low to the ground, its spacious, beautifully proportioned rooms were ornamented with handcarved wainscot, cornices, and mantels; the exterior was of expertly finished tabby, and at either end was an open portico with columns of Italian marble. An unusual architectural feature was the series of floor-length windows across the front, while the entire back of the house was a solid wall—perhaps an early experiment in the modern idea of solar heating.

The Troup residence, a large house constructed, like Ashantilly, entirely of tabby, was designed by that gifted young Englishman, William Jay, who drew the plans for the famous

Habersham and Owens-Thomas places in Savannah. An apprenticed architect in London, young Jay came to Savannah in 1818, and although less than twenty-five years of age he soon made a name for himself along the coast, and designed some of the most beautiful buildings in the region. The Troup house was the town residence of Dr. James McGillivray Troup, planter-physician, who was one of the most prominent men of McIntosh County. The Darien physician served as justice of the county, as commissioner of the McIntosh County Academy, as president of the bank, mayor of Darien, and as state senator.

It was one of Dr. Troup's daughters, Clelia, who married Daniel Murray Key, a grandson of Francis Scott Key. A son of this marriage, Francis Murray Key, grew up in the coastal region, and as a young man went to the Philippines and later to South America, where he spent the rest of his life. In 1952 his son, Francis Scott Key, came to the United States and visited relatives and friends as he traveled along the Georgia coast.

In addition to their townhouses, the well-to-do families of Darien had summer places at Baisdens Bluff, a resort a few miles east of town. Here many of them spent the hot months to escape the "fierce disease of the coastal lowlands," while others journeyed farther from home. The *Gazette* announced that the paper would be carried at John Niblo's in New York for those residents of the coast who were summering at Saratoga or other resorts "at the North." During these months business in Darien was almost nonexistent. Many of the offices and stores closed for the summer, and from May first to November first the bank opened at eleven o'clock and closed at one.

The first frost was the signal for Darien to rouse from its summer hibernation; and the returning life of the town was described in the columns of a November copy of the *Gazette*: "During the last ten days the weather has been cool and pleasant, attended occasionally by our good friend and physician Jack Frost; and those who were placed on beds of languishing, from the disease peculiar to the climate, are now we are happy to say, fast recovering their health from the gloom and despondency that surrounded them. Many of our citizens who journeyed hence for the benefit of the health of themselves and families have returned with all the glowing pictures of the rose in their features and countenances. Business again begins to rear its drooping head from the withered condition with which it is usually afflicted during the summer season."

Autumn brought the big logs down river, and the Altamaha was reported in good boatable order. The sawmills on the bluff advertised for sealed proposals to supply them with timber up to ten thousand logs. Instructions for preparing the great cypress trees for cutting were published. "To get cypress timber with ease, the trees should be deaded one year before hand, by pealing the bark off 8 or 10 inches wide when it strips well; the best time to peal the trees is the full moon."

From its beginning the settlement of Darien had given religion and education a prominent place in the development of the community, and as the town grew it became the religious and educational center of the Altamaha region. The Darien Sabbath School Society was organized February 10, 1820, and "the school under patronage of said society" was opened in the Darien Presbyterian Church on the following Sunday, February thirteenth.

The church announced the rental of pews for "eighty, one hundred, and one hundred twenty dollars according to location, and any person desirous of a choice will have preference by giving the greatest sum over the aforesaid assessment." "Things not in order" were listed: "To stand before the Church door before services. To salute persons coming in by bowing, smiling, &. To allow your children to be stuffing themselves all the time with apples, sweet cakes, candy, or anything else. Sleeping in Church. To stand around the door gazing at the Ladies as they are leaving the Church to see who conducts them."

One of the cultural organizations was the Darien Library Society to which subscribers paid quarterly dues of five dollars; and the most prominent educational institution was the Academy, with its "principal seminary for day students and boarders at Baisdens Bluff, and several minor Institutes fixed in different parts of the county." There was a school at the Masonic Hall which offered trigonometry, composition, and the art of surveying for fifteen dollars per quarter; geography, English grammar, and arithmetic for twelve dollars; while reading, writing, and orthography could be had for ten dollars.

The opening of a new private academy was announced "under the care of a graduate of Princeton College; and should circumstances warrant, the services of an amiable and accomplished Lady in all the branches of a polite English Education and in the French Language can be immediately procured." Other advertisements offered lessons in fencing and dancing; and Mrs. Jones respectfully made known to inhabitants of Darien that she would "devote her time to the instruction of young Ladies on the Piano Forte, and having studied under some of the first professors at the North she flatters herself that her system will ensure success."

In addition to the commercial, religious, and educational life of Darien there were boating parties and regattas and meetings of the agricultural and sporting clubs. Washington's birthday was celebrated each year "with becoming respect and mirth," and the Fourth of July was properly celebrated by a program of events which started at four o'clock in the morning.

We are given a detailed account of one such celebration with Thomas Spalding, Esq., as President of the Day and Dr. James Troup as Vice-President. "The dawn of day was ushered in by repeated discharges of cannon and musketry and the Flag of freemen was unfurled to the morning breeze by the shipping in port." At 4:00 A.M. the Darien Volunteers, completely equipped, in uniforms with blue pantaloons, assembled at their parade grounds where they performed many handsome evolutions. There followed parades, speeches, and the reading of the Declaration of Independence at the Presbyterian Church. At 3:00 P.M. a "superb dinner" was served at the Mansion House. The newspaper did not give the menu, but did given an account of the program which preceded the dinner. "The Toasts (gentlemen only of course), which were interspersed with cheers, songs, and music, were thirteen by the citizens and nine volunteer toasts. The list of toasts by the citizens, or scheduled toasts, were to The Day, George Washington, The President, etc., with the thirteenth, To the American Fair—Matchless in virtue, may the principals inculcated by our free Constitution absolve them of all domestic imperfections."

The Darien *Gazette* was published weekly, first by Millen and Maxwell, and later by Charles F. Grandison. A double sheet measuring twelve inches by eighteen, the paper kept its readers abreast of the news not only of town and state but of national and international importance. In the spring of 1821, unusual weather made the headlines in the local columns. On March tenth the editor reported "streets and housetops covered with Snow about 2½ inches in thickness. We do not recollect to have seen so great a quantity here since 1802." And three weeks later—"Frost! We had hoped as Spring Advanced with her enlivening hand that Wintry scenes would have disappeared from our view like the blooming rose of morning doomed to wither with the declining sun of evening, but the contrary is the fact. Frost, the destroyer of our fruit and vegetable fields, has blasted the fair prospects."

Regular features of the newspaper were its columns of *American Intelligence* and *European Intelligence*. Under *Important News from Charleston* early in the year 1820, "the brig *Cervantes* arriving in 38 days from Gibraltar brought the pleasing certainty of the Ratification of our Treaty with Spain which cedes the Floridas to the United States," and in July 1821 an article headed "The Floridas Are Ours" gave a detailed description of the ceremonious exchange of flags at St. Augustine. Also in 1821 the *Gazette* published the inaugural address of President Monroe upon his reelection, and in the same issue an account of the ratification of the treaty with the Creek Indians. In another 1821 edition the paper recounted at great length the death of Napoleon Bonaparte.

In August 1821 the readers were informed that a large supply of cents or copper coins were ready for distribution from the mint of the United States in Philadelphia. It was stated that these coins would be issued to any reasonable amount in exchange for an equal amount of specie, and not less than a keg containing from 150 to 180 dollars transported by land or water at the expense and risk of the government.

The often repeated statement that the Bank of Darien was once the largest south of Philadelphia has been a subject of doubt and dispute, and it may or may not be true; but the bank in this port town was for a time the leading financial institution of the state. The history of the Bank of Darien, though brief, is interesting, spectacular, and tragic. Half state-owned and thus partially controlled by the state government, with a branch in Milledgeville (then the capital of Georgia) and half a dozen branches in other parts of the state, the bank was a center of political controversy throughout the twenty-two years of its existence.

Although some existing government records show that large amounts of federal funds were for a time on deposit in the Bank of Darien, records of those early days of banking in the United States are fragmentary and incomplete owing to the loss and destruction of valuable papers in war and by fire. Research into government reports and into old records of contemporary state banks, into private and official papers on file in the Library of Congress and in state historical societies, fails to produce figures with which to compare other banks of the day with the Bank of Darien. However, with its various branches and large state, federal, and private deposits, it seems that there may be some foundation for the claim that the bank of the little river town on the Altamaha was indeed for a time the largest south of the main branch of the Bank of the United States in Philadelphia.

The years 1823 and 1824 were disastrous ones for the town of Darien. During this period the region suffered from all three of the ancient enemies of the coastland—erosion, hurricane, and fire. Baisdens Bluff Academy was undermined and carried away by the river, and the hurricane of 1824 brought severe damage to the town and tragic loss of life and property on nearby plantations. The paper reported total destruction of many buildings, and expressed the opinion that less than half a dozen houses in Darien had escaped serious injury. The Eastern Saw Mill was in ruins; two schooners were blown ashore; the rice fields were inundated; the cotton crops ruined. A few weeks after the hurricane a notice in the *Gazette* invited friends and acquaintances of the storm sufferers to "join a procession to the church where the Reverend William McWhir would hold services," adding that the church would be "open to all persons desirous of uniting in the solemnities of the day whether owning pews or not."

Fire was an ever-present hazard in the coastal region. With the combination of dense woodlands, high winds from the sea, the age-old English custom of heating houses by open fires, and inadequate fire-fighting equipment, a blaze once started often spread out of control and left great damage and destruction in its wake. There were two disastrous fires in Darien in 1823 and 1824—one at the Upper Steam Saw and Rice Mill, the other a "great conflagration along the waterfront which destroyed Moore's wharf, the Exchange dock, another wharf, a large five-story tabby building; in all sixteen or seventeen buildings from Bolton's fire-proof range to Hunter's brick and stone bldg. Fortunately high tide enabled shipping at wharves to haul into the stream." (The newspaper recalled another fire in which two-thirds of Darien was laid in ashes in 1820.)

In this same year of 1824 the large government deposits were withdrawn from the Bank of Darien, and the series of unfortunate circumstances affected the bank to such an extent that it was forced to discontinue specie payments for a short time. The town suffered a general depression. With the comment that "no whitening canvas cheer the eye, no noisy waggon bells strike on the ear," an editorial headed "Darien has declined and Why?" offered such reasons as "lack of capital, ruinous system of credit, the need for improvement in navigation of the Altamaha, and the poor condition of the roads leading to Darien." Many planters and merchants of the state were using the more distant ports

of Augusta and Savannah because there were better roads to
those cities.

Darien managed to survive its calamitous experiences, and although the bank never regained the prestige it had enjoyed for
the few years of its meteoric prosperity it did recover from the
disastrous year of 1824. The mills were rebuilt; the Upper Steam
Mill was made fireproof with a five-story brick building for the
ricemill and a separate building for the sawmill. Work was done
upon river and roads, and since the hurricane had brought such
heavy losses in cotton the Union Agricultural Society was organized to help stimulate interest in other crops. The society
included the counties of Bryan, Camden, Glynn, Liberty, McIntosh, and Wayne.

In spite of local troubles news of general interest found its way
into the papers in 1824. It was noted that a Gas Light Company
had been formed in New York and that it was anticipated the
whole city would be lighted with gas in a very short time. Noah
Webster, Esq., was announced to be on the eve of his departure
for England and France, where he was "about publishing his
Dictionary on which he has been engaged upwards of twenty
years." The editor of the *Gazette* noted that a railway had been
suggested for facilitating transportation from Worcester to Boston, but he had doubts of its practicability.

In a front-page article the newspaper voiced concern over the
new fashion of cravats for men. The *Medical Adviser* was quot-
ed as proof that the cravat had a tendency to produce apoplexy
by pressing upon the jugular veins. "Why," asked the writer,
"does Lord Byron wear no cravat? Because Byron knows that
the operations of the mind may be impeded by pressure upon the
jugular veins." The article ended with a warning to gentlemen of
fashion: "of all introductions in dress the cravat is the worst—
both unseemly and dangerous."

In March 1825 there was widespread excitement over the
Marquis de Lafayette's visit to Savannah. Each community had a
mounted militia of gentlemen who rode their own horses and
furnished their own regimentals, and there was a friendly rivalry

between the Darien Hussars and the Liberty County Troop of Light Dragoons. Both organizations were in Savannah for the reception of Lafayette, and the mayor and a number of prominent citizens of Darien also attended the festivities where Dr. Troup's brother, Governor George M. Troup, gave the welcoming address.

In 1828 a group of coastal planters of Scottish descent met at the Mansion House and organized the St. Andrews Society of Darien with John Couper of St. Simons Island as president and Thomas Spalding of Sapelo as vice-president. Wearing the plaids of their clans the group pledged itself to uphold the high ideals of the society: "To cherish the recollections of our homes and the birthplace of our fathers—to promote good fellowship among Scotchmen and their descendants in this adopted country, and to extend to unfortunate Scotchmen and their families assistance and council in case of necessity."

The *Gazette* was replaced for a time by the *Darien Telegraph*, and in some rare copies dated 1834 and 1835, lumber, shipping, and agriculture were still of first importance in the river town. General's Cut Ferry announced permanent service across the Altamaha between Darien and the public landing in Glynn County with a ferry boat for conveyance of mail and passengers and safe flats for carriages and horses, and with accommodations made for horses at the landing.

An original copy of the semi-annual report of the Bank of Darien for October 1836 at the Georgia Department of Archives shows the total assets to be more than a million and a half dollars, but the panic of 1837 brought real disaster to the bank. It forfeited its charter in 1841 and closed in 1842. Businesses failed; the newspaper exhorted subscribers to pay their bills and finally announced itself "out of paper, out of ink, out of patience." By midcentury the town of Darien was at the end of its era of great prosperity. Contrary to the prediction of the *Gazette*, railroads were proving their practicability and were taking over much of the inland shipping, but no railroad had been built through Darien. The sawmills were still operating, and the nearby plantations still shipped produce from the Darien wharves, but the town could no longer hope to rival Savannah as a port.

Then came the tragic 1860s and that night of horror in 1863 when the entire town was put to the torch by a force of freedmen and runaways. Most of the inhabitants had refugeed to Baisdens Bluff, but when day broke over the Altamaha few buildings had survived the holocaust. Beautiful Ashantilly was far enough from town to have been spared, and the Oglethorpe Oak that, according to tradition, once sheltered a whole company of British soldiers under its spreading boughs, miraculously lived through the fire, its seared branches to grow green again by the time the descendants of the hardy Highlanders had rebuilt their town on the bluff.

Although Darien was rebuilt from the ashes and enjoyed a brief return to prosperity in the years following the War Between the States, its importance as a business and shipping center gradually diminished. The Oconee boxes no longer floated down river with their loads of cotton; the golden streams of rice no longer poured into ships' holds; the songs of the boatmen no longer rang over the water. For a time the logs continued floating down the river and the banks echoed to the strident whine of the saws, but as the forests of virgin timber were cut the sawmills became less profitable and were finally abandoned and left to fall into ruins. Although a railroad was eventually built through Darien, it came half a century too late, and was not long-lived.

But the old town never lost its atmosphere of historic culture and tradition. The Ashantilly house stood for years before it was partially destroyed by fire. Restored in part, it stands near St. Andrews Cemetery, which surrounds the Spalding family burying ground. Some of the old summer homes still stand at Baisdens Bluff, with great oleander branches reaching to their second-story verandas. And there is always the river. The same old Altamaha flows between the high bluffs and the spreading marshlands, its waters busy with fishing boat and pleasure craft and the going and coming of the shrimp fleet.

In the center of the little town, near the old Oglethorpe Oak, a marble and bronze monument decorated with the thistle of Scotland and the Cherokee rose of Georgia pays homage to "the Highlanders of Scotland who founded New Inverness in 1736. Their valor defended the struggling colony from the Spanish invasion. Their ideals, traditions, and culture enriched the land of their adoption."

In 1961 the site of old Fort King George was acquired by the Georgia Historical Commission. Archaeological explorations have disclosed a number of relics of Spanish, pre-colonial, and later periods, which are displayed in the visitors' center constructed at the site by the commission.

A dozen miles northwest of Darien on the old Barrington Road is the spot where the Lost Gordonia of botanical fame was first discovered. On his expedition in 1774 William Bartram, the naturalist, classified and named this new shrub. He had seen it on a previous trip into this section made in 1765 with his father, John Bartram, but as this was in the autumn when the plant was not in bloom, they had not been able to classify it. The new shrub was described as a flowering tree, growing fifteen or twenty feet high, with large white blossoms similar to camellias but having a delightful fragrance. Bartram describes in his *Travels* the location in which the plant was found as being on the northeast side of the Altamaha near Fort Barrington. This early colonial fort was renamed Fort Howe during the Revolution, but was afterward again called Barrington. No trace remains of the old fort, but the site is in the western part of McIntosh County.

Bartram classifed the shrub as the head of a new species of Gordonia which he honored with the name of the illustrious Dr. Benjamin Franklin, *Franklinia Alatamaha*. Although he says there were two or three acres in the vicinity where the plant grew abundantly, Bartram wrote that he had never seen it in any other place and had never since in all his travels seen it growing wild. Subsequent search for the shrub by other botanists has failed to find any trace of it in the location where it was first discovered. All the plants now existing are said to have been propagated

Bartram's "Lost Gordonia"

from the specimen sent back by Bartram to his botanical gardens in Philadelphia.

On his expedition William Bartram landed at Sunbury, attended church at "Medway," visited "Darian," went hunting and fishing on "Sapello," and visited James Spalding on St. Simons

Island. In his enchanting *Travels*, published in 1792, Bartram wrote so beautifully of his excursion by boat and by horseback along the coast that his descriptions are said to have been the inspiration for some of the poems of his contemporaries, most famous among them Wordsworth's "I Wandered Lonely as a Cloud."

7   The River Plantations

The Altamaha River, which figured so prominently in the colonial history of Georgia, was originally known as the "A-lat-amaha," but the extra "a" has long since disappeared and the name of the stream is pronounced as though the first syllable were "all." The lilting Indian name of the coastal river has been further shortened by poets from time to time, the best-known example perhaps the *Altama* of Goldsmith's *The Deserted Village*. Young Goldsmith, a friend of Oglethorpe in the general's old age, no doubt heard of the Georgia river in gatherings such as Boswell describes when he and Dr. Johnson "dined at General Oglethorpe's where we found Dr. Goldsmith."

Although the coastal country of the province of Georgia was well settled by 1760, the territory below the Altamaha had remained undeveloped. When the colony had been established upon land in the southern territories of Carolina, it was "from the northern part of the stream or river commonly called the Savannah unto the most southern stream of a certain other water called the Alatamaha." The Altamaha divides into several branches and flows into many streams as it nears the sea; and although Oglethorpe in fortifying the coast chose to interpret the most southern stream to include all of the Golden Isles, there had been no settlements on the mainland south of Darien.

As more colonists came into the coastal territory both South

Carolina and Georgia felt justified in claiming the region below the Altamaha; South Carolina because it had been included in her original charter, Georgia because it joined her southern boundary. In 1762 the governor of South Carolina made grants in this territory, but the Georgia governor petitioned the Crown for the disputed land, and in 1763 it was added to the province of Georgia by royal proclamation. Old maps and deeds show several hundred thousand acres granted to Carolinians, before the dispute was settled, with large grants to Henry Middleton, Henry Laurens, and other prominent South Carolina planters. Some of these men were allowed to retain the property upon condition that they clear and cultivate it as required by Georgia regulations. Before any extensive cultivation was undertaken the colonies were at war, and it was a number of years after the American Revolution before the region was fully developed.

And so it came about, during the late 1700s and early 1800s, that a group of South Carolina planters came to coastal Georgia, planters who had already prospered along the Ashley and the Cooper, the two rivers which South Carolinians claim flow together to form the Atlantic. Since little was known in those early days about fertilizer and the rotation of crops, the custom of multiple plantation ownership had developed as new lands were cleared when the fields became impoverished. The experienced rice and cotton planters of the older colony saw new opportunities in the rich alluvial soil of the Altamaha delta; and so a part of the old Debatable Land, the no-man's-land south of the Altamaha, became a land of great plantations whose owners were not only among the most prominent planters of South Carolina, but were some of the wealthiest and most influential men of the South and of the nation.

Just below Darien was the famous Butler Island rice plantation, property of Major Pierce Butler, whose wife was a daughter of Thomas Middleton, younger brother of Henry Middleton. Along the south branch of the river was the great Hopeton Plantation, which belonged to John Couper of Georgia and his friend and business partner James Hamilton. Next to the Couper-Hamilton property were three plantations, Elizafield, Grantly, and Evelyn, owned by Dr. Robert Grant, planter-physician of Sand Pitt, South Carolina. All of these planters also had property upon the island of St. Simons. Adjoining Dr. Grant's tracts were Broadfield and New Hope, which belonged to English-born William Brailsford of Charleston. The Butler, Couper-Hamilton, Grant, and Brailsford places were the largest and best known of the Altamaha River plantations.

The fertile delta lands were ideally situated for growing rice: far enough from the sea for the water to have lost the strong salt that would have damaged the grain, yet near enough for the ebb and flow of the tide to be an advantage in flooding the low-lying fields. Rice had been a profitable crop in South Carolina for more than a century, and the owners of the Altamaha River plantations brought with them hundreds of slaves experienced in the complicated work of the rice fields. Vast acres of marshland were drained, ditches and canals dug, dikes and levees built, sluice-gates and locks constructed. Strong embankments had to be thrown up completely around the river islands, as they often lay two or three feet below the crest of the water at high tide. The plantations were stocked with cattle, sheep, hogs, and poultry; there were mules for plowing and for drawing the farm wagons, but oxen were the principal work animals on the coastal plantations. Their patient strength was useful for logging and pulling stumps, for work in the marshy lowlands, and for operating the cane and rice mills described as "cattle impelled."

Rice was planted in March, April, and May, and the fields were flooded at full moon and new moon when the tides always run high. A big event of the plantation was "claying" the seed rice. The grain was spread upon the floor of the rice barn and covered with a thick mixture of clay and water. Then the slaves, young and old, had a "shout"—a sort of dance where they shuffled barefoot over the rice, clapping, singing, and chanting. Visitors to the plantations wrote of having seen similar performances when traveling in Egypt. When the shout was over the grains of seed rice were covered with the heavy clay which would keep them from floating until they took root.

As soon as the grain was sowed the sluice-gates were opened

Rice preparation on the Georgia coast in the early years of the twentieth century

and the tide was allowed to cover the fields. Then the gates were closed and the rice was left to sprout. The fields were drained when the green shoots showed above the shallow water—a pretty sight, the acres of new green, the banks blooming with wild violets and with a tangle of yellow jasmine and wild blackberry. Constant work was required to keep the fields clear of "careless grass" and weeds, to give the rice its exact amount of water, to keep canals and ditches dug out, and locks and sluice-gates in repair against the continual force of the tide.

As the grain ripened there was the added task of trying to protect it from the flocks of little rice birds that descended at dawn upon the fields. Boys stationed on the banks with improvised noisemakers were often joined by the young men of the family for the early morning sport of shooting, as the birds were considered a delectable breakfast dish, delicious morsels crisply browned and served with buttered grits and hot biscuits. When the rice was fully matured it was cut and loaded upon flats, long raftlike boats that could be poled along the canals or drawn by oxen from the tow-paths upon the banks. After the harvest had been gathered in, the whole plantation celebrated with a feast and "jubilee," followed by a well-earned rest.

Although the cost of preparing the land for cultivation is said to have run as high as $1,000 an acre, there were fortunes to be made in the coastal country during the first half of the nineteenth century. In addition to rich ricelands the properties below the Altamaha had forests of the live oak, cypress, and white pine that were in demand for shipbuilding; and the acres cleared by cutting the valuable timbers made fertile fields for cotton, cane, grain, vegetables, and fruits. Oranges were one of the profitable crops of the early days. Most of the plantations had groves from which the fruit was shipped by the schooner load to northern markets; but a succession of unprecedented freezes that damaged the trees about the time that the industry was being developed in Florida finally put an end to oranges as a money crop in Georgia.

The description of a river plantation advertised for sale in the Darien *Gazette* gives an idea of the estates along the Altamaha: "a shad fishery excelled by none; a peach orchard of rare fruit—yield 500 to 1,000 gallons; a good sawmill and a cotton machine; 2 or 3 convenient landing places; handsome beach in front of dwelling and a bold river half a mile in width." Each of the large plantations was developed into a well-organized community where hundreds of people were supported by the bounty of the land. Besides the cotton gin and the sawmill, there were mills for threshing rice and grinding cane; and owners of smaller farms nearby often took their products to the large plantation gins and mills instead of to the public ones at Darien and Savannah. There were blacksmith shops where horses were shod, vehicles kept in repair, and farm implements made, and carpenter shops where utility furniture was built. A cooper made casks, kegs, and barrels; a tanner cured hides for harness and for work shoes. There were the cotton house, sugar house, and rice barn; the cattle barn and dairy; the smokehouse, poultry houses, and stables for the carriage and saddle horses. There was a plantation hospital, a central commissary for provisions, and an ice house to store supplies of ice brought by boat from the North.

Although the coastal plantations were remote from large centers of population the owners were in constant communication with their factors or business representatives in Savannah and Charleston. These agents handled the sales of cotton and rice for the planters and did marketing for the plantations for a commission of 2.5 percent. Lists of supplies ordered from the factors show that sugar and "superfine flour" were bought by the barrel, candles and soap by the forty- and fifty-pound box, salt by the bushel; coffee was ordered in seventy-five-and hundred-pound lots, tea eight and ten pounds at a time. Other items included a dozen gallons of brandy; letter paper by the quire, together with bunches of quills and packets of ink powder; thread was ordered by the pound and needles by the hundred; "segars" by the thousand. There were usually orders for dozens of yards of dress material for the ladies, and for the planters' use the list sometimes included a "fine Beaver Hat" or a "cock'd Hat & 2 yards Black Ribband for a cockade."

The houses built upon the river plantations in the early 1800s were larger and more individual in design than the simple cottages of some of the earlier settlers of Georgia. Made of ax-hewn timbers upon high tabby foundations, they had graceful flights of steps and double doors wide enough for hoop skirts. English planters from Barbados had been an important part of the early life of South Carolina; and the houses and customs of the planters who came to Georgia showed some of the influences of the colonial plantations of the West Indies. There were floor-length windows shuttered against the sun, and verandas were often enclosed by the West Indian "louvres," similar to the venetian blinds of today. Like the Carolina river estates, the plantations along the Altamaha had an inconspicuous land approach; a sandy trail through the woods led from the big road to a tree-bordered avenue, that familiar hallmark of the southern plantation. The houses were surrounded by acres of lawns and gardens and flowering woodlands reminiscent of the gardens and parks of country places in England.

The landed proprietors of South Carolina maintained their townhouses in Charleston and their country seats upon their river plantations; and so, accustomed as they were to the fashionable life of the Carolina city, the planters furnished their homes in the wilderness of Georgia with ancestral mahogany, fruitwood, and walnut; with hangings, ornaments, paintings, and libraries imported from the Old World. Into the new land they brought old traditions, old customs, plants and cuttings from old gardens, old recipes, old wines. They brought the distinctive speech of the Carolina low country, and its cadence still lingers on the Georgia coast.

Migrating with the seasons like their Indian predecessors, each family had at least two residences, some three or more. In addition to their St. Simons property most of the planters along the Altamaha had vacation places upon the "salts" near Brunswick, at the mineral springs of Wayne County, or in the Sand Hills resort near the village of Tebeauville (Tebōville), now included in the town of Waycross. The men made frequent trips to Charleston, New York, Philadelphia, and London, and they were often accompanied by the whole family with several servants in attendance. The plantation families entertained with the old-time hospitality, visiting back and forth by boat and by carriage. Banquet boards were lavishly spread, and wine cellars were stocked with the choicest products of the Old World and the New. The great chimneys of the detached kitchens had niches beside the fireplaces where casks of wine were mellowed; and many a keg of wine and brandy, aged by a year's voyage on a sailing vessel, was welcomed at the end of the twelvemonth with a celebration by the owner and his friends.

Following the English customs of the day the plantation families had their lawn fêtes and picnics, their musicales and quadrilles. They formed Shakespeare clubs where they wore improvised costumes and read plays aloud, each member taking a part. Just as their English forebears had enjoyed water parties on the Thames, so the people of the Georgia river plantations enjoyed boating parties upon the Altamaha, rowing and singing at night on the moonlit water. And by day there were expeditions for fishing, shrimping and crabbing, and for gathering the "Ogeechee limes" that hung in clusters from the branches of trees along the water's edge. Although legend has it that the "limes" had been brought into the coastal region by the Spaniards, they were in fact the fruit of a species of black-gum tree that grew beside the rivers. Preserved whole, the Geechee limes made a piquant accompaniment for the game that was so abundant in the woodlands.

An important part of the work of the river plantations was boat building. Since most of the travel and all transportation of crops and supplies were by water, each estate had a number of boats in the charge of the head boatman or stroke oarsman, who was one of the most powerful and intelligent of the hands. Besides the flatboats for hauling, there were sloops and longboats for family use. The longboats were cypress dugouts "tastily finished," manned by four, six, or more oarsmen and capable of carrying a number of passengers. The skilled crews considered themselves superior to the other workmen and there was keen rivalry between boats of the different plantations. Each crew had its own songs, and an arriving boat could be identified by the singing of the oarsmen.

Most of the coastal planters were enthusiastic boatmen, always ready to pit the skill of their crews against those of neighboring plantations. These races were often followed by a feast upon a flatboat tied at the dock, with the losing owner furnishing the accompanying wines. The outstanding social events of the year were the regattas to which hundreds of visitors came, not only from the Georgia coast, but from all up and down the eastern seaboard. From the vantage point of gaily decked pleasure boats they watched the races between dugout canoes entered from the various plantations, with cash prizes that sometimes ran into five figures. The racing dugouts, made from whole tree trunks thirty, forty, and even fifty feet long, were hollowed until their walls were scarcely more than an inch thick. Manned by their crews of slaves, stroked by the rhythm of the rowing chantey, with the master of the plantation in the coxswain's seat, these huge shells sped through the water with amazing speed, doing the mile in little more than six minutes. Following the races, neighboring plantations threw open their doors to the visitors, and there were celebrations both in the big house and in the quarters.

Since many of the children of the large plantations were taught at home until they were old enough to go away to school, it was the custom for a tutor to be engaged by several families within easy riding or boating distance of each other. The tutor lived with each family in turn, holding classes in the schoolhouse upon the plantation where he was staying. Although the girls and boys learned their three R's from their tutors, they were trained in the ways of young ladies and young gentlemen by the upper servants. The butlers were men of intelligence and personality, dignified, efficient, competent, trained to the perfection of English butlers. They and the indispensable South Carolina "maumas" had the responsibility and management of the other house servants, of domestic affairs, and in fact usually of the entire household. They were strict disciplinarians and their word was law with the younger generation. The coachmen had charge of the stables, and under their critical eyes both girls and boys learned to ride. The head boatmen taught the boys to row, to fish, and to swim; while the seamstresses and head cooks trained the young ladies in the domestic virtues.

Some of the plantations were in the charge of overseers, but most of them were under the supervision of the owners themselves with the assistance of their headmen or "drivers," highly trained blacks who were selected for their intelligence and ability for handling workmen. The plantation day started at six o'clock, and at nine there was an hour's break for breakfast. In the big house breakfast was set out in the dining room in the English manner or served in the bedrooms for any of the ladies or visitors who wished it. There was a light lunch at noon and the work day was over by three.

At four o'clock in the afternoon the main meal of the day was served. This was a formal seated dinner, and the candles were usually lighted before the last course was finished. Dinner was followed by an evening of conversation or entertainment. In most houses it was the custom to have a late supper set out informally in the dining room, the time varying with the season of the year. The plantation house was rarely without visitors, since people were continually "coming to stay," as on the country estates in England. After the English geologist Sir Charles Lyell visited the Georgia coast in 1846, he commented in his book *Second Visit to the United States* that there was a "warmth and generous openness of character in the southerners which mere wealth and a retinue of servants could not give."

Dinner-party invitations, delivered by hand, read "from four to ten," and most of the guests arrived by boat with portmanteaux containing formal attire to be donned after the long ride on the river. If the distance was great they stayed overnight, but for those who were going home, parties at plantations along the Altamaha sometimes had an atmosphere reminiscent of Cinderella's ball. Often at the height of the merrymaking the sound of the waiting oarsmens' conchs brought the guests dashing for their boats—not a warning at the approach of midnight, but at the approach of low water. For boats must be through General's Cut before ebb tide caught them in the shallow passage. There was a legend that the cut had been dug in a night by Oglethorpe's men, and many a crew caught there at low tide had reason to wish that the general had ordered it dug a few feet deeper.

At Christmas there was a week's holiday on the plantations.

No sleigh bells tinkled over snow, but a great Yule log blazed in the fireplace while doors and windows stood open in that charming custom that still prevails in parts of the rural South. Red-berried cassina and blue-berried cedar, glossy leaves of magnolia, and green fans of palmetto adorned the houses. Smilax festooned doorways and mantels and encircled silver punch bowls, while the traditional English plum pudding was decorated with holly from the plantation woodlands.

The out-kitchens were full of singing and laughter and appetizing smells of roasting turkey and duck and suckling pig, of baking fruitcakes, pies and puddings. The whole household must superintend the cutting of the great tree which would be loaded with gifts for the plantation hands, who would start coming at dawn with their shouts of "Christmas gift." The young men displayed their prowess with the rifle as they vied with each other in shooting down bunches of mistletoe. Competition was keen, for the best shot was accorded first kiss under the mistletoe at the Christmas ball.

The storybook life of the river plantations was brought to an end by the War Between the States. Fortunes disappeared during the four corrosive years of war, and the old way of life was no longer possible. Cotton prices were low, and the cultivation of rice was too complicated to be profitable with the postwar labor conditions. Helplessly, the planters saw the disintegration of the very fabric of their lives. Many of the owners, grandsons of the original planters, regretfully left their ancestral estates and went to the cities where they made connections with the shipping, lumber, and cotton businesses for which their experience had best fitted them. Some of those who returned to their homes and replanted their fields gradually gave up the struggle, and the cultivation of rice on the coastland was finally abandoned when the great tidal wave of 1898 broke through the dikes and destroyed the crops. The rice fields reverted to marshes which today abound with wild duck and marsh hens, and hunters are grateful for the old canals that make the marshlands accessible to their boats.

Butler Island

Butler Island, important in the history of the Old South, was the first of the early river plantations to revive cultivation of the marshlands in the twentieth century. One of the leading rice plantations of antebellum Georgia, the 1,500-acre island was originally developed by Major Pierce Butler of South Carolina. Irish-born Pierce Butler, third son of Sir Richard Butler, had come to the colonies when a young man in his twenties as an officer in the British Army. In the South Carolina newspapers of 1771 we find the announcement of the marriage of "Major Pierce Butler of His Majesty's 29th Regiment to Miss Mary (Polly) Middleton, daughter of the Thomas Middletons of Prince William Parish."

Two years later Major Butler gave up his military career, resigned his commission, and turned his interests to planting and politics. At the onset of the Revolutionary War he represented South Carolina in the Continental Congress, but it is said that he declined to sign the Declaration of Independence "on the grounds that he had come to America in the service of His Majesty George III." He did sign the Constitution, and was one of the first South Carolinians elected to the United States Senate, where he "flamed like a meteor." He is described variously as "something of a martinet . . . a man who thinks for himself . . . a wealthy, somewhat dictatorial aristocrat, most elegant in person and deportment, with the blood of the Irish earls in his veins." In old papers Senator Butler is reported dining with the president and enjoying Sheridan's *School for Scandal* from the presidential box in a New York theater. When President Washington visited the South, Pierce Butler helped to entertain him in Charleston and accompanied him from Charleston to Savannah.

When the Butlers were in South Carolina they spent part of their time on their Maryville Plantation and part in Charleston, where the major was on the vestry of St. Michaels Church. Their young daughters were taught at home while their son, Thomas, spent his school years in England. After nineteen years of marriage, Mary Middleton Butler died, and some of her husband's letters (now in the British Museum) reflect his grief and his anxiety for the well-being of his daughters and his "dear and tenderly loved son Thomas." Later, disapproval of Thomas's marriage caused estrangement between Pierce Butler and the son for whom he had felt such deep affection.

Major Butler was among the first of the South Carolina planters to become interested in the region south of the Altamaha, and it was largely through his influence that other South Carolinians bought property in Georgia. Butler's first purchases had been made in 1774, but no improvements were undertaken on his Georgia holdings until some years after the close of the Revolutionary War. Development of his Hampton sea-island-cotton plantation on St. Simons Island preceded that of the Butler Island rice plantation. Both plantations were conducted with military efficiency and both were enormously profitable and increased the already ample fortune of their owner.

In the early 1800s Pierce Butler made Philadelphia his permanent home; there he served for years as a director of the Bank of the United States. But as long as he was physically able he continued to spend part of each year in Georgia where managers were in charge of the plantations.

Major Butler died in 1822 and is buried in the churchyard of Philadelphia's Christ Church. His "planting interests in Georgia" were left by will to be held in trust for his young grandsons, Pierce, John, and Thomas Mease, provided they adopt the surname Butler. Thomas Mease died in boyhood; John declined to change his name. The surname Butler was readily adopted by the major's namesake, 15-year-old Pierce, who was deeply attached to his grandfather. Consequently the Georgia plantations were inherited by young Pierce Butler, who later deeded half of the property to his brother, John, upon his adoption of the surname Butler.

In 1834 Pierce Butler II was married to the English actress Frances Anne (Fanny) Kemble, daughter of the Shakespearean actor Charles Kemble and niece of the "immortal" Mrs. Siddons. Fanny, scarcely out of her teens, had made her brilliant debut in Covent Garden in the role of Juliet, and was the toast of London society when she met young Pierce Butler during an American tour. He was handsome, aristocratic, wealthy, and he and the irresistible Fanny Kemble were married when she was in her early twenties and at the height of her popularity.

When Pierce Butler and his bride settled in Philadelphia the young actress was hospitably received, but she amused herself and offended her husband's friends by writing and publishing frank and witty criticisms of her hosts and hostesses. The best Philadelphia's social and cultural circles could offer appeared crude and amusing to brilliant, spoiled, impetuous Fanny Kemble Butler.

It was the custom for Pierce Butler or his brother to make annual visits to Georgia in connection with the management of their plantations, and in December 1838 Mrs. Butler went south with her husband. Accompanied by their daughters, Sally age three and Frances less than a year, and an English nursemaid, the Butlers spent the winter months on the rice island.

If Fanny Kemble Butler had been unhappy and dissatisfied with her life in Philadelphia, she found life in the South even less to her liking. The pampered and fashionable young woman who had been educated in Paris, who had lived in the world of Mendelssohn, Liszt, and Browning, in whose home Tennyson, Thackeray, and Edward Fitzgerald had been frequent visitors, was profoundly bored by the rural society of the Georgia coast. There was no large plantation house on Butler Island, and, uncomfortably domiciled in the overseer's cottage, Fanny was depressed by the low-lying rice fields. The young Englishwoman hated the idea of slavery, and she encouraged the Negroes to bring their complaints to her. It was here on Butler Island that Fanny Kemble Butler started writing her *Journal of a Residence on a Georgian Plantation*.

In spite of her dissatisfaction with life in general, the sensitive, temperamental Fanny with her inherent love of nature was captivated by the wild beauty of the coastland. After pages of com-

Frances Anne Kemble

plaint and despair over her situation, the mercurial writer would burst into a lyrical description of the exquisite evergreens, myrtles, magnolias, and gardenias. The island was further beautified by a double row of fragrant orange trees that grew for miles around the levee which protected the fields from the river. Unable to enjoy her favorite exercise of horseback riding in the restrictions of the rice island, Fanny learned to row, and had her own "darling little canoe which rejoiced in the name of the *Dolphin*" in which she spent many an hour on the river under the "unspeakable glory of the Southern heavens."

Throughout the whole time that the Butlers stayed in the South, Fanny had such passionate quarrels with her husband and the overseers about the management of the plantations and handling of the slaves that she even "suspected herself to be an intolerable nuisance." The marriage of the Pierce Butlers was stormy and short-lived, but although she never returned to Georgia the young Englishwoman was to have a permanent and devastating influence upon the destiny of the region. Her *Journal*, published years later at the beginning of the War Between the States, is believed by some historians to have swayed public opinion in England and in America against the South.

During the war Butler Island was deserted except for some of the slaves who remained in their homes. Although Pierce Butler was a native of Philadelphia, he loved the family plantations and had many friends on the Georgia coast. Personally and financially interested, his sympathies lay with the South, but he was powerless to do anything in the interest of the people and property in Georgia until after the war. In 1866 he and his daughter Frances, then a young woman in her twenties, who shared her father's interest in the southern property, came to Butler Island to attempt the formidable task of restoring the rice plantation to a profitable basis.

Like her famous mother before her, Frances Butler kept a diary, or journal, and we are indebted to the Frances Butlers, mother and daughter, for many of the descriptions that help to reconstruct the life of coastal Georgia before and after the war. Although the daughter's journal did not contain the exquisite word pictures nor the barbed wit of the gifted Fanny's, it showed her to have the commonsense, understanding, and sense of humor necessary for the almost insurmountable problems connected with the attempt to rehabilitate the plantations.

The Butlers were gratified to find many of their former slaves

still living on the island, and to discover that they had guarded
and cared for the stock so well that they had a large flock of
sheep and a fine herd of cows. They were touched when Uncle
John and Maum' Peggy made the boat trip up from St. Simons to
bring a sack containing ten silver half-dollars that a Yankee captain had paid for some chickens the first year of the war. The old
overseer's cottage on Butler Island was empty, but most of the
furniture had been carried inland for safe keeping, and was soon
back in place. With the help of her German maid, Frances Butler
made the rooms attractive with fresh covers and white muslin
curtains. The orange trees were in bloom, and the acre of fenced
ground around the cottage was beautiful with roses, with orange, fig, and peach trees, and a "superb magnolia."

That year the rice fields of Butler Island produced the best
crop that was made in the region, but Pierce Butler did not live
to enjoy his hard won triumph. He died suddenly in August
1867. After her father's death Frances Butler carried on his work
of reclaiming the Georgia property. In the years of reconstruction, labor problems became increasingly difficult, but the owners of Butler Island were able to afford to hire Irish laborers from
the North to come down each year for the necessary work of
banking and ditching the rice fields.

For four years Pierce Butler's daughter, and her German maid,
managed the plantation alone. She usually spent the hottest part
of the summer in Philadelphia or in England, but the rest of the
year she made her home in Georgia, where she had a pleasant
life visiting back and forth with old friends of her family, some
of whom were attempting to restore neighboring property, while
others lived in nearby Savannah or in South Carolina. Friends
from the North and from England came to visit and were entertained as in the old days by hunting, fishing, and rowing.

In the summer of 1871, while she was in England, Frances
Butler was married to the Reverend Mr. James W. Leigh, the second son of Lord Leigh. Young James Leigh, who had visited the
Georgia plantations on trips to the States, was deeply interested
in the South and its problems, and some of his letters make valu-

able additions to his wife's journal. When the couple came to America they brought English laborers and established them upon Butler Island. A small neighboring river island that was part of the plantation had been rented to a planter who was experimenting with Chinese labor, and James Leigh commented humorously that their property "now represented Europe, Asia, Africa, and America."

Like the early Georgia colonists, the owners of Butler Island found that British laborers were not fitted for the work of the coastlands, and the imported workmen were returned to England. In spite of the large sums of money and the decade of heartbreaking effort that had been invested in the Butler property, the plantation was never restored to its former prosperity. After the winter of 1876 the Leighs placed Butler Island in the hands of a manager and went to England to live. A hurricane in 1878 left the rice crop a total loss, and it was finally decided that the plantation could not be operated profitably.

Left untenanted for many years the island was purchased in the 1920s by Colonel Tillinghast L'Hommedieu Huston, part owner of the New York Yankees in the days when Babe Ruth was making baseball history. Colonel Huston and his family built a comfortable two-storied white clapboard house upon the site of the overseer's cottage where Fanny Kemble Butler had been so unhappy. In reclaiming the island plantation Colonel Huston first developed it into a dairy farm with a few experimental acres planted in citrus fruits and vegetables; and, later, experiments were begun in raising iceberg lettuce. Major Butler's old tidewater system was found to be useful for irrigating the fields, and the experiments proved so successful that lettuce was established as the main product of the plantation. Modern improvements were made in the irrigation and drainage system, but many of the original dikes and canals of the old rice fields were put back into use. The water was controlled by sluice-gates that could be opened at high tide to flood the fields or to water them by an overhead sprinkler system; as the tide ebbed the fields were automatically drained.

After Colonel Huston's death the plantation was operated by his estate until it was sold in 1949 to Richard J. Reynolds. Further improvements were made, and additional acreage planted, and the cultivation and shipping of lettuce grew into a thriving industry. The island that played its dramatic part in the history of the Old South became a part of the history being made by the farmers of the New South. Once again spring was a busy time for old Butler Island Plantation; lettuce was harvested from March to May, the same time that the seed rice was clayed and planted in the early days. The plantation lay on either side of the highway just below Darien; and the grounds of the plantation house, behind their graceful clumps of bamboo, had the appearance of a sunken garden lying below the levee that protects the island—the old embankment where the orange trees once grew. A remnant of the old brick kiln and the vine-covered ruin of the chimney of an old rice mill are landmarks of the days of the famous Butler rice plantation.

In 1954 the historic island, together with neighboring small islands and marshlands, became the property of the State of Georgia and is today part of the Altamaha Wildfowl Area.

Altama

Altama's story is the story of the great Hopeton Plantation. For Altama land was once Hopeton land, and the Altama house was built by James Hamilton Couper, who was for forty years master of Hopeton. Hopeton-on-the-Altamaha was a model plantation and experimental farm of the nineteenth century, a center of interest for farmers and scientific agriculturists from all parts of the United States and for visitors from other countries as well. In the opinion of the editor of the *Southern Agriculturist*, Hopeton was decidedly the best plantation he had ever visited and he "doubted whether it could be equalled in the Southern states."

Although cultivation was begun upon the property before 1800 no residence was built at Hopeton for many years after the land was cleared. Part of the great Couper-Hamilton interests, it included a tract recorded on a South Carolina grant dated April 1763 to "William Hopeton Esq. 2000 acres situated on So. side of River Alatamaha," additional mainland acreage, and the river island known as Carrs. The owners of Hopeton, John Couper and James Hamilton, two of the most prominent of the early coastal planters, both made their homes upon their cotton plantations on neighboring St. Simons Island; and it was after John Couper's eldest son, James Hamilton Couper, became master of the river plantation that the house of Hopeton was built.

From earliest childhood it was obvious that James Hamilton Couper was a boy of unusual ability and outstanding intelligence. He was sent to New England to school at the age of eight, and, fulfilling all the hopes and ambitions of father and god-father, was graduated with honors from Yale in 1814 when scarcely out of his teens. After he had worked for a year or two under the guidance of the two older men, profiting by their wisdom and experience, young James was given complete charge of Hopeton Plantation in 1816.

The most methodical and systematic of men, James Hamilton Couper kept daily records of every detail connected with the management of the plantation; and some of his ledgers are treasured in historical libraries today, valuable sources of research for students of nineteenth-century plantation economy. The books are not only examples of James Couper's admirable system of accounting, but are works of art, their pages of copper-plate script illustrated with pen-and-ink sketches tinted in pastels and watercolor, buffs and pinks, greens, sepias, and blues for the fields of cotton, rice, cane, corn, and vegetables.

His journal of 1818, which may be the first complete yearly record after he assumed management of Hopeton, has on the title page "Notes on Agricultural and Rural Economy," followed by a quotation from Cicero which gives an insight into Couper's philosophy of life: "Omnium autem rerum, ex quibus aliquid acquiritur, nihil est Agricultura melius, nihil uberius, nihil dulcius, nihil homine libero dignius." Used often in his writing and in speeches before the agricultural societies, this favorite quotation of young Couper was often simplified for the benefit of those less erudite than he: "There is nothing superior, nothing more fruitful, nothing more worthy of a liberal mind than the pursuits of agriculture."

In 1825 James Couper spent several months traveling in the British Isles and in Europe with special interest in Holland, where he made a study of water control. Later this knowledge was put to practical use in an improved diking and drainage system in the Hopeton rice fields. As the cultivation of sugarcane became increasingly profitable, a sugar mill, boilers, and a steam engine were imported from England, and one of the most complete sugar works in the country was erected at Hopeton.

Soon after his return from Europe young Couper bought his father's share in the plantation, and after his godfather's death he managed the Hamilton interests for the heirs. In 1827 he was married to sixteen-year-old Caroline Wylly, daughter of the Alexander Wyllys of St. Simons Island. Now that there was a mistress as well as a master of Hopeton, a plantation house was necessary. The young couple lived in one of the estate cottages, "a mere pigeon-hole," until a huge old tabby sugar house was remodeled into a fine three-storied mansion designed by James Couper himself, who was an amateur architect of unusual ability. The house of Hopeton stood on rising ground near the bank of the broad canal that ran into the Altamaha a quarter mile away; the grounds were beautifully landscaped and planted with every flower and shrub indigenous to the region. The house was furnished with family heirlooms and imported pieces, and with paintings and steel engravings collected in Europe. The library shelves held a superlative collection of books, considered one of the most carefully and brilliantly chosen private libraries in the country.

In the nineteenth century many prominent European scientists and writers made extensive tours of the United States and published accounts of their travels. Since Hopeton Plantation was one of the important places and James Hamilton Couper one of the best known men of the New World, a number of these European travelers made the difficult journey to the Georgia coastland to visit in the Couper home. They traveled by boat to Savannah, then by boat or stagecoach to Darien, where they were met by a longboat from the plantation. Then would come an eight-mile row up the river with the singing of the boatmen echoing from the evergreen forests on either side, singing which one of the visitors, Captain Basil Hall, thought "not unlike that of Canadian *voyageurs*, but more nearly like that of the Bunderboatmen of Bombay." Guests were enchanted upon their arrival at Hopeton as the boat turned into the canal between the rice fields and they saw the house standing in the midst of its flowering gardens and woodlands like an English country place on the Thames.

We have a charming picture of the Couper family from the pen of another visitor, Frederika Bremer, the nineteenth-century Swedish novelist, author of half a score of books. Described by Hawthorne as "a little fairy person, worthy of being the maiden aunt of the whole universe," Miss Bremer found the Couper household delightful. In her *Homes of the New World and Impressions of America* published in Stockholm, she said it was a "home full of gay youthful countenances, six boys and two girls, the youngest the image and delight of her father. Mrs. C. is the youthful, pretty, and happy mother of this handsome flock of children, and Mr. C. reminds me of Waldo Emerson in urbanity and grace of conversation."

An extraordinary man, James Hamilton Couper has been described as "a pioneer in the agricultural and industrial development of Georgia and the South; one of the greatest men Georgia ever produced; and one of the leading private citizens of America, possessing as much knowledge as an encyclopedia." His interests and talents "embraced the universe." As an able microscopist in the days when microscopes were rare even in universities and medical schools, Couper made valuable contributions to the world of science. He was a recognized geologist, archaeologist, and conchologist, and his ability as an architect was demonstrated in Savannah's beautiful Christ Church which he designed. He was keenly interested in the history of the state, and his assistance to George White in the writing of his *Historical Collections of Georgia* and to William B. Stevens in his *History of Georgia* was gratefully acknowledged by the authors.

Through his interest in geology Couper became acquainted with Sir Charles Lyell, and when the renowned geologist visited the United States he and his wife were invited to stay with the Coupers. In the account of his travels published in London in 1849, Sir Charles wrote at length of the visit to Hopeton, where he made a "geological examination of the southern and maritime part of Georgia near the mouth of the Altamaha."

Visitors at Hopeton were always impressed with two of the Coupers' servants whose fame still endures along the coast. They were the legendary Abraham-Fire-All, culinary disciple of Cupidon of "Chocolate," and African Tom, headman of the plantation. In an article, now in possession of the Georgia Historical Society, Couper described Tom as a Foulah from Kianah in the Kingdom of Massina, who had been captured when he was a young boy and sold into slavery in the Bahamas. His African name was Sali-bul-Ali, and he was a strict Mohammedan; he read Arabic and had a Koran in that language, but did not write it. Like his friend Bul-ali of Sapelo, he was a man of industry, honesty, and intelligence, and in his master's opinion was capable of conducting the entire plantation without an overseer.

In addition to his business and scientific interests Couper found time to indulge his hobby of boat racing. He designed his own racing dugouts and superintended their construction; he trained his crew of eight oarsmen himself and, as he often said, "a finer one never rowed." His *Becky Sharp*, *Walk-Away*, and *Sunny South* were usually found at the regattas along the coast, more often than not in the lead, with the master of Hopeton seated behind his crew as they timed their stroke to their favorite "Slippers, Shoes, and White Stockings."

After James Hamilton Couper had managed Hopeton for forty years he drew plans for a smaller house where he and his wife could retire from the heavy responsibilities of the large plantation. The site selected for their new home was a wooded slope within two miles of the river for which the place was named—Altama, the name used by Goldsmith for the Altamaha.

A two-storied tabby house surrounded by fenced lawns and gardens, Altama was completed in 1857. As a farewell to Hopeton, the Coupers entertained with a houseparty for more than a dozen guests, three from England, others from Savannah and neighboring island and mainland plantations. After the festive week was over, the great house of Hopeton was closed and the plantation was placed in charge of Couper's younger brother, William.

With more leisure to devote to his own affairs, James Hamilton Couper spent much of his time on research and experiment and on the extensive correspondence that he carried on with experts in the various fields of science in which he was interested. He also took an active part in promoting education in the southern states, and especially in founding the University of the South at Sewanee, Tennessee. He was one of the trustees of the university and was on the committee that prepared its constitution in 1858.

James Hamilton Couper was bitterly opposed to secession, but when war came all of his sons went into service; the two oldest were killed, the youngest taken prisoner. His fortune gone, his heart and health broken, the master of Altama suffered a paralytic stroke from which he never recovered. After his death in 1866 the fields of Hopeton and Altama were never successfully cultivated again. The Hopeton house was empty and falling into decay, but in the years following the war one of the sons, James Maxwell Couper, spent some time at Altama and made every effort to restore the old way of life. While Frances Butler Leigh and her husband were living at neighboring Butler Island the two plantations had some of the old-time boat races and festivities; but, like the Leighs, the Coupers realized that the property could not be operated profitably, and they eventually left the coast and made their home in Atlanta. Many of the fine pieces of furniture, the books and paintings, that had graced both Hopeton and Altama and some of the high bookcases that had been built by slaves for the old Hopeton house were taken to Atlanta and placed in the Coupers' residence there. The coastal property passed into the hands of the Hamilton heirs, and in the following years the house of Hopeton burned.

In 1898 the entire Hopeton-Altama property was bought by a Shaker colony from Union Village, Ohio. The Shakers, or "shaking Quakers," who had prospered so greatly in their agricultural colonies in Ohio, considered the coastal region ideal for farming and stock raising. Newspapers of the day reported that they had bought several large tracts in the vicinity, intending eventually to move all the Shaker communities to Georgia.

The Altama house was the home of some eighteen or twenty of the "brothers and sisters," but since part of their creed was to live separate from the world, outsiders caught only occasional glimpses of the men in their somber garments with their hair cut in bangs across their foreheads and of the women in their sedate dress with modest bonnets and neckerchiefs. They imported purebred cattle, repaired plantation buildings and sold the machinery from James Hamilton Couper's sugar mill which was falling into ruins. They reclaimed the rice fields and in 1899 harvested a $10,000 crop of rice. No new converts to Shakerism were made, and in 1902 the colony sold their Georgia property and went back to Ohio.

Owned next by John Crow, then Frank Caldwell, both of Ohio, Hopeton-Altama became the property in 1914 of William duPont of Wilmington, Delaware, who gave the entire place the name Altama. Extensive improvements were made, including the addition of a third story to the old Couper house. Until Mr. duPont's death in 1928 he and his family enjoyed the plantation as a winter home and private game preserve.

In 1933, when the property was bought by Cator Woolford of Atlanta, the grounds were landscaped and the Play House and swimming pool were built. In 1940 Mr. Woolford was host to a houseparty of descendants of James Hamilton Couper, and grandchildren, great-grandchildren and great-great-grandchildren came from far and near. Mr. Woolford died in 1944, and in 1945 the Altama property was acquired by Alfred W. Jones of Sea Island.

The house built by James Hamilton Couper in 1857 had gone through many changes, the most extensive being the third story added by Mr. duPont in 1914. In the mid-1950s it became apparent that all of the heating, plumbing, and wiring would have to be replaced along with other major repairs. Since the place was not being used as a home, it was reluctantly decided in 1959 to raze the old house and at the same time to build a small addition to the Play House as a weekend retreat.

Altama is now owned jointly by the second generation of the Alfred W. Jones family. In 1976 the plantation was deeded to Marianna Jones Kuntz, A. W. Jones, Jr., Katharine Jones O'Connor, and Howard Coffin Jones.

Altama consists of 70 acres in the home site, 1,000 acres of river swamp, 1,000 acres of abandoned rice fields, and 4,000 acres of high land largely planted in pines to carry out a forestry program begun in the late 1950s.

The ruins of James Hamilton Couper's sugar mill still stand; traces can be seen of irrigation ditches and sluice-gates in the former rice fields; and the old canal banks make convenient roads. A few gardenias from the Hopeton gardens still bloom in the undergrowth.

Elizafield

Elizafield Plantation, just below Hopeton, was on a tract of land whose romantic history reaches far back into the mists of the past. Some students of Indian lore say that it was the site of the ancient Creek village of Talaxe; and some historians believe that it was the location of the mission-presidio of Santo Domingo established in 1604. A large octagon-shaped tabby ruin still standing has been an object of interest for years. Pieces of nineteenth-century machinery found among the ruins are proof that the building was used as a mill for threshing rice or grinding cane when the plantation of Elizafield was situated here two centuries after the founding of Santo Domingo. But although examination by experts produced no evidence that it was of Spanish origin there are those who still believe that the mill was built on the ruins of the mission of long ago.

Cleared in the early 1800s by Dr. Robert Grant, wealthy planter-physician from South Carolina, the land called Elizafield was destined, during more than half a century, to see his children, his grandchildren, and his great-grandchildren. A native of Leigh, Scotland, young Robert Grant, when scarcely out of his teens, had come to Carolina, where he became a prominent surgeon as well as a prosperous rice planter. He and his wife, the former Sarah Foxworth, lived at Waterfield Plantation near Sand Pitt, South Carolina, before they came to the Georgia coastland to make their home. Their extensive property along the Altamaha was divided into three parts—Grantly, Evelyn, and Elizafield. For years Grantly and Evelyn were merely vast acres of rice fields with their ditches, banks, and canals; and of cotton and cane fields, with their settlements for the hands. Elizafield, named for Dr. Grant's mother in Scotland, was the home plantation of the family. And upon the island of St. Simons the Grants had a summer place called Oatlands, where they spent the hot months when the "fever" lurked in the rice fields.

In 1811 Oatlands was the birthplace of the son who was to become master of Elizafield. Named for his father's close friend, Dr. Hugh Fraser of South Carolina, Hugh Fraser Grant grew up to love the river plantations and to become one of the leading rice planters of the Georgia coast. And what a satisfaction it must have been to Dr. Grant and his old friend when young Hugh married Dr. Fraser's daughter, Mary.

In 1833 Dr. and Mrs. Grant retired to their St. Simons place, and the river plantations were divided between their sons, Charles and Hugh. Evelyn became the property of Charles while, for a quarter-century, Elizafield was the home of Hugh and Mary Fraser Grant and their family.

The original house was destroyed by fire, but young Grant rebuilt at once on the same foundations. Set back at some distance from the river on the bank of a deep canal, the Elizafield house was designed in the typical southern colonial manner with a double flight of buttressed steps leading to an open portico with great square columns two stories high. In the spacious rooms there were Brussels carpets and crystal chandeliers, imported silver and china, and hangings of brocade and damask.

Approached by the traditional tree-bordered avenue, the house was surrounded by fenced lawns and gardens. There was a grape arbor and an orange grove, and an orchard famous for its nectarines and peaches. To one side stood the children's schoolhouse, a replica of the big house, with miniature columns and portico. At the rear were the quarters for the house servants. Here lived Maum' Rebecca, Mrs. Grant's personal maid and head seamstress for the family. Here, too, lived the coachman, Frederick Proudfoot, and his wife, Maum' Ann, the children's nurse; and Sukey, cook superlative, and her assistant, Martha, whose preserves and jellies reached an enviable point of perfection. And here lived Caesar, that important member of the household, butler and major-domo of Elizafield—Caesar, whose manner achieved that perfect balance between deference and dictatorship, that unshakable poise and dignity which characterized the well-trained plantation butler.

The Grants and their six children, five daughters and one son, spent the summer months at their place, the Parsonage, on the "salts" near Brunswick, and at their Sand Hills cottage near Tebeauville, with frequent visits to Grandma and Grandpa Grant on St. Simons Island. Dr. Robert Grant died at the age of eighty-one "revered and beloved by his family, respected and esteemed by all who knew him"; and Grandma Grant came to Elizafield, where she spent the remaining five years of her life. In a quiet wing of the house she had her own rooms where the children loved to visit; and the younger ones liked to ride with her in the phaeton as the gentle old horse jogged along the shady winding roads of the plantation. She was indeed a favorite with the children for sometimes she allowed them to hold the reins, and besides Grandma always carried peppermints in her reticule.

As the older daughters grew up there were trips to New York and to Europe; there were houseparties at Elizafield and visiting back and forth with the young people at Hopeton and Altama on the one side and at Broadfield and Hofwyl on the other, with friends in Darien and Savannah and on the island plantations. On fine afternoons the young ladies and their visitors were content to play a quiet game of lawn croquet or, in hoopskirts and ruffles and carrying parasols, to promenade along the wide banks of the canal. But in the evenings there were gatherings for music and dancing; and among visiting boats at the Elizafield landing there was usually one from Retreat Plantation on St. Simons—the boat of young Mallery King, who had his own pet name, "Jenty," for pretty Eugenia (Jinny) Grant.

As the 1860s drew near and life on the plantations began to lose its lightheartedness, parties and dances gave way to serious and troubled gatherings. Although Hugh Fraser Grant's health had begun to fail he was enrolled in the Glynn County Reserve, and when war did come and young Hugh Fraser, Jr., left to join the army, much of the responsibility for the safety of the household fell into the hands of Caesar, the butler. When the approach of gunboats down the coast made it no longer wise for the family to remain at Elizafield, Caesar was a "tower of strength." Under his supervision boxes and barrels of china, glass, and silverware were carefully packed in rice straw and Spanish moss and buried in the garden. Clothes and a few personal belongings and household necessities were packed. Trunks and boxes, coops of poultry, and provisions from the smokehouse were loaded on wagons. Then Caesar shepherded family and house-servants into carriages and carry-alls, and the cavalcade set out on the long journey to Tebeauville, where they and many of their friends found sanctuary during the war years.

News of the men in the army came from time to time. Young

Captain Mallery King had Jinny's promise to wait until his return, and he wrote hopefully of an expected leave. When word
came that he was at Kennesaw Mountain near Atlanta and that
he would be able to come to Tebeauville long enough for a wedding, there were hurried preparations. Firm in the traditions of
the Grants, Caesar hitched up a wagon and set out on the long
drive to Elizafield to dig up the china that was always used at
family festivities. The clouds of war were pushed back for awhile
as old friends gathered to celebrate the wedding and to drink the
young couple's health and happiness with the toast that is still
remembered in the family—"A Grant to a King." And refresh-
ments were served on the flower-wreathed English china that has
been used at the wedding receptions of daughters of the family
from that day to this—the china that Caesar dug up from the
garden at Elizafield in 1862.

Finally the war was over, but the Grants never returned to
Elizafield. The family went to Savannah to live, and management
of the plantations was put in charge of an overseer. For a few
years Mallery and Jinny stayed at the old home place, and their
children were the fourth generation to live on the Grant plantation; but when the Kings moved to St. Simons Island, the
Elizafield house was left unoccupied. The plantations were proving unprofitable and soon the fields of Elizafield, Evelyn, and
Grantly were no longer cultivated. The sluice-gates fell into dis-
repair; the tides overflowed the ditches and canals; the marshes
reclaimed the rice fields. Marsh grass covered the lowlands and
dense undergrowth covered the lawns and crowded out the gardens and orchards. The plantation buildings fell into ruins. The
big empty house went up in flames, and finally as the years
passed, nothing remained of Elizafield but a few tabby foundations and ruins and myriad beautiful memories. In the twentieth
century, descendants of Hugh Fraser Grant arranged for the remains and markers of Dr. and Mrs. Grant to be removed from
the family burial ground at Elizafield to the churchyard at Christ
Church, Frederica.

But the saga of the land was not yet at an end. In the 1930s

Cator Woolford presented 350 wooded acres of the old Eliza-field plantation to the State of Georgia to be designated Santo Domingo State Park. A decade later the historic property was made available by the legislature for the establishment of Boys Estate, Georgia's town just for boys.

A dream-come-true for a group of Glynn County business and civic leaders, Boys Estate was founded in 1945 with a board of trustees composed of prominent Georgia citizens. Under the guidance of J. Ardell Nation, the boys set up their city government and did a superb job of running their community. Like Boys Town in Nebraska, the estate elected its own city officials and had its own chamber of commerce. Each boy did his share of the work, and they lived together in groups with housemothers in charge of the cottages. With a deep understanding of boys, the men responsible for Boys Estate knew that many a youngster would prefer insecurity for himself rather than be parted from his dog. So an integral part of the town was Dogs Estate, where Rags could share the life of his young master. Other animal companions enjoyed the hospitality of the youthful town; friendly donkeys helped with the chores, and a sorrel horse drew the surrey-with-the-fringe-on-top that was provided to show visitors over the estate. Boys Estate entered a new phase in 1976 when admission was opened to girls, and the name was changed to Youth Estate.

Hofwyl

Hofwyl Plantation, on the same side of the river as Hopeton and Elizafield, was owned and cultivated by five generations of the family who cleared the land. In 1802 the William Brailsfords came from South Carolina to Georgia. He was born and educated in England; she was the former Maria Heyward of the great rice planting "dynasty" of Carolina. They bought Broughton, the Laurens' rice island in the south branch of the Altamaha, and the nearby river plantation New Hope on the mainland. No sooner had they repaired the buildings and settled their fieldhands upon the island than Broughton was devastated, with great loss of life and property in the hurricane of 1804. After this tragic misfortune the Brailsfords determined to give up their island plantation and to make their home on the mainland.

Across from Broughton and adjoining New Hope was an uncleared tract of land called Broadface upon surveyors' maps. This property was still owned by the state, and the Brailsfords bought it to add to their mainland plantation. Workmen and implements were carried across from Broughton to "Holla Over," the landing place on the mainland. Trees were felled for the corduroy road which was laid from river to house site. Sturdy tabby foundations were made of shell and sand from the river bank mixed with the water that flowed from newly dug wells. The high-spirited Brailsfords declared that the place must have a new name; Broadface would never do for a family with wide faces such as theirs! So the land known as Broadface was rechristened Broadfield.

The plantations of their friend Major Butler had escaped the full force of the hurricane, and the hospitality of his St. Simons place was extended to the Brailsfords until their Broadfield house was built. Finally it was completed, and William and Maria Brailsford and their six children moved into their new home on the Altamaha—a wide-spreading two-storied house with great chimneys at either end, hand-hewn timbers above, tabby walls below. A carriage drive led through the center of the first story to a courtyard in the rear. Giant trees surrounded the grounds, and wide stretches of rice fields lay between house and river—fields that produced such a fine quality of grain that, according to government record, the superior "Broadfield Rice" on the Charleston market took its name from the Brailsford plantation.

A decade and a half after they had moved into their Broadfield home, the Brailsfords' daughter Camilla was married to Dr. James McGillivray Troup of Darien. Then in 1824 hurricane winds once more roared in from the Atlantic and this time destroyed the Troups' house in Darien. Once again a member of the Brailsford clan had to build anew; this was the beautiful house that William Jay designed, and the first child born in the Troups' new home was their daughter Ophelia in 1827. Here and in their summer place at Baisdens Bluff six of James and Camilla Troup's eleven children grew up, two sons and four daughters.

As the years went by Camilla Brailsford Troup fell heir to Broadfield, and when her daughter Ophelia was married her dowry was the lower half of the property. Ophelia's husband, George Dent, was the son of Commodore Dent, retired commander of the *U.S.S. Nautilus*, a Carolinian who owned land in McIntosh County. George had been educated in Switzerland, and sentiment for his boyhood school led the young couple to give its name, Hofwyl, to their plantation. The remainder of the river property was divided among the other Troup children, and another generation cultivated the lands of William and Maria Brailsford.

During the War Between the States George Dent and his fifteen-year-old son James went into the army along with other men of the coastland while the remaining members of the family joined the refugee colony at Tebeauville. The year 1865 saw husbands and sons plodding homeward, and women and children returning to the deserted plantations. The houses that still stood were rifled and despoiled, fields laid waste, fences down, cattle strayed, horses gone. Even the courage and high spirits of the Brailsford descendants faltered under the shattering blows of war and reconstruction. The men of the family thought it might be wise to follow the example of other planters and go into industry rather than fight the desperate battle of recovery, than try to wrest a living from their devastated lands.

But Matilda, eldest of the Troup daughters, felt a fierce protective love for the river plantations of her grandparents. Faced with the almost insurmountable task of restoring order out of the chaos wrought by war, Matilda took everything into her inexperienced hands. Most of the buildings were uninhabitable; so she settled herself in one of the cabins on the Broadfield Plantation and supervised the planting and harvesting, the repairing of sluice-gates, the clearing of ditches and canals. And gradually family, servants, and land responded to the indomitable courage of Matilda. As the seasons came and went, again came planting, flooding, and harvesting of rice in the marshlands; planting, chopping, picking cotton on the highlands. The plantation began to recover some of its former life. Buildings were repaired. Tables were again bountifully set. The original plantation house had burned, but the renovated overseer's house made a comfortable home for the Dent family.

Young James Troup Dent shared his aunt's deep love and understanding of the land, and when he in turn became master of Hofwyl, the plantation was once more a pleasant and comfortable home for the Brailsfords' descendants. With changing times the production of rice was proving unprofitable; so the old rice fields were abandoned and more land was cleared and planted in cane, cotton, corn, and grain.

James Troup Dent had pondered long on the problem of malaria which so sorely beset the coastal people. He did not agree with the idea that a miasma from the marshes caused the chills and fever that drove the owners from their plantations each summer. After years of observation and study, the master of Hofwyl agreed with the new idea that the swarms of mosquitoes which plagued the lowlands during the hot months were bearers of the dread malaria. He had such confidence in this theory that, in the summer of 1903, he determined to put it to the test of practical experiment. Instead of moving to their summer place, Carteret, on the salts near Brunswick, the Dents made preparations to spend the summer at Hofwyl. Every window and door of the plantation house was carefully screened, and every possible precaution was taken against mosquitoes. And in spite of the misgivings of their friends the family spent a healthful summer at home.

Convinced at last, others began to realize the importance of protecting their houses against the malarial mosquito, and the necessity of taking steps for its extermination; and succeeding summers saw more and more families staying safely at home. Many of the coastal people today think of Hofwyl Plantation as the pioneer of its region in the successful fight against malaria.

The plantation was inherited by Gratz, Miriam, and Ophelia Dent, the children of James Troup Dent and the fifth generation of the family of William and Maria Brailsford. During the depression in the 1930s, when large property owners were "land poor," Hofwyl was operated as a dairy with a herd of purebred Guernsey and Jersey milch cows grazing in the lush pastures of the old plantation. In the following years, as coastal property was again in demand, Hofwyl's valuable acres were once more an asset to her owners.

Over the years, as Hofwyl passed from one generation to the next, the ties between the land and its people seemed to grow ever stronger. Giving in abundance in return for the work and the love of its owners, the old river plantation came to have a personality of its own, to have a sort of serenity and confidence, a sense of protectiveness toward the people who lived upon it.

The giant live oaks that watched the generations come and go always had their special place in the affections of Hofwyl's owners. When storm, that ancient enemy of the coast, roared in from the sea and the great boughs creaked and groaned and sometimes crashed to the ground, there was grief as for a stricken friend. But the old plantation lived through tempests and war, through good times and bad. Old trees fell, but young trees grew sturdy and tall; the harvest was gathered, but the fields grew green again.

In the last quarter of the twentieth century, historic Hofwyl Plantation entered a new era. Ophelia Dent was the last of the Brailsford descendants to live at Hofwyl. At her death in 1973 the 1,268-acre antebellum plantation was left by will to the State of Georgia, the property to be used for "scientific, historical, educational and aesthetic purposes." Miss Dent also left a trust fund, the interest to go toward maintaining Hofwyl "for public enjoyment."

In June 1979 Hofwyl-Broadfield Plantation was opened to the

public. Under the administration of the Recreation and Historic Sites Division of the Georgia Department of Natural Resources, the visitation program includes interpretive exhibits of plantation life as shown by slides, paintings and old photographs; with occasional special programs demonstrating such old-time tasks as dipping candles and weaving baskets of broomstraw and palmetto.

A tour of the grounds, left in their natural state, offers visitors the opportunity of observing the vegetation and animal life of the marshes that were once acres of rice fields. The plantation house has been left just as it was in Miss Dent's lifetime, with furnishings collected by five generations of her family. Of special interest is a picture of Ophelia Dent's maternal great-aunt, Rebecca Gratz, who was the inspiration for Sir Walter Scott's "Rebecca" of *Ivanhoe.*

As related in the book, *Rebecca Gratz,* by Rollin G. Osterweis (1935), the beautiful Rebecca, daughter of one of Philadelphia's "merchant princes," was disappointed in love and thereafter devoted her time and resources to a life of good works among the city's unfortunates. A close friend of the Gratz family, Washington Irving, while visiting Sir Walter Scott, described to the author the beauty and self-sacrificing life of the young Philadelphia woman. Later, Irving received a copy of Scott's *Ivanhoe* inscribed by the author, "I hope you recognize your Rebecca."

Visitors who are privileged to see old Hofwyl Plantation as it has been over the years owe a debt of gratitude to two Brailsford descendants—both women. In 1865 Matilda Troup accomplished the all but impossible task of inspiring the family to restore their ancestral land after the chaos of war. More than a hundred years later Ophelia Dent left her beloved home for the enjoyment of others.

8 St. Simons Island

Old St. Simons and Frederica

S t. Simons Island is the only one of the Golden Isles that has never been privately owned. Approximately the size of Manhattan Island, it has been inhabited down through the centuries by various groups of people. The discovery of widely separated burial mounds indicates that there were several settlements here in prehistoric times, and the Creeks are known to have had more than one village on this island which they called Asao. The Spaniards established three missions on Asao in the 1500s; one, the mission of San Simon, gave the island its name.

When James Edward Oglethorpe selected San Simon, or St. Simons, as the strategic place to fortify against Spanish invasion, he had a fort constructed on the west side of the island where a bend in the river formed a natural vantage point. One of the largest British fortifications in colonial America, the fort was a protection not only for the other colonies but for the town within its walls; and town, fort, and river were all called Frederica in honor of Frederick, Prince of Wales.

North of Frederica was a sentry station in the charge of Richard Pike and called Pikes Bluff, and on the northwest tip of the island was the New Hampton outpost, where a garrison of soldiers and their families lived. A temporary fortification at the south end of the island, Delegals Fort, under the command of Lieutenant Philip Delegal, was succeeded by the larger Fort St. Simons, which was connected with Frederica by a military road. The anchorage for the British ships was downriver from Fort Frederica at a bluff named for Captain Gascoigne, master of the *Hawk*. A few miles east of Frederica was the German Village, settled by a group of Salzburgers who had come to Georgia in search of freedom of worship.

The town of Frederica had a population of almost a thousand, and around Fort St. Simons there was a settlement of several hundred inhabitants, where a lookout was constantly scanning the horizon and a sentry stood ready to ride to Frederica with news of any strange sails that might appear.

Fort Frederica was garrisoned by "The Regiment of Foot for the Defense of His Majesty's Plantations in America," and the walled and moated military settlement grew into one of the most important towns in the colony. On either side of streets "regularly laid out and margined with orange trees," the temporary palm-thatched shelters of the first colonists were replaced by substantial dwellings, some of them handsome two- and three-storied houses built of brick and tabby; for among the settlers were bricklayers and masons as well as carpenters, cabinetmakers, and locksmiths. There were well-filled storehouses, well-supplied trading posts and shops of various kinds, for the colonists included blacksmiths, silversmiths, and watchmakers; millers and merchants; bakers and brewers; tailors, tanners, and shoemakers. Lists of these first citizens show families of four, five, and six children; and the schoolteacher was an important member of the colony as was the "Publick Midwife."

Minister to the spiritual needs of the first residents of Frederica was Charles Wesley, younger of the two brothers, ministers of the Anglican church, whose names were later to become synonymous with Methodism. John, in his early thirties, served the Savannah church while Charles, still in his twenties and newly ordained, had come to St. Simons as Oglethorpe's secretary and as minister for the settlement at Frederica.

Worship services were held under the great live oaks until a suitable building could be erected. The first "tabernacle" at Frederica was the North Storehouse, completed in April 1736. Records of 1739 report that the South Storehouse was finished, a building "sixty foot long by twenty foot wide, three stories, the two lowermost . . . for provisions and the uppermost a Chappel."

Although Charles Wesley did not stay long in the colony of Georgia, and his brother made only an occasional visit to Frederica, both men had a part in the early life of St. Simons.

What a picture the imagination draws of Frederica! A bustling military post built in a clearing hewn out of this insular "forest

Charles Wesley preaching to the Indians

primeval," its streets peopled by British Regulars in their red coats and three-cornered hats; by Highlanders in plaids and bonnets; by Indians in moccasins and breech-clouts; by trader, merchant, artisan; by townspeople with their sprinkling of courageous pioneer women, bravely flaunting the ruffles and "ribbands" that caused their pious young pastor such grave misgivings. And in the midst of it all was the aristocratic James Edward Oglethorpe, experienced military man and member of the House of Parliament.

Public farmlands were cleared and planted, and the fields yielded abundantly in the semitropical climate. Each colonist had a homestead of fifty acres, and there was a royal grant of three hundred acres "to be cultivated as maintenance for a minister and other Religious uses." Colonists of independent means received large grants of land, and farms and plantations were developed in the vicinity of the town.

Oglethorpe himself had a home near Frederica, on a tract known as "The Farm," or "The General's Farm," where he lived in an English cottage called Orange Hall, set in a grove of live oaks and with a garden and an orchard of oranges, figs, and grapes. Nearby was Harrington Hall, the home of Captain Raymond Demere, who had served for ten years "with my Lord Harrington in Spain."

Early records show a five-hundred-acre grant to Captain Gascoigne and describe his plantation a few miles downriver from Frederica, "near the station where his ship usually rides." Near the Gascoigne Plantation was Hawkins Island, the property of Dr. Thomas Hawkins, Frederica physician and regimental surgeon. Captain George Dunbar, a ship commander, and John Terry, silversmith, and recorder of Frederica, had grants on Dunbar Creek, where Terry planted hundreds of orange trees and called his plantation Orange Grove.

Daniel Cannon, master carpenter who built many of the houses at Frederica, owned a tract at the northeast end of the island, which was known as Cannons Point. Archibald Sinclair, tithingman at Frederica, had a plantation on Sinclair Creek, later called

Village Creek; while John Lawrence, another of the early settlers, was granted land nearby. Substantial grants were made to Lachlan McIntosh and to Patrick (later Sir Patrick) Houstoun, an officer in Oglethorpe's Regiment.

Both England and Spain coveted the coastal territory, and when war was declared between the mother countries, the Spanish and English colonies grew openly hostile. The situation came to a head when an Englishman named Jenkins, caught by the Spaniards in the region set apart as the Debatable Land, was punished by having one of his ears cut off. This incident led to hostilities which came to be known as the War of Jenkins' Ear. Although this was a minor part of the conflict in Europe, the far flung little colony of Georgia was fighting for its very existence; and Oglethorpe proceeded to start offensive moves against the Spaniards in Florida. When the Spanish fort at St. Augustine proved impregnable, Oglethorpe's forces withdrew to their island stronghold, strengthened their defenses, and waited for the expected invasion.

When the sails of the Spanish armada of half-a-hundred galleons appeared over the horizon, History itself galloped beside the sentry as he spurred his mount up the military road to warn the garrison at Frederica. Oglethorpe gave orders for the guns of Fort St. Simons to be spiked, for the fort to be abandoned, and for the inhabitants of the settlement to move to the protection of the larger fort at Frederica. The Spaniards took possession of the south end of the island, and as a detachment of Grenadiers advanced for the attack on Oglethorpe's stronghold, they were met by a platoon of soldiers from Frederica. After skirmishes between the troops, the British retreated and let it appear that they intended to offer no further resistance. The story is told that the Spaniards proceeded to stack arms and prepare a meal, unaware that the surrounding woods concealed the English forces together with Scouts, Rangers, Marines, Highlanders from Darien, and a band of friendly Indians from whom the colonists had learned woodland warfare. According to tradition, a Scotch bonnet raised cautiously from the undergrowth was a signal for the first shot to be fired on the unsuspecting Spaniards. In the surprise attack, the superior Spanish forces were completely routed in the historic Battle of Bloody Marsh.

The remnants of the Spanish troops withdrew to the south end of the island where, drawn by Oglethorpe's shrewd strategy into an overestimation of British strength, they destroyed Fort St. Simons, took ship, and sailed back to St. Augustine, leaving the British in undisputed possession of the coastal territory. On the departure of the enemy, Oglethorpe issued a proclamation for a day of public thanksgiving—Georgia's first Thanksgiving day, July 25, 1742. The victory over the Spaniards was acclaimed in Great Britain and in the colonies, and Oglethorpe received congratulatory letters from a number of the provincial governors.

In 1743 General Oglethorpe returned to England, leaving Fort Frederica for a time in charge of his aide, Captain Horton, who was promoted to the rank of major. In the peaceful years after the treaty between Spain and England, when there was no need for a strong fortification at Frederica, most of the troops were withdrawn or disbanded, and the reduced garrison that remained was under the command of Captain Raymond Demere, who continued to make his home on the island. With the withdrawal of troops, most of the Salzburgers and others of the early settlers left for homes on the mainland.

Grants made while the Trustees were directing the fortunes of the colony of Georgia were restricted to "tail-male," or inheritance by the grantee's eldest son. After the Trustees relinquished the charter of the colony in 1756, grants were made in fee simple, or ownership of land with unrestricted rights of disposition. After some of the original land holders left the island, their property was regranted, and additional acreage was granted to military and civilian colonists.

In 1758 fire destroyed a number of houses in Frederica, and the fort and remaining buildings were neglected and falling into ruins in 1760 when a large part of the property was acquired by Donald Mackay, a prosperous merchant of the colony. His business partner was James Spalding, a young Scotsman from County Perth, and the company of Mackay and Spalding, branch of a London firm, was known throughout colonial America. Cargoes were shipped from England to the central storehouse at Frederica, and from here goods were carried by boat and pony train to the widely scattered Indian trading posts operated by Mackay and Spalding.

In the *Georgia Gazette* of March 28, 1765, it was announced that the General Assembly had passed an act for repairing the barracks in Frederica Town, but in 1767 the last detachment of the depleted garrison was withdrawn.

In 1772 James Spalding, who was then a member of the House of Assembly and a justice of St. James Parish, was married to Margery McIntosh, a granddaughter of his business partner, Donald Mackay. The first home of James and Margery Spalding was "The General's Farm," and it was here, in the English cottage built for Oglethorpe, that their son, Thomas, was born, he who became known as the Laird of Sapelo.

With the establishment of the prosperous mercantile house of Mackay and Spalding, business activity had been renewed on the island. When William Bartram visited here in 1774 he found many of the "spacious and expensive buildings of Frederica in ruins, but a number of neat houses in good repair and inhabited, and St. Simons seeming to be recovering, owing to the liberal spirit of J. Spalding, Esqr., who is President of the island."

Throughout the Revolutionary War, St. Simons was left uninhabited. James Spalding was a noncombatant, but he remained loyal to the Crown, and moved with other loyalists to Florida. Most of the island residents joined the patriot army. After the war Frederica, formerly in St. James Parish, was made the seat of Glynn County, named for John Glynn, British supporter of provincial rights.

When James Spalding returned to find his storehouses in ruins and his business gone, he turned his interests to agriculture. One of the first successful planters of the new long-staple cotton imported from the Indies, Spalding recouped his fortune and became one of the largest landowners in the county. Included in his property was a tract at the sound end of the island, where young Thomas Spalding and his bride spent the first months of their married life in a cottage that has been described as a duplicate of General Oglethorpe's Orange Hall.

Captain Demere's son, Raymond, Jr., also returned to the island after the war and added further acreage to the family property. Other planters bought land on St. Simons, and in the late 1700s and early 1800s there were a number of plantations raising the crop that made agricultural history and that caused the little coastal island to be known all over the world as the "famous long-staple cotton island of St. Simons."

Few of the planters were wealthy, but there was luxury and comfort and the gracious pleasant life of the Old South, when one successful crop of sea island cotton might bring its owner a hundred thousand dollars. They had fine horses and handsome carriages and comfortable houses; they traveled in the British Isles and on the continent of Europe, ordered books from Philadelphia and London for carefully selected libraries, and had family portraits painted by Thomas Sully of Philadelphia and by journeyman artists or "house painters."

The island planters were men whose ancestral background and culture gave them common interests, and whose nationalities and experiences made as cosmopolitan a group as could be found anywhere in the world. English, Scottish, Irish, and French, they included professional men, Oxford graduates, statesmen, military men—all individuals of wide experience, intensely interested in affairs of the world as well as in those of their own new country. Primarily agriculturists, they were also sportsmen, epicures, and students. Their interests embraced philosophy, religion, arts, and sciences; the semiseclusion of their surroundings gave them leisure for reading, study, and discussion. The hospitality of the island plantations was a byword throughout the country, as remarked in a newspaper of the day: "If the health of the St. Simons planters should keep pace with their hospitality they will each see their hundredth year."

Although the postwar years brought a period of great prosperity to the St. Simons plantations, only a handful of inhabitants remained in once busy Frederica, and in 1797 the county seat was moved to the town of Brunswick on the mainland. Known as Old Town, Frederica's wharves were still in use, and when regular mail service was established it was the "post town" for the island. But over the years, even the ruins of the old military town gradually disappeared, since much of the material from the abandoned buildings was carried away to be used in other construction. Tabby and brick from Frederica were used in building the first St. Simons lighthouse, established in 1811.

In the latter part of the War of 1812, when the British invaded the Georgia coast, some of the residents of St. Simons left for places of safety on the mainland and English troops occupied the island for three weeks. Plantations were plundered and equipment, food supplies, cotton, cattle, and slaves were carried away. As soon as hostilities ended, life on the plantations was resumed and the island again enjoyed a period of peace and prosperity. Moribund Frederica was still the post town and the gathering place for Fourth of July celebrations, boat races, picnics, and other island festivities.

It was in the year 1820 that the Glynn County census first listed the name of James Frewin, who with his family played an important part in the future of Frederica. For more than a hundred years the site of the old town was to be owned by the Frewin-Stevens families.

James Frewin, a native of London who had served for a number of years in the British Navy, came to the United States in 1815 when he was thirty-seven years old. He lived first in Baltimore, then in Savannah, where he was naturalized in 1819. Shortly afterward he settled on St. Simons Island, where he was to spend the rest of his life.

Frewin bought property in Frederica and with his wife, the former Sarah Dorothy Hay of Sunderland, made his home in the old town. Here, according to an 1824 issue of the *Darien Gazette*, "Captain Frewin kept a little battery tavern and store near the river." An entry in an 1825 Glynn County deed book refers

to Frewin as a "mariner" following a "seafaring life," which indicates that he also pursued the nautical calling for which his
Navy experience had fitted him. Perhaps he operated a coast-
wise boat on the inland waterway, or he may have shipped, from
time to time, on one of the vessels that plied, with cargo and passengers, between Georgia and England.

James Frewin's property consisted of "lots in Frederica, dwelling house, store, one riding chair, one wagon, horses, cattle,
poultry, hogs, etc." until 1828 when he bought, at a sheriff's sale,
"all that parcel of land at Frederica . . . known as the Old Fort
together with the improvements thereon consisting of a large
and commodious dwelling house." Over the following years,
Frewin bought other property, including lots in Frederica from
James A. D. Lawrence, William Moore, and John Cole; a lot,
livestock, and furniture from Mrs. Mary Abbott, and "three
acres adjoining Frewin land" from James Gowen.

In 1838 the Frewins visited relatives in England and, on their
return, brought Mrs. Frewin's eighteen-year-old, orphaned niece
and namesake, Sarah Dorothy Hay, to live with them at Frederica. Miss Hay was later married to Captain Charles Stevens.

Charles Stevens, born in Denmark in 1816, came to the United
States when he was twenty years old. He landed first at New Or-
leans, lived for a time in Savannah, then settled on St. Simons
Island, where he made Frederica headquarters for the shipping
trade in which he was engaged. His sloop *Splendid*, schooner
Florida, and, later, schooner *Southern Belle* carried freight on
the inland waterway, touching at ports between Savannah and
St. Marys.

In addition to his shipping interests Captain Stevens, after his
marriage, became a landowner and planter. He bought a number of lots in the old town as well as property in the Frederica
area, including three hundred acres from Christ Church. Eventually the Frewin-Stevens families owned practically all of the
land originally included in the town of Frederica and a large
acreage in the vicinity.

For a time Charles and Sarah Dorothy Stevens and their growing family lived in a house built on the foundations of the old fort, but after their home was almost demolished by storm in the 1850s they built farther back from the river.

Members of the Frewin and Stevens families continued to visit from time to time in England, where the eldest Stevens daughter, Annie, was educated. According to the family Bible, Mrs. Frewin died in 1854; since she is not buried in the cemetery at Christ Church, Frederica, it is believed that she died while visiting English relatives.

In the summer of 1861 Confederate troops were stationed at the south end of St. Simons Island to guard the entrance to Brunswick harbor. In December, when the coast was blockaded by Federal gunboats, residents of the island were ordered evacuated. Since all of the younger men had left their plantation homes to join the Confederate Army, the older men, women, children, and slaves hurriedly packed necessities, buried silver, and closed houses. A few prized articles of household furnishings, clothing, foodstuffs, and people were crowded onto boats and rafts, leaving many valuables behind.

The Confederate troops were evacuated in February 1862, and the soldiers were ordered to blow up the lighthouse to keep the light from being of aid to the blockaders. With St. Simons and Brunswick in Federal hands, the island was used as a concentration area for freed slaves from the mainland, or "contraband," as they were called.

When the residents of St. Simons were evacuated, Charles Stevens, who was then forty-five years old, refugeed with his wife and seven children to Wayne County, but eighty-five-year-old James Frewin refused to leave his home. Even when the island was occupied by Federal troops, Frewin and his friend Cole stayed at Frederica. Before the Stevens family left, a signal was agreed on, and sometimes at night, when a lantern flashed the message that the area was clear of troops, Captain Stevens would row over to Frederica for a visit with his uncle.

On January 30, 1863, the surgeon of a Federal ship on blockade off St. Simons wrote in his journal: "Paid old man Cole a visit; found an old man sick at the house who is going to his last home, being beyond all medical skill." The next day the young doctor "stopped at Mr. Cole's place and found that the old man had gone to that 'bourne from whence no traveler returneth.'" This was James Frewin, who is buried in Christ Church cemetery.

Charles Stevens's schooner, *Southern Belle*, hidden in a creek near Darien, was discovered and confiscated by the crew of a Federal boat. In 1864 Captain Stevens, a noncombatant, was taken prisoner. When he refused the offer of Federal officers to act as pilot for their boats patrolling the inland waters of the coast, he was taken, as a prisoner of war, to Fort Delaware, where he died in 1865. A monument to his memory stands in the family burial plot in the cemetery of Christ Church, Frederica.

After the war, when some of the island planters and their families returned to their homes, Captain Stevens's wife leased her land to be farmed, but it was an unprofitable venture. In 1867 she was commissioned postmistress of the Frederica post office, where she served for a number of years.

James Frewin's property was left by will to the children of Charles and Sarah Dorothy Stevens. Captain Stevens left no will, and his property was divided among his children. Part of the land is still in the possession of his descendants.

That portion of the Frewin-Stevens holdings originally included in the town of Frederica was inherited by Stevens's daughter, Belle, later Mrs. William Taylor. In 1903 Belle Stevens Taylor deeded the "old fort and sixty feet of land in all directions" to the Georgia Society of Colonial Dames of America. The historic ruin, which had deteriorated over the years, was repaired and preserved by contributions from members of the society, and attempts were made to have the site named a national shrine.

In 1941 a group of interested citizens organized the Fort Frederica Association, and funds were raised for the purchase of the acreage adjoining the fort. The Society of Colonial Dames deeded the plot of ground on which the ruins of the old fort stood, and the entire area was presented to the National Parks Service.

In 1947 the tract was formally dedicated as the Fort Frederica National Monument, one of America's few pre-Revolutionary shrines and one of its most beautiful national parks.

In November 1951 work was begun on excavation of foundations of the old town. Through research into the history of Frederica and study of records and plats in colonial reports, Margaret Davis Cate, local historian and Parks Service historical collaborator, was able to point out the exact spot at which to start excavation. After the accumulated earth and leaf mold of two centuries had been dug away, new and exciting discoveries were made with every swing of the pick, every turn of the spade.

The first excavation disclosed foundations of a building identified as a three-storied, partitioned house, or duplex, known to have been occupied by Dr. Thomas Hawkins, Oglethorpe's regimental surgeon, and Samuel Davison, tavernkeeper. Further excavations uncovered foundations of additional houses, the ruins of a blacksmith shop and brick forge, and the foundations of the storehouses that were Frederica's first "chappels."

Six filled in wells were discovered, one packed to the brim with refuse that contained articles of inestimable value to archaeologists and historians. Among the whole and fragmentary articles found in the excavations were pieces of hand-etched glassware, goblet stems with teardrop intact, and numerous fragments of porcelain and Delft. There were a few eighteenth-century English pennies and German coins, and an engraved nameplate that had belonged to Captain Horton, discarded, no doubt, when he was promoted to the rank of major upon being placed in command of the troops at Frederica when General Oglethorpe returned to England in 1743.

In 1954 the site of the Battle of Bloody Marsh was acquired by the Fort Frederica Association, to be added to the National Parks System. In 1958 the Fort Frederica Museum and Visitor Center was dedicated in ceremonies that included more than a hundred descendants of original settlers and soldiers of old Frederica.

Ruins of the barracks, Fort Frederica National Monument

In 1961 people throughout the state were saddened by the sudden death of Margaret Davis Cate, who willed her valuable collection of historical material to the Fort Frederica National Monument. Through the efforts of the Fort Frederica Association, a memorial wing to house the collection was added to the museum building, and in 1964 the Margaret Davis Cate Memorial Library was dedicated. In 1977, when the Park Service was not prepared to have the material available to the public for research, the Cate Collection was placed on permanent loan to the Georgia Historical Society in Savannah where it is accessible to researchers.

From the time Fort Frederica was added to the parks system, it has attracted thousands of visitors annually, with the number increasing each year. Here on the bank of the Frederica River may be seen contours of the old earthen breastworks and the grassy slope of the moat that outlined the eighteenth-century fortified town. Tabby ruins of the old fort, remnants of the barracks, crumbling brick tombs in the old burial ground, and excavated foundations of some of the original buildings are all that remain of the colonial military town established by James Edward Oglethorpe in 1736.

Fort Frederica

Christ Church, Frederica

Following Charles Wesley's return to England, other clergy-men were sent to Frederica by the Society for Propagating the Gospel in Foreign Parts. Best known, perhaps, was the Reverend Bartholomew Zouberbuhler, who served the entire colony of Georgia from 1743 to 1766.

When St. Simons became an agricultural island in the late seventeen and early eighteen hundreds, the plantation families felt the need for a place of worship. In 1807 Christ Church, Frederica, second oldest Episcopal church in the Diocese of Georgia, was organized by a group of island planters.

Named as wardens of the newly organized church were Dr. Robert Grant of Oatlands Plantation and William Page of Retreat, while vestrymen were George Abbott of Frederica, John Couper of Cannons Point, Raymond Demere, Jr., of Mulberry Grove, James Hamilton of Hamilton Plantation, and Joseph Turner, collector of the ports of Frederica and Brunswick. The act of incorporation in 1808 declared these men "to be a body corporate by the name and style of 'the church wardens and vestrymen of the Episcopal Church of the town of Frederica, called Christ Church.' "

The state legislature, petitioned for land on which to erect a church building, granted one hundred acres of the commons of Frederica and three lots within the town, these "glebe lands" to be rented and the income used for the church. The list of subscribers toward support of the church includes the names of many coastal planters whose descendants are still communicants of Christ Church, Frederica.

The Reverend William Best of Savannah was the first rector of the parish, and early services were held in the home of John Beck, one of the original subscribers. For use of his house Mr. Beck was paid one dollar a week, with an additional fifty cents a week for cleaning and preparing for services. The Beck house stood on the site of Oglethorpe's old place, Orange Hall, the only home the general ever owned in Georgia.

Before funds could be raised for the erection of a church, the coastal planters suffered reverses due to the restrictions and embargoes that preceded the War of 1812. It was decided that "in consequence of the present embarrassed situation of the country, it is not the proper time to engage in such an expensive undertaking as the building of a church and supporting a clergyman."

Construction of a church was postponed for a number of years, but the Reverend Edmund Matthews, D.D., came to serve the parish in 1810 and remained until his death in 1827. It was during his ministry that the first church was built in 1820. The little house of worship, a simple square building painted white with green shutters and a belfry atop, was set in a grove of historic live oaks, those "first temples" under which the Wesleys preached to the colonists.

In 1823 Christ Church, Frederica, with Christ Church, Savannah, and St. Pauls, Augusta, organized the Diocese of Georgia.

"Well supported and well attended," Christ Church, Frederica, was the center of religious life for the entire island. We have a description of Sunday services from the pen of Caroline Couper Lovell, great-granddaughter of John Couper. We are told that the congregation started arriving "by gig and chaise" as early as nine in the morning to attend the eleven o'clock service. "The ladies gathered for gossip until 'Dearly Beloved' was uttered by the rector. . . . The men, upon arriving, seated themselves outside on benches under the trees, received their mail which was brought to them by the postmaster at Frederica, read letters and discussed the latest news. . . . The children played in the shade until all were summoned to worship."

An important event in the early life of the little church occurred in 1831 when the convention of the diocese met for the first time in Christ Church. Delegates from the parish were wardens Colonel William W. Hazzard of West Point Plantation and Thomas Butler King of Retreat, and vestryman Dr. Thomas F. Hazzard of Pikes Bluff.

Another milestone for the church was the celebration in 1836 of the centennial of the island's first religious services. Principal speaker for the occasion was Thomas Spalding of Sapelo.

People like to tell about the time when a swarm of bees contributed to the upkeep of the church. A letter to the Trustees from one of the first settlers at Frederica mentions "a great plenty of Bees on the island," and they must have been still plentiful a century later. The rector of Christ Church, so the story goes, was preparing to ask the parishioners for funds for some needed repairs to the building when a swarm of bees was noticed around the belfry. Upon investigation, a large store of honey was found, enough to be sold for all that was needed for repairs and for the addition of a vestry-room as well. Thereafter, the church was often called the "Bee Hive Church" and the Ladies' Missionary Society was known as the "Bee Hive Society" or the "Busy Bees."

In 1837, perhaps because of financial reverses caused by the "panic" of that year, the vestry received authorization from the legislature to sell land belonging to the church. According to a "History of Christ Church" compiled in 1910 by the Reverend D. Watson Winn, parts of the glebe lands were sold in the 1840s, and, according to a deed in the possession of descendants of Captain Charles Stevens, a tract of "300 acres known as Church Lands, except 5 acres retained for Church use" was sold to Captain Stevens on April 1, 1851. This may have been the 300 acres set aside when the town of Frederica was laid out "to be cultivated . . . for religious uses."

After the War Between the States, returning residents of St. Simons found that Federal occupation of the island had left their church in ruins—altar broken to pieces, pews burned, window panes out, organ smashed. The church funds had been lost in a Savannah bank that was ruined by the war, and the parishioners who had returned to their devastated plantations had no resources with which to rebuild their church or to support a clergyman. Evening prayers were read each Sunday in the home of Horace Bunch Gould of Black Banks Plantation, one of the first planters to return after the war.

The story of the present church is the story of Anson Greene Phelps Dodge. In the late 1870s, when mills were operated on the island by the Dodge lumber interests, young Anson Dodge visited St. Simons. He was attracted to the island and its people,

Anson Dodge, first rector of Christ Church, and his first wife, Ellen

and sympathized with the communicants of Christ Church in their brave attempt to hold their parish together.

The present church was built as a memorial to Anson Dodge's first wife, Ellen, who died in India while the young couple were on a wedding journey around the world. Her body was returned to St. Simons Island and entombed in a vault beneath the chancel of the new church, to await burial in the same grave with her husband.

In addition to planning the church and providing funds for its construction, Anson Dodge attended theological seminary and in 1884 became the first rector of the present Christ Church. He built a home nearby and for the rest of his life worked untiringly in the Diocese of Georgia, establishing a number of churches in the coastal area. He also founded an orphanage, the Dodge Home for Boys, which remained in existence for well over half a century.

After Anson Dodge's death in 1898, Charles Spalding Wylly, in his *Annals and Memoirs*, paid tribute to this "priest of the Episcopal Church, who rebuilt the broken church and endowed with his fortune the Diocese of Georgia, and left memories, chapels and churches which attest and bear witness that at Frederica there lived and died a man who forgot himself in his love for God and his fellowman."

During Dodge's ministry in Christ Church Parish, his young son by a second marriage was killed in an accident. The little boy, his mother, the former Anna Gould, and his Grandmother

Christ Church, Frederica

Dodge are buried near the tomb of Anson and Ellen in the family plot close to the church that was built through the generosity of its first rector.

Hardly larger than a chapel, the house of worship has a serene and simple dignity with its high-spired belfry and its narrow stained-glass windows. In the old churchyard are monuments marked with the names of Page, King, Grant, Couper, Fraser, Wright, Gowen, Abbott, Gould, Frewin, Stevens, Demere, Cater, Postell, Wylly, and of many others who have had a part in the history of St. Simons Island. The Hazzard family vault, dated A.D. 1813, stands in ruins as it has stood since 1863, when it was desecrated during Federal occupation of the island.

A granite slab marks the grave of Lucien Lamar Knight, first state historian of Georgia, where he "wished to sleep in the long peace of Eternity under the boughs of the Wesley Oak and by the waters of the murmuring Altamaha."

St. Simons in the Last Century

The years following the War Between the States were difficult ones for the families who returned to their homes on St. Simons Island. On every plantation there were freedmen who were willing to work for their former owners for the small wages the planters were able to pay, but none of the island families could afford to hire the workers necessary to operate a large cotton plantation. Much of the land that had supported the planters' families and "people" in abundance lay uncultivated. The lumber mills that opened in the 1870s provided welcome employment for a number of island men, both white and black. With regular service between St. Simons and the mainland supplied by the *Ruby*, mail and passenger boat for the mill colony, the island became a summer retreat for Brunswick families.

As the summers came and went, St. Simons grew to be one of the best-loved resorts of Georgia. A permanent village at the south end of the island attracted a few new residents, and some of the families connected with the lumber industry remained after the mills were closed. Summer hotels were constructed and boardinghouses were opened, and people from other parts of the state built summer cottages to which they returned year after year. Visitors now arrived aboard the *Emmeline* and the *Hessie*, those two boats that were remembered with nostalgia for many a year.

In the early resort days, the summer people were met at the pier by horsedrawn surreys, but as the number of vacationers increased rails were laid and a trolley drawn by a pair of donkeys carried visitors to hotel, boardinghouse, or beach cottage. Transportation was accelerated when the donkeys were replaced by a little steam engine that went puffing along showering sparks indiscriminately on the stiff-brimmed straw hats of gentlemen passengers and the ruffled parasols of the ladies.

When St. Simons Island was made more accessible with the opening of the Torras causeway in 1924 and of the airport a decade later, the resort became known to people in other sections of the country. But although the causeway increased the number of visitors to "The Island," as it is affectionately known throughout Georgia, St. Simons remained until 1941 a sleepy little place with only a few hundred permanent inhabitants.

At the beginning of the Second World War, a Naval Air Base and Radar School were located there, and with two shipyards in Brunswick and a lighter-than-air base in the upper part of the county hundreds of newcomers came into the coastal region. There was a new invasion of Yankees, young heroes who cocked their caps at a jaunty angle and were confident that they were the original discoverers of the coastland and its charms. They were delighted with its semitropical beauty and its inhabitants, and the coastal people found themselves, rather to their surprise, liking the invaders. Golden sands, palm trees, and moonlight cast their age-old spell, and wedding bells were soon ringing for many of the bachelors.

The increased wartime population brought St. Simons its first public school. High school students continued to attend Glynn Academy in Brunswick, but a modern elementary school was built for younger children on the island. War's end found many of the new families reluctant to leave St. Simons. Permanent homes were built in the village and in the adjoining East Beach residential area, and new subdivisions were developed. Instead of a summer resort, the island found itself a thriving community. Soon there were new churches and stores, an enlarged amusement center, a new post office, and a school of art. The old island was launched into a new era.

The causeway that connects St. Simons and the mainland stretches across a five-mile network of the Marshes of Glynn with its tidal creeks and rivers—Terry Creek, Back River, Little River, Mackay River, and the Frederica River, a part of the Intracoastal or Inland Waterway. The causeway constructed in 1924 was rebuilt a quarter-century later with the wooden bridges replaced by electric drawbridges. Gone are the days of the narrow road with its rickety old bridges lined with fishermen, where a man turned a handcrank to open the drawbridge, and where the tollhouse keeper greeted vacationers by name, welcomed them back each summer, and peered into the car in friendly consternation, complaining that there were so many dogs and cats he couldn't count the people. Gone are the long quiet months of off-season when summer cottages were closed and there was nothing to do but fish and crab and enjoy endless hours of lazy sunshine. There is no off-season now.

Each year brings more permanent residents to St. Simons, more subdivisions and shopping centers, more traffic on the narrow, tree-lined roads. But in spite of the increased population and the many visitors, there is still an atmosphere of seclusion and relaxation. One of the island's charms is the casual indifference with which the vacationer is accepted. There are amusements and diversions at hand, but the visitor is not exhorted to enjoy himself. He can fish or crab or swim or just sit. She can wear the latest in fashionable beach attire or a pair of old jeans—it is a matter of complete indifference to St. Simons.

A day of barefoot adventure may be spent on the pier at the end of the village street. The shrimp fleet chugs past at dawn to string itself across the near horizon like an Old World etching. If the trout are biting, the pier will be lined with anglers, shoulder to shoulder. Other times it is occupied by a sprinkling of crabbers, fishermen, and children enjoying the sun and the sea breeze. Porpoises roll in the surf; a sand crab scuttles across the beach; children dig in the sand under the pier; an artist sets up an easel nearby; a Coast Guard boat knifes its way along the channel.

Your neighbor may be a five-year-old, big eyed over the barnacled blue-clawed monster caught in his crab trap; or a bewhiskered octogenarian chuckling over the zebra-striped sheephead lured by his fiddler-crab bait; may be a vacationing schoolteacher or a coed with all but nonexistent bathing suit; a shabby fisherman hoping for a good catch to sell to the market, or an equally shabby visiting tycoon in faded jeans. The fisherman who has been to St. Simons only a few seasons fishes from pier, bridges, water's edge, or fishing camp. The old-timer is apt to disappear for a few hours up one of the creeks or rivers, and come in with a sunburn, a proud grin, and an incredible string of fish—but try to find out where he caught them!

When the Coast Guard Station, dedicated to "those who died on Georgia's coast," was opened in 1937, the island noted with interest that the government had chosen to drop the final letter from St. Simons; and soon afterward it was noted that the cancellation stamp on island mail had also discarded the "s." The Coast Guard and even the United States Post Office were granted the privilege of calling themselves whatever they pleased, but St. Simons had always been St. Simons and had no intention of changing. After several years in which the new "St. Simon" spelling was unanimously ignored by visitors and residents alike, the missing letter was officially restored.

Few visitors leave the island without photographing, sketching, or painting the lighthouse. Commissioned in 1872 to replace the original one destroyed in the sixties, it is among the most impressive on the Atlantic coast. Tall, perfectly propor-

Lighthouse and Keeper's Cottage, now the Museum of Coastal History, St. Simons Island

tioned, gleaming white, it has the same simple and dignified beauty that characterizes the Washington Monument. For more than half a century the light was operated by kerosene; in 1934 electricity was installed. No lighthouse is complete without its ghost, and the one on St. Simons is no exception. The tread of descending footsteps was a familiar sound to keepers of the light before an automatic system was installed. And stories are told of one of the most faithful of the early keepers who was said to return to lend a hand in time of trouble.

Since 1971 the keeper's cottage at the foot of the light tower has been the Museum of Coastal History sponsored by the Coastal Georgia Historical Society. The cottage, reputed to be the oldest brick building in Glynn County, is on the National Register of Historic Places.

St. Simons Island is relatively free from the hurricanes that harass parts of the eastern coast. But, on occasion, the red flags of storm warning go up; the rising wind sends dirty gray clouds scudding across a lowering sky, and waves break ominously on the shore. The ocean is no longer friendly, but malevolent. Small craft scurry for dock, and the island battens itself against the elements. Visitors nervously pack their belongings, and old timers cock an eye at the sky and allow "it looks like we're in for a little blow."

But damage seldoms runs to more than a few shingles and shrubs, and the sun is soon shining again.

9   St. Simons Plantations

Hamilton

Hamilton Plantation, on the bank of the Frederica along the southwestern side of St. Simons Island, was the home of James Hamilton, Esquire, prominent planter and shipper of the coastal region. When he and his friend John Couper chose, near the turn of the eighteenth century, to live upon their island plantations, the two properties formed a nucleus for a community of gentlemen planters which was to develop into one of the leading social and cultural sections of the South. Although there were already a few large plantations on St. Simons, most of its acreage had been divided into numerous small holdings, and the following decade saw these properties merge into some twelve or fourteen plantations that were devoted almost entirely to the cultivation of cotton.

James Hamilton's property included land originally granted to Captain Gascoigne of His Majesty's *Hawk*, and the plantation was recognized as one of the first where long-staple sea island cotton was grown along the coast soon after the Revolution. On this property, too, the government cut live oak timbers that went into that famous fighting ship, the *Constitution*, "Old Ironsides," pride of the Navy.

Described as a Georgia planter and shipper, a South Carolina merchant-planter, and a London merchant, James Hamilton was away from his island home for a part of each year because of his business connections; but in spite of his wide interests he helped to build the early life of the community. He served as one of the first vestrymen of Christ Church, and took an active part in civic affairs of island and county. His wharf at Gascoigne Bluff, where the British fleet had anchored in Oglethorpe's day, was the main shipping point for the island; here ships from other ports came for their cargoes of cotton and lumber. Perhaps more farsighted than some of the planters, James Hamilton, having made a fortune from his southern plantations, disposed of a large part of his coastal property and moved to Philadelphia, where he lived for the rest of his life. When he died, it is said, he left to his grandchildren an estate valued at more than a million dollars.

After James Hamilton left St. Simons, the plantation on the Frederica became the property of his namesake James Hamilton Couper, and for a number of years was managed by Captain John Fraser, husband of James Couper's sister Ann, the Frasers with their large family of children making a lively, hospitable home of the beautiful estate. Set well back from the river, the plantation residence was not a mansion, but a house of simple colonial architecture with shuttered front veranda and high, latticed foundations. Surrounded by a hedge of flowering yucca, it overlooked the broad Frederica and the great expanse of marshland. The wide lawns sloped down to the banks of the river, and shell walks led through formal gardens to rose garden, cutting garden, and herb garden—all divided by picket fences and boxwood hedges. When the young Pierce Butlers were in Georgia in 1839 they were entertained by Captain and Mrs. Fraser, and Fanny Kemble described Hamilton Plantation as "by far the finest place on the island."

The property was later managed by James Hamilton Couper's youngest brother, William Audley, whose descendants still cherish a silver pitcher that commemorates the part their ancestor played in the rescue of survivors of an explosion that occurred in 1850 on a steamer near the Hamilton dock. Most of the passengers were thrown clear of the boat, as they happened to be gathered along the rail enjoying the pleasant sight of the Couper children playing on the lawn with a pet fawn. Dozens of survivors, many of them badly burned, were brought to the plantation, where William Audley Couper turned the cotton barn into an improvised hospital, using bales of cotton for emergency beds. In appreciation of the kindness and hospitality shown them, the grateful passengers sent their host the engraved pitcher, which has been handed down as a treasured heirloom through the generations.

In the 1860s, Hamilton, like other coastal plantations, suffered the brutal indignities of war, but the following years brought a new era to the splendid old place. Bought by a lumber company in the 1870s, the old plantation saw a settlement of newcomers move into the vicinity of the mills which were built along the banks of the Frederica. In the forests of St. Simons and neighboring islands great oaks and virgin pines crashed to the ground under the axes of timber crews, and for more than a quarter-century the river echoed to the raucous buzz of the saws, while barges, loaded with lumber at old Gascoigne Bluff, busily plied the waters of the Frederica.

The new community was known as "The Mills," and its story is told in a remarkable unpublished scrapbook which is treasured by the St. Simons Library. Made by a former resident of the island whose family divided their time between New England and St. Simons during the mill era, the scrapbook tells how Norman W. Dodge, son of philanthropist William E. Dodge of New York City, and Titus G. Meigs also of New York, bought the Hamilton plantation for the Dodge-Meigs Lumber Mills. A church and a schoolhouse were built, and houses for the officials and workers of the mill colony included quaint Ivy Manor and charming Rose Cottage with its thousands of roses. There were cottages with scrollwork and gingerbread trim, and latticed summer-houses, and rustic arbors covered with wisteria and honeysuckle vines. There were pomegranate hedges, chinaberry trees and fig trees, shell walks, flower beds, and white picket fences.

Amateur plays were given in the old Hamilton warehouse at the end of the wharf at Gascoigne Bluff, and the great plantation barn became the general store for the mill community. The old Hamilton house was occupied by various families, and at one time was a boardinghouse; and its enclosed basement floor was used for dancing classes. The old place burned about 1885. Over the years the mills on the Frederica passed to other owners, and eventually there were four different mills, the Big Mill, the Planing Mill, the Cypress Mill, and the Lower Mill. As the timbers were cut out, the lumber supply diminished until finally in the early 1900s the St. Simons mills were shut down. After the mills were closed, some of the old fields were put under cultivation by a produce dealer; but the buildings had fallen into disuse and the grounds, overgrown and neglected, were littered with rubbish and debris and with rusting pieces of discarded equipment when, in 1927, the place became the property of Eugene W. Lewis of Detroit.

Like his close friend Howard Coffin, a pioneer in the development of automobiles and aircraft, Eugene Lewis was also the founder of the Industrial National Bank of Detroit. The Lewises had become interested in coastal Georgia on their annual visits to the Coffins on Sapelo Island, and when they bought the St. Simons property they planned to restore and enlarge a house built in the mill era, to clear and beautify the surrounding grounds, and to enjoy the place as a winter home. The rambling two-storied white clapboard house, remodeled and furnished with early colonial pieces, made a charming and appropriate residence; but as the new owners learned more about the history of their property they came to feel a responsibility to the old place— an urge to recreate something of its proud past.

The former name of Hamilton Plantation was restored, and, as Eugene Lewis writes in his *Yesterday on Hamilton and St. Simons Island, Georgia*, although he "had no idea of engaging in agriculture when the property was purchased, tradition, precedent, and the sentiment in the locality" induced him to try the experiment. And so the Lewises labored mightily: he to restore the land to its former productiveness, and she to restore the lawns and gardens to their former beauty.

Since they decided to limit the crops to vegetables, the fields where some of the original sea island cotton had been grown were planted in Boston head lettuce, peas, cucumbers, peppers, tomatoes, eggplant, cabbage, and cauliflower. An irrigation system was installed to pipe water from the artesian wells, and the fertile land yielded abundantly. At harvest time a hundred workers were employed—many of them descendants of former slaves on the plantation—and twelve to fifteen thousand crates of vegetables were shipped to northern markets.

While the master of the plantation concerned himself with what he called his vegetable acres, the mistress was busily superintending the restoration of the grounds. A quantity of ancient ballast discovered in the sand and mud near the dock provided historic stones for a delightful rock garden. Handmade English brick by the thousands, reclaimed from the ruins of old buildings, were used in garden walks, terraces, and for the floor of a slave cabin built in 1805, which was refinished and furnished as a recreation room. A rustic bridge across a shady brook led to a picturesque bamboo corridor, while flower-bordered gardens surrounded lily pools and swimming pool. The spacious lawns with their spreading trees were further beautified with palms and shrubs, and with masses of oleanders which were all propagated from seven original bushes found still growing upon the plantation. Old Hamilton, rescued from oblivion, was again one of the finest places on the island.

Another opportunity to be of service in preserving the early history of his plantation was presented to Eugene Lewis in connection with the rebuilding of *Old Ironsides*. When the historic ship went into dry dock in 1927, its restoration was made possible by funds raised by popular subscription, the greater part contributed by school children throughout the United States. Lewis, with his deep personal interest in the ship which contained timbers cut a century and a half before upon his Georgia property, took a leading part in the project in his home state of Michigan. Twice during the rebuilding of the ship he visited the yards in Boston, where he was told that some of the original live oak was still sound and would probably be good for another half-century. When the reconstructed frigate made a tour of the coast she received an enthusiastic welcome in her home waters in Georgia.

The first few seasons were prolific ones for the fields of old Hamilton Plantation. Then came the depression, "an era," says Eugene Lewis, "which was no time for a banker to be a gentleman farmer." Cultivation of the Hamilton fields was still carried on, but on a smaller scale, and shipment to distant markets was discontinued.

For a score of years Hamilton, part-time home of the Lewises, dispensed the gracious hospitality of antebellum days until war again brought an end to its plantation life. Once more labor conditions made the operation of large estates impractical, and in 1949 the plantation house with its surrounding grounds became a conference center for the Methodist church. Called Epworth-by-the-Sea after Epworth, England, birthplace of John and Charles Wesley, it is a beautiful and appropriate memorial with its spacious lawns, its shady brooks and lily pools, its bamboo walk and grassy retreats, its chapel, its palms and flowers and moss-draped trees.

The approach to the walled estate winds through a grove of spreading live oaks and gnarled old cedars past the grounds of the Cassina Garden Club, where two restored slave cabins stand in a nineteenth-century garden. Nearby a county park offers tables for picnicking and a marina for boating and fishing. On holidays water traffic on the Frederica is congested along old Gascoigne Bluff, the favorite course for racing boats, just as it was when slaves manned the oars of the dugouts and their rowing chanteys rang across the marshes.

Cannons Point

Cannons Point Plantation, home of the John Couper family, was located on the northeast part of St. Simons Island. Some of the old coastal places grew to have a personality of their own, formed by all the lives that touched them; but the Couper plantation was a setting for the magnetic personality of its owner. A man of distinction was John Couper, Esquire. Well over six feet in height, with keen blue eyes and red hair, he was cultured, charming, witty, a great raconteur and a famous host. With the sense of humor and spirit of mischief that had been his chief characteristics as a boy in Scotland, he used to claim that he had come to this country for the good of his native land. And indeed the fun-loving boy must have been a sore trial to his dignified Presbyterian minister father. John Couper might chuckle over the memory of throwing snowballs at a newly wedded couple as they emerged from his father's kirk in Lochwinnoch Parish, but Preacher Couper saw no humor in the escapade. After a succession of such pranks it was probably not hard for young John to persuade his father to allow him to come to the new colony as so many of his fellow Scotsmen had done, and where he was to live zestfully for three quarters of a century.

When he was only sixteen years old John Couper arrived in Georgia as an apprentice to the Savannah branch of an English business firm which soon afterward moved to Florida for the duration of the Revolutionary War. Ten years later young Couper went into business in Sunbury, where he became a prosperous merchant and a justice of Liberty County. He married Rebecca Maxwell of the Midway community, and their first child, James Hamilton Couper, was born in Sunbury. After the Couper-Hamilton partners bought their coastal properties, John Couper's interests turned to agriculture, and he and his wife made their permanent home on St. Simons.

The Couper property included widely scattered tracts, some on the northeast part of the island, some along the eastern side, and others at the south end; but John and Rebecca Couper selected Cannons Point for their homesite. The Point, the land originally granted to Daniel Cannon, carpenter at Frederica, lies between the Hampton River and Jones Creek, and it was here overlooking the river that the Coupers built the house in which they were to live for half a century. Referred to in Fanny Kemble's journal as a "roomy, comfortable, handsomely laid out mansion," it was further described by another visitor as a "fine three-storied mansion with a veranda running all around and a large portico on either side."

With a natural aptitude toward scientific agricultural experiment and the traditional green thumb of the Scotsman, John Couper became one of the leading agriculturists in the world. Cannons Point was not only one of the finest cotton plantations, but one of the most unusual and interesting places in the South. James Hamilton, whose business interests took him to the far corners of the world, sent cotton seeds and plants to John Couper for experiment on the St. Simons plantation; and under the expert and intelligent care of this master of agriculture, long-staple sea island cotton was developed to perfection. Couper was also one of the first coastal planters to experiment successfully with the cultivation of sugar cane.

In the gardens of the Cannons Point Plantation grew every fruit and flower, every shrub and tree that could be induced to thrive in its surroundings. There were groves of lemons and oranges, and there were date palms imported from Persia. When Thomas Jefferson was president he was interested in experimenting with the culture of olives in the United States, and he advised John Couper to order some olive trees from Marseilles. Acting upon Jefferson's advice, Couper imported two hundred trees, and since olives thrive near the sea in soil rich with the calcium of shell, the grove at Cannons Point yielded well and a fine quality of oil was pressed from the fruit.

In spite of his absorbing interest in agricultural experiment, John Couper found time for varied outside activities. One of the most influential citizens of early Georgia, he served as a member of the legislature, and in 1798 was a representative from Glynn County to the convention that drew up the state constitution. He was one of the first vestrymen of Christ Church, president of the Union Agricultural Society, a lifelong member of the St. Simons Hunt Club, and the first president of the St. Andrews Society of Darien. The first St. Simons lighthouse was built upon land sold for one dollar to the government from the Couper tract at the south end of the island, site of old Fort St. Simons. Although he was a man of universal interests, said to have known more prominent men in the United States and in Europe than any other man in the South, most of John Couper's busy life was spent at his plantation home, where he delighted in his family and friends, in his gardens, his books and paintings, and his view of the river.

From time to time early-nineteenth-century newspapers carried items of interest from the Cannons Point Plantation. In an old copy of the *Georgia Gazette*, under the heading "Rapid Vegetation," we are told that "Some English Peas brought by a British brig from Liverpool were planted by Mr. Couper of St. Simons Jan. 10. On the 27th of Feb. that gentleman sent the captain of the brig a peck of fine peas from the same seed." And in the columns of the Darien *Gazette*: "There is an old liveoak stump on Mr. Couper's plantation (St. Simons) from which the original sternpost of the *Constitution* was taken. Shortly after the capture of the *Guerriere* by that vessel a Bay Tree sprung up from the centre of the old stump—and has continued to flourish ever since—and as an evergreen may be seen at all times of the year constantly increasing in beauty and strength. We are told that Mr. C. guards it with uncommon care." A later newspaper relates that Mr. Couper was so impressed by the symbolism of a bay laurel crowning the Constitution Oak that he expressed his thoughts in an article and some original verse which brought interested letters from many people in this country and abroad. As a number of the writers requested souvenirs, the genial master of Cannons Point had paper weights, inkwells, vases, and other small articles carved of wood from the famous stump to be sent to all who wished them.

Far from being the dour and penurious Scotsman of tradition, John Couper was one of the jolliest and most generous of men, the kind of individual who might have been described by Dr. Johnson as the "most unscottified of his country's men." His quick wit and humor, his wide knowledge of nature, of literature, and of life, and his inexhaustible store of anecdotes made him a delightful companion. Visitors came from far and near to see his orchards, fields, and gardens, and stayed to enjoy his witty and learned conversation and his lavish hospitality. The fabulous dishes concocted by Sans Foix of Cannons Point are legendary. This famous cook's method of preparing a boned turkey that retained its original appearance was a secret never revealed; a spotless white cloth always at hand concealed the mystic rites from anyone who dared invade the sanctity of the kitchen. The master of Cannons Point taught his fiddler Johnny to play the pipes for the entertainment of visitors; and once when a committee was meeting to discuss the purchase of an organ for the church the incorrigible Mr. Couper arrived with his man Johnny, complete with bagpipes, and suggested him as a substitute for the organ.

The five Couper children were taught at home until each in turn went away to school; but even when some of the sons and daughters were absent the house at Cannons Point was always full. When the Basil Halls visited the Coupers their little daughter Eliza "was much pleased with the number of children at Cannons Point and not five minutes after her arrival went scampering about the passages with them." Relatives and friends came to spend a week with the hospitable family and were made welcome for a year, while their children shared the tutor who taught two generations of young Coupers.

Although the Couper boys spent their school and college years away from the plantation, all three inherited their father's love of agriculture. In a letter to his family in Scotland, John Couper humorously outlined plans for one of his sons: an education in New England followed by a period of study in Europe, after which he was to return to St. Simons "to plant cowpeas and pumpkins as his father has done."

As for the girls, they received the usual education for young ladies of the day. When the eldest daughter was enrolled in Miss Datty's Boarding School in Charleston, her curriculum included French, drawing, music, and dancing; and her love of pretty clothes is seen in bills for "disbursements made by Miss Julia Datty on account of Miss Ann Couper." One such bill lists eight pairs of shoes at a dollar and a quarter a pair, innumerable gloves at fifty cents a pair, a net handkerchief at two dollars and a half, and a tortoise-shell comb three dollars. "Ribbands" were a large item, as was embroidery silk.

In 1816 Miss Ann was married to Captain John Fraser of the British Army, and the couple lived in London for a few years. Some of her letters enclosed curls from the heads of their first two babies, curls that still gleam brightly between the time-yellowed pages of the letters. She enjoyed London social life, and still with her girlhood love of pretty clothes, wrote her mother in 1820, "I am in want of a Pelisse silk velvet but the price is so enormous in this Country. Knowing that those articles are comparatively cheap with you I must beg if convenient you will send me twelve yards of Royal Purple—also one pair white, one pair black silk stockings."

Even after the older Couper children were grown, the household at Cannons Point grew larger instead of smaller. When the Frasers returned to the United States to live, they remained for some years with the Coupers, and several of their nine children were born at Cannons Point. Also the place was a second home for the eight children of the James Hamilton Coupers of Hopeton. A mutually enjoyed companionship existed between John Couper and his grandchildren. Descendants tell how the master of Cannons Point, a lover of nature in her every mood, would march around the veranda during the wildest storms, arm-in-arm with one of his young granddaughters who shared his exultation in the elemental fury of the wind; and he and his grandsons were sometimes the despair of John Couper's eldest son, dignified James Hamilton Couper, whom they called "the old gentleman."

The respect which the world of agriculture felt for the experiments made by the master of Cannons Point was not always shared by his own household. During a time when every known variety of grape had been imported from Europe in an attempt to revive the region's early interest in winemaking one of the children wrote plaintively to an absent member of the family that the garden was "very grapy."

In spite of all the experiments, cotton remained the principal source of income at the Cannons Point Plantation. The exposed situation of the fields improved the quality of the cotton, but at the same time made it more vulnerable to the tropical hurricanes that sometimes struck just before the crop matured or before the mature cotton could be picked. John Couper had been able to take in stride the loss of a hundred-thousand-dollar crop in the hurricane of 1804 and to recoup the heavy losses suffered by embargoes and seizure of a large number of his slaves by the enemy in the War of 1812. In the hurricane of 1824 the "loss at Cannon's Point was incalculable, as the sea broke in and deluged the whole Point, sweeping away buildings, undoing the labor of years"; and when loss of the 1825 crop by an unprecedented plague of caterpillars was followed by a drop in cotton prices, the Cannons Point Plantation found itself in serious financial difficulties.

Since the acres that had supported scores of people were now scarcely making expenses, the planter was faced with the problem of providing for all of those who were dependent upon him, his family and his "people," as he always called his slaves. With wry humor he commented in a letter, "8% compound interest I found to be the real perpetual motion." A practical man, a man of sound judgment and calm wisdom, with the philosopher's reasonable attitude toward the triumphs and disappointments of life, he saw that he must relinquish the greater part of his coastal holdings. After the larger part of his property was sold to his partner, James Hamilton, a letter to his brother in Glasgow is typical of those characteristics which distinguished the man: "I saw no hope of paying my debts and retaining my property. . . . I thought it best during my life to meet the storm." And just as John Couper had marched exultantly in the teeth of the gales that swept in from the sea, so he met the storms of circumstance—a "man of cheerful yesterdays and confident tomorrows."

Their financial problems solved, the Coupers retained their beloved Cannons Point, where they lived happily past their golden wedding anniversary. After his wife's death in 1845, John Couper spent his remaining years with his eldest son's family at

Hopeton Plantation. He died in 1850, having lived for ninety-one years in what he always considered the best of all possible worlds. He and his wife are buried in old Christ Church Cemetery on St. Simons as are many members of his family. John Couper's epitaph, all but indecipherable in the time-stained marble of his monument, says "his long life was devoted to the duty of rendering himself most acceptable to his Creator by doing the most good to His creatures."

The plantation at Cannons Point continued to be planted in cotton and was used as a summer home for the James Hamilton Couper family. And so another generation of young people grew up in the beautiful old place, with the long happy days for horseback riding, boating, and picnicking, and the moonlight nights for music and dancing.

After the war Cannons Point Plantation was rented to various tenants, but there was no successful cultivation of the land that had once been famous for its abundance. In 1876 when the Reverend James Leigh was at Butler Island, he and James Maxwell Couper of Altama spent a day at Cannons Point. The house was untenanted, and the fields and gardens were overgrown. Old Rina, one of the family servants, was delighted to have company, and she served a meal of Scotch broth, cold beef, duck, potatoes, hominy, and rice. The two men wandered about the deserted place and talked about old times, and James Maxwell Couper dug some rosebushes and bulbs from his grandfather's garden to take back to Altama. The bulbs were later transplanted to the garden of the Couper residence on Ponce de Leon Avenue in Atlanta, where they multiplied and bloomed fragrantly each spring for half a century. When the Atlanta house was razed to make way for progress, the bulbs were moved again and planted in the gardens of old John Couper's great-great-grandchildren, from where some of them finally found their way back to Altama through a gift to the owners of the plantation.

Cannons Point eventually passed into other hands, and the fields were again cultivated to some extent. It is related that the olive trees were still bearing, and that oil made from the fruit was exhibited at the Exposition of 1898. We are also told that the remaining part of the old *Constitution* stump was sent to Atlanta to be displayed at the Exposition. The Cannons Point house burned near the turn of the century, and all that remained of the Couper home was the kitchen fireplace and chimney where Sans Foix cooked his fabulous meals. Great oleanders bloom around the crumbling foundations of the old house; a few silver-green olive trees may still be found in the tangle of undergrowth; and the long fronds of John Couper's Persian date palms rustle in the breeze from the Hampton River.

For years the Cannons Point property was owned by the Strachen family of Savannah, but since 1971 the old plantation has belonged to the Sea Island Company. Preliminary archaeological work has located historical sites to be preserved in event of future development.

Hampton

Hampton, owned by Major Pierce Butler of South Carolina, was one of the most widely known of the old St. Simons plantations because of its association with those two turbulent personalities, Aaron Burr and Fanny Kemble. Located across a narrow creek from Cannons Point, the plantation included 1700 acres on Hampton Point, the site of Oglethorpe's New Hampton outpost.

In 1758 the tract was granted to Henry Ellis, Georgia's second royal governor. The next owner was Philip Delegal followed by John Graham, who sold to Pierce Butler in 1774.

For his St. Simons plantation Major Butler acquired additional acreage adjacent to Hampton Point as well as the neighboring island of Little St. Simons. But no improvements were made on the property until several years after the close of the Revolutionary War.

In 1785, as shown in the eighteenth-century records, Pierce

Butler mortgaged his Georgia holdings to Jan Gabriel Tegelaar of Amsterdam, Holland, for 150,000 guilders. More than one historian has speculated that unsettled postwar conditions in the United States caused Butler to turn to Europe for funds to begin improving his property. Within a short time financing was arranged in South Carolina, and in 1791 the mortgage was paid and the land was free of debt.

In the meantime hundreds of workers and large quantities of materials, supplies, and livestock were transported by boat and barge from South Carolina to Georgia. With the vast amount of clearing, planting, and building to be done, Hampton was years being developed into one of the finest and most prosperous sea island cotton plantations on the Georgia coast. A letter written by Major Butler in 1794 says that his settlement at Hampton was "still in its infancy" but was expected to be completed within a year or two.

The Butler residence, or "Big House," was described by a visitor as "an imposing mansion, luxurious and hospitable"; and the comfortable guest cottages nearby were always ready to be placed at the disposal of friends. Skilled workmen were brought from Butler's South Carolina plantation to construct these and other buildings; old letters mention as many as half-a-dozen dwelling houses as well as an overseer's house, summerhouses, workshops, barns, stables, dairies, and other plantation buildings. The grounds were laid out into formal gardens and a sunken garden, and beautified with orange trees and hedges of oleander and boxwood.

The major, austere and dignified autocrat that he was, differed in every way from his easy-going, unpretentious neighbors; and the strict military regulations and discipline at Hampton were in marked contrast to the leisurely atmosphere of the other plantations. Hospitality was dispensed with unwonted formality, and the casual visitor arriving by boat must state his name and business to a warden or *vidette* at the dock before being escorted to the Big House. Managed with the regimental efficiency that was part of Pierce Butler's nature, Hampton was a model community that produced everything needed in the daily life of its inhabitants.

Since he was a prominent figure in the public life of the nation, Major Butler entertained many distinguished persons at Hampton. He often extended the hospitality of the plantation to business, social, and political friends when he was not in residence, confident that they would be cared for by his retinue of efficient servants in the manner for which the place was famous.

In 1804 Vice-President Aaron Burr, a former colleague of Pierce Butler's in the Senate, spent some weeks at Hampton soon after his duel in which Alexander Hamilton was killed. In the senator's absence Burr was entertained by residents of St. Simons and of towns on the mainland.

In a letter to his daughter written while he was at Hampton, Burr said that the plantation "affords plenty of milk, cream and butter; turkeys, fowls, kids, pigs, geese and mutton; fish of course in abundance; figs, peaches, melons, oranges and pomegranites." Further comforts were Madeira wine, brandy and porter; and his neighbor, Mr. Couper, had sent "an assortment of French wines, all excellent, and an orange shrub which makes a most delicious punch." This last was no doubt some of Mrs. Couper's orange cordial for which the "receipt" still exists. In delicate, faded script Rebecca Couper directs the reader to "put into three quarts of brandy the chips of 18 Seville oranges and let them steep a fortnight in a stone bottle close stopped. Boil two quarts of spring water with a pound and half of the finest sugar near an hour very gently. Clarify the water and sugar with the white of an egg, then strain it through a jellybag and boil it near half away. When it is cold strain the brandy into the syrup."

It was in this same year of 1804 that Hampton experienced the terrible hurricane that would have taken the lives of more than a hundred hands but for the quick thinking of Morris, one of the headmen of the plantation. In charge of the workers in the fields on Little St. Simons, Morris saw signs of the approaching storm and managed to get everyone into the hurricane house before the full force of the hurricane struck. In gratitude for his bravery, Major Butler offered Morris his freedom; when this was declined, Morris received a generous cash reward and a silver tankard engraved:

To Morris
from
P. Butler
For his faithful, judicious and spirited
conduct in the hurricane of September 8th, 1804, whereby the lives
of more than 100 persons
were, by Divine per-
mission, saved.

The coin-silver trophy was handed down to the eldest son in each generation of Morris's family. The fifth holder of the "Butler Cup" was Morris Seagrove of Brunswick, Georgia, who, having no son, returned the tankard to a Butler descendant then living in England. In recent years the heirloom has been returned to Georgia to be displayed in a coastal museum.

Hampton remained one of the finest and most luxurious plantations on the coast as long as Major Butler used it as a part-time home, but when his health prevented the annual visits to Georgia, the place was no longer maintained on the former lavish scale. The plantation continued to be a profitable enterprise but it ceased to be the model of efficiency of other days.

The young Pierce Butlers came down from Butler Island to Hampton in the early spring of 1839, and although Fanny Kemble Butler made little effort to enter into the social life of the community, she found a congenial friend at the neighboring plantation of Cannons Point. For even the critically discriminating Fanny could not resist the spell of John Couper's personality.

The young Englishwoman was both entranced and repelled by life at Hampton. She was excited over the wealth of wildflowers and wrote enthusiastically of the beauties of the island seen on her daily horseback rides. To pampered and fashionable Fanny Kemble St. Simons must have seemed little more than an elemental wilderness but that strain of wildness that was a part of her nature made her enjoy it in spite of herself. On her saddle horse Miss Kate or the spirited Montreal she spent hours each day in the woodlands that she thought even more beautiful than her beloved English parks.

But at Hampton young Mrs. Butler was incensed by the waste and decay on the once magnificent plantation. In the years since Major Butler's last visit the Big House had become sadly run down, the gardens overgrown and neglected. Fanny believed that the "ruins of the old dilapidated planter's palace" would hardly stand long enough to be carried away by the erosion that had already claimed the orange grove that had once stood between house and river.

After spending seven weeks at Hampton the Butlers returned to Philadelphia, where their marriage eventually ended in divorce. Fanny never returned to Georgia; but the old Butler house had been built to endure and is mentioned in a letter from Sally Butler almost twenty years later when she was at Hampton with her father, who often brought one or both of his daughters South with him. At this time the Couper family from Hopeton were vacationing at Cannons Point, and Sally had good times with them and with young people on the other plantations.

The ruins of the deserted house still stood when Frances Butler and her father came to Hampton in the spring of 1866, but all of the grandeur of the old plantation had completely disappeared. When the Butlers moved down from the rice plantation, bringing their household goods by raft, they found that Hampton, like other St. Simons places, had been despoiled during Federal occupation. The only habitable dwelling, a cottage entirely stripped of furniture, was refurnished and made comfortable and attractive with fresh curtains and slipcovers. Frances Butler described the cottage as having "four rooms down and two up, with a hall ten feet wide in the center and a veranda with Venetian shades running around it."

Since an old mule cart was their only conveyance, Pierce Butler bought his daughter a saddle horse, and she had two pet bear cubs, the "funniest, jolliest little beasts imaginable." With the neglected gardens cleared and trimmed, orange trees and shrubs in bloom, and the woodland a tangle of blossoms, the younger Fanny found the beauties of the island as enchanting as her mother had.

The Butlers found a number of their former slaves still living on the plantation. There were Uncle John and Maum Peggy (who had brought the silver half-dollars to Butler Island) and there was the old man, Carolina, who had been Major Butler's body-servant; and Preacher John who had lived at Hampton from its beginning and who saw the fifth generation of the family when Sally Butler Wister came to visit with her little boy.

Bram was employed to replant the fields and had no trouble with the hands as eight members of his own family were working under him. The first year the cotton crop did well but the next year, after Pierce Butler's sudden death, the crop was destroyed by army worms in a single night.

Frances Butler, first alone except for her housekeeper and later with her husband, the Reverend James Leigh, continued to spend part of the year at Hampton. But, after ten years of effort, it was obvious that profitable operation of the place was impossible. The ruins of Major Butler's old house burned in 1871.

Pierce Butler died intestate and, when his estate was finally settled, Sally Butler Wister's share was the principal part of Hampton Plantation, which eventually passed by inheritance to her son, Owen Wister, novelist.

Frances Butler Leigh's share of her father's property included Little St. Simons, which was sold in the early 1900s to a pencil manufacturer for the red cedar growing in abundance on the island. It developed that many of the cedars were so twisted by the ocean winds that they were not suitable for the manufacture of pencils, and after all usable trees were cut Little St. Simons became a private vacation retreat for the owner's family and friends.

Left almost entirely in its natural state, the island attracts such a wide variety of sea and land birds that it is known as one of the finest bird-watching areas on the Atlantic coast. In recent years Little St. Simons has been opened to reservations for day or overnight visitors who are transported aboard boats that dock near the site used by Hampton Plantation boats in antebellum days.

Hampton lay undisturbed for almost three quarters of a century before there was any sign of life beyond the brilliant flash of a bird's wing or the motion of a deer in the undergrowth. As the old place gradually returned to the semitropical wilderness from which it came, time completed its cycle; in World War II there was a lookout on the lonely tip of St. Simons Island where Oglethorpe stationed his New Hampton outpost two centuries before.

In the late 1970s it was announced that the Hampton property would be developed as a residential subdivision with paved streets leading to building lots. Some of the ruins of Major Butler's eighteenth-century buildings would be leveled.

Because of the significance of the site as one of the few antebellum plantations that had never been disturbed, a limited archaeological survey was allowed before extensive clearing was started. From March 20 to May 19, 1978, members of the Anthropology and Archaeology Department of the University of Florida excavated the historic site at Hampton Point.

Evidence was found of occupation of a prehistoric village and nomadic camp site, indicated by pottery shards of the Pine Harbor/Savannah II period; there was also evidence of Spanish contact in the sixteenth-century mission days. Artifacts from plantation times included fragments of royal pattern and bake creamware, of direct painted pearlware, porcelain, and earthenware tile, with innumerable fragments of wine bottles.

Ruins of the Butler residence, or Big House, showed it to have been of typical low-country construction, with four fallen brick chimneys and supports of a wide veranda around three sides. Nearby was the ruin of the customary detached kitchen.

Still standing were remnants of the walled formal gardens with ruins of two summerhouses of tabby. The site of the overseer's house was marked by a tall brick chimney, a bricklined

well, and the remains of a detached kitchen. Other ruins surveyed included a large stable complex with walls to ten feet high,
at least two slave settlements of the four mentioned in old com-
munications, and a number of unidentified structures, probably
guesthouses, workshops, and other plantation buildings.

Some of the ruins of once-beautiful Hampton Plantation were
left standing, others were removed to clear the land for development. As noted in the archaeological report: "Hampton's ruins
attest to its former magnificance." *Sic transit gloria mundi.*

Retreat

Retreat Plantation, on the south end of St. Simons Island, was
the property of Major William Page, a friend of Major Butler,
who had come from Pages Point, South Carolina, and had purchased island and mainland acreage along the Georgia coast in
the early 1800s. The St. Simons property which Major Page
called Retreat was formerly the plantation where the Thomas
Spaldings of Sapelo had lived when they were first married. Major and Mrs. Page had only one child, a daughter Anna Matilda.
The family lived in the house that was a replica of General
Oglethorpe's old Frederica place, Orange Hall, a roomy eighteenth-century English-style cottage sturdily built to stand the
West Indian gales that sometimes blew in from the sea. The
Pages planned to build a larger house overlooking the water of
channel and sound, but the years went by and they were com-
fortable in their simple home.

As young Ann Page grew up she shared her mother's love for
homemaking and gardening, and inherited her father's genius
for managing the affairs of the great plantations. Pretty and
lovable, she was a favorite with everybody and a sought-after
belle of the coastal region. In 1823 a young lawyer from Massachusetts, Thomas Butler King, came South on a visit, and was
so charmed with the coastland that he decided to make his home

in Georgia. One of the chief charms must have been Ann Page, for in December 1824 the editor of the Darien *Gazette* broke into plaintive verse:

"We Bachelors
Whom love abhors
And whom each fair despises
May envy those
More lucky beaus
Who woo and win those prizes
That we in vain
Have strove to gain
Through endless days of sorrow
Yet we may pray
If not today
Our times may come tomorrow
Married: At Retreat, St. Simons Island, on the 1st. inst.
by the Rev. Edmund Mathews, Thomas B. King to
Anna Matilda, only daughter of Major William Page."

Within little more than two years after their daughter's marriage, Major and Mrs. Page both died, and Ann Page King inherited the coastal property. After spending a few years at Retreat the Thomas Butler Kings and their growing family lived on one of the mainland plantations, Waverly, near the present town of Kingsland. Young Mr. King was already becoming interested in the statesman's career that was to be his life's work; and when a depression in cotton prices made operation of their several plantations impractical the family disposed of most of the mainland property and moved to the St. Simons place.

Like the Pages before them, the King family lived in the house built in the 1700s by the Spaldings, the charming English cottage of handhewn timbers with shuttered veranda and gabled roof. They set out an avenue of live oaks leading to the site selected for the plantation mansion, and a drive bordered by water oaks led to the cottage, which stood some distance to the right of the intended house site. One can imagine the plans Butler and Ann

King must have made for a larger house, but the years at Retreat were too filled with living to leave time for the building of mansions. Meanwhile there was a guesthouse for overnight visitors, the daughters were happy in their dormer-windowed bedrooms, and the sons had their own "Grasshopper Hall." Clustered around the cottage, besides the annexes for extra sleeping quarters, were hothouses, summerhouses, the customary detached kitchen, and the schoolhouse where lessons were taught until the children were old enough to go East to study—the girls to finishing schools, the boys to Yale and Princeton.

Other buildings in the little settlement around the dwelling were the plantation hospital and the famous four-storied cotton house that was used as a guide for ships during the years when there was no lighthouse on the island. There was the tabby barn, and there were the servants' quarters. Favorite among the younger servants was Neptune Small, who although not much older than the boys themselves kept a stern eye on the young gentlemen in Grasshopper Hall. There were Juno, Minerva, and Adelette, and Naynie who reigned supreme at Retreat. Naynie, who had taken care of Ann Page King when she was a baby, was to live to help "raise" the third generation.

The real beauty of Retreat was in its surrounding gardens. The spacious grounds were laid out in formal gardens in which bloomed almost every flower and shrub known to the region; there were nearly a hundred varieties of roses, but never a flower without a fragrance. A "cedar pleasaunce" formed a windbreak between house and beach, and shell walks led through the delightful maze of the Kings' famous arboretum. A "plantation" in the English manner, the arboretum contained specimen trees and rare shrubs, many of which had been brought in tubs on sailing vessels from foreign parts, gifts from friends of Thomas Butler King.

Many stories are handed down of houseparties and dances, of amateur theatricals, of banquets and musicales and weddings of the daughters of the household. With the King family of nine children, the sons handsome and gallant, the daughters beautiful and talented, life was lighthearted and charming at Retreat. And truly a retreat his home must have been to Thomas Butler King. Son of a family of Massachusetts statesmen, the master of Retreat became a prominent figure in affairs of government, affairs that often took him across the continent and to foreign countries.

A member of the House of Representatives for more than a decade, and chairman of the House Naval Committee at the time that *Old Ironsides* was first rebuilt, Thomas Butler King was presented with an ornamental vase made from some of the ship timbers that had come from St. Simons Island. Fashioned in the design of the famous Warwick Vase the handsomely carved urn is still treasured by the Kings' descendants. When California was ceded to the United States by Mexico, Thomas Butler King was appointed by President Taylor to inspect the territory. Later he served for a time as collector of the port of San Francisco. In his absence the management of the plantation fell into the competent hands of his wife, who was as well known for the superi-

The Warwick Vase

ority of the cotton grown in the fields of Retreat as for the perfection of the roses grown in her famous gardens.

What an amazing woman Anna Page King must have been! With her large family of children, the management of the vast acres of the plantation, the personal care which she gave to her many slaves, the hours spent with her flowers and shrubs, her home still had a reputation for an ease and grace of hospitality which has long outlived the house itself. Prominent men of this and other countries, friends and associates of Thomas Butler King, were frequent visitors, and when Audubon visited there he was "fain to think he had landed on one of the fairy islands said to have existed in the Golden Age."

The years at Retreat were gracious and happy ones, an existence almost ideal until 1859, when the eldest son, Butler, and his mother died within the year. When the clouds of war began to gather and the storm broke over the nation, it shattered the foundations of Thomas Butler King's life. Here was a war between the government to which he had given a lifetime of service and his beloved Southland in which the happiest moments of that lifetime had been lived. A heartbroken father saw his remaining sons go to war, one never to return. At the same time an important mission for the Confederate government required his presence in Europe. Small wonder Thomas Butler King's health failed, and he was laid to rest in 1864 beside his wife in Christ Church cemetery.

The other members of the household had refugeed to their place "The Refuge" in Ware County, and Retreat stood deserted during the war years. In the nightmare days of Reconstruction the old homestead was confiscated by an individual of carpetbagger fame. When it was finally restored to its owners the fields were unplanted, fences down, livestock and equipment gone. But the Mallery Kings decided to come with their family to live at Retreat in an attempt to bring the old place back to some of its former productiveness. The Kings' three young daughters, Mary Anna, Frances Buford, and Florence Page, were just the age to find high adventure in their life on the neglected plantation.

There were other young people whose families were trying to restore their property, and there were boys and girls at the Mills on the old Hamilton Plantation.

Of course Neptune and some of the other servants had come back to the island with the family, and the three girls never tired of hearing them tell about life at Retreat before the war. They shuddered delightfully over tales of the "Ghost with the Long Arms" that used to walk beneath the live oaks and of the dire calamities that befell those to whom it beckoned. They thrilled over the romances of the four lovely daughters of the household: of Hannah, who married William Audley Couper and was for a time mistress of Hamilton Plantation on the Frederica; of Florence, for whom the youngest of the three girls was named; of Virginia, whose pet name was Appeleeta; and of Georgia, who sang like an angel. They liked to hear how visitors approaching the river landing would silence their boatmen's songs to listen with delight to the sweet girlish voice drifting over the water.

The girls liked to hear, too, the stories Neptune told of the war years. Like many servants of the Old South, he had gone to war with Lord King, and when the young captain fell in the battle of Fredericksburg, Neptune had carried him in from the battlefield and had brought his body back to Georgia. He then made his way back to the battlefront to be with the youngest son, Cuyler, whom the family called "Tippecanoe." The two were together throughout the war, both homesick for their peaceful island, and when the moon was full Neptune would remind the boy "High water on the bar, Marse Tip."

The stables that had housed the carriage and saddle horses were empty now, so the girls persuaded Neptune to show them how to yoke Tom and Jerry, the team of gentle oxen. There were places they wanted to go and an ox cart was better than walking, and soon the three pretty girls in their strange equipage were a familiar sight on the island. The unusual conveyance often brought excitement—such as the time one of the oxen decided to lie down while the girls were attending church, and it took the efforts of most of the men of the congregation to haul him to his

Neptune Small (right) recounting his adventures in the Civil War

feet, get the yoke and reins untangled, and start the young ladies on their way home. Another time when the girls were visiting some young people on a neighboring plantation the oxen were tied to the porch railing. The visit lasted too long even for the patience of Tom and Jerry, and a crash brought everyone to the porch to find that the oxen had determined to pull loose and go home, carrying part of the railing with them.

And so for a few years young feet again danced over the mellowed old floors of Retreat; Japanese lanterns flickered over the lawns; song and laughter drifted over the water. But although the King girls had some happy times in the years they spent on the old plantation, these were heartbreaking years for Mallery and Eugenia. Their youngest child, Thomas Butler King III, died when he was scarcely more than a baby. And the difficulties of restoring the plantation were proving insurmountable. Adequate help was not to be had; the crops were disappointing, with cotton prices low. Finally Mallery King reluctantly gave up the attempt to revive Retreat, moved his family back to the mainland, and took up other interests. After standing empty a few years the plantation house and the cotton house went up in flames one night as the wind blew in across the channel. Later a part of the old plantation became the Sea Island Golf Club, and the spreading acres of Retreat again offered pleasure to visitors from far and near.

A quarter of a century after the romance-haunted old house burned, the last chapter in its history was being written in New England in the native state of Thomas Butler King. In the town of Attleboro, Massachusetts, in 1929, an antique dealer bought at auction an old clock with wooden works that had a card inside its back cover which read "U.S.S. Ethan Allen on blockade Jan. 10, 1863." The G.A.R. Dining Club of Attleboro undertook to trace ownership of the clock. With the help of Charles C. Cain, Jr., publisher of the Attleboro *Daily Sun*, Navy Department records were searched, and it was discovered from an old ship's log in the Washington Archives that the *Ethan Allen* on that date in 1863 had been at St. Simons Island, Georgia. Subsequent investigation established the fact that the clock had been taken from the Kings' house at Retreat Plantation. It was arranged for a delegation of citizens from Attleboro to make the trip to Georgia to return the clock to descendants of the King family.

In May 1930 the group from Massachusetts arrived by boat at Savannah, where they received a hospitable welcome. They proceeded by car to Brunswick, where they found the city decked out in bunting and holiday mood to greet them. As the motorcade of visitors and their Georgia hosts reached the grounds of old Retreat, Navy cruisers and Coast Guard boats, with flags waving and pennants flying, steamed into the harbor. With Howard Coffin, founder of Sea Island, as master of ceremonies, Congressman Martin of Massachusetts eloquently presented the clock; Senator George of Georgia, with equal eloquence, accepted it for the King descendants who, in turn, presented it to Mr. Coffin to be placed in the Sea Island Golf Clubhouse. Music was furnished by descendants of slaves of the plantation. The beautiful bass voice of Neptune's son Clarence and the high sweet soprano of his daughter Cornelia drifted over the water, and the old clock ticked the minutes away as serenely as though it had not been gone from its island home for almost three score

Ceremony held upon the return of the clock to Retreat Plantation

years and ten. A few years later an unfortunate fire broke out in the clubhouse and, before it could be extinguished, the historic old clock had been destroyed.

The approach to the Sea Island Golf Club skirts the original avenue of trees, leading past the ruins of the slave hospital. The central part of the clubhouse itself is the old tabby barn. In a shady grove by a lily-covered small pond is the little cemetery where plantation slaves and their descendants have been buried since 1800. The inscription on the bronze tablet which marks the tombstone of Neptune Small tells its own story of the devotion of this man to the family which held him in the highest affection and esteem all of his long life. Looking up the grass-grown avenue between the ancient live oaks, one half expects to see the gardens of old Retreat Plantation through the spreading moss-hung branches.

Long View

Long View, near Cannons Point, was the part-time home of Mrs. John McNish and her daughter, Mary Jane. Mrs. McNish, the former Ann Mary Johnston, was the daughter of Thomas and Mary Dews Johnston of the Hermitage Plantation on the Little Ogeechee River near Savannah [not to be confused with de Montalet's Hermitage Plantation on the Savannah River]. Thomas Johnston, a native of Scotland, was related to John Couper of Cannons Point Plantation. When Ann Mary, age thirteen, and her sister, Jane Elizabeth, age twelve, were orphaned, they were taken into the hospitable Couper home, where they grew up as daughters of the household.

When Ann Mary was seventeen years old, John McNish of Galloway County, Scotland, came to St. Simons Island as clerk and bookkeeper for John Couper and his partner, James Hamilton. Within a few years the young Scotsman had settled in Savannah, where he became a prosperous cotton merchant.

In 1819 John McNish and Ann Mary Johnston were married in the Couper home "without much parade or show." McNish's wedding gift to his bride was a dainty set of pearl and amethyst jewelry, made in Paris and consisting of a necklace, two bracelets, earrings, brooch, and tiara. The exquisite set, in its original case, is still treasured by descendants of the couple, and individual pieces have been worn by brides of each succeeding generation.

For their home in Savannah itemized bills of lading still in existence show quantities of silverware, "41 and ¾ yards Brussels carpet and a fancy hearthrug to suit," and other furnishings ordered by John McNish from London and Liverpool. The handsome pieces of hollow ware and flat silver, all marked with the thistle of Scotland, are still in the possession of the family.

After their marriage, John and Ann McNish divided their time between their townhouse in Savannah and the Hermitage Plantation, which they shared with Ann's sister, Jane Elizabeth. Two children were born to the couple, a daughter, Mary Jane, and a son, William Couper, named for his grandfather, William McNish, and for John Couper of Cannons Point. Little Couper McNish died in October 1826, at the age of eighteen months. John McNish died in December of the same year.

After her husband's death, Ann Johnston McNish built the Long View house on four acres of Cannons Point land leased from John Couper for a yearly rental of one dollar. Here Ann and her young daughter could be near the Coupers, and Mary Jane could know the pleasant island life that Ann had enjoyed as a girl. Except for Mary Jane's boarding-school years in Philadelphia, the McNishes still lived at the Hermitage. But they were often at Long View, which was staffed and kept in readiness for their arrival.

A letter from Ann McNish, written from Long View in 1836, shows her love for the place and her pleasure in the surroundings. She reports "the little birds well and happy and the plants growing. Anet and Fox [horses?] much pleased with the fresh springing grass, and Betty, the cow, and baby doing well." She also tells of preparations for the celebration of the centennial of the founding of Frederica, with John Fraser as master of ceremonies and with a ball, "of course," included in the plans.

In 1843 Mary Jane McNish was married to Leighton Wilson Hazlehurst, the son of Robert and Elizabeth Wilson Hazlehurst, whose families were among the earliest settlers of Glynn County.

In the 1860s Long View, like other places on St. Simons, was left unoccupied. Ann Johnston McNish spent the war years with Mary Jane and her family at their summer home in Wayne County, where she died in 1869.

Lawrence

The tract of land known as Lawrence, adjoining Cannons Point Plantation, was granted to John Lawrence, one of the early settlers of Frederica. After passing into other ownership, the property came back into the family when it was acquired by A. D. Lawrence, who sold it to John Couper of Cannons Point in 1801. In the late 1820s and early 1830s Couper's son-in-law, Captain John Fraser, and his family lived at Lawrence.

In 1866 the property, along with Cannons Point, was sold by the Couper family to A. Griswold of Newport, Rhode Island. Lawrence was later owned by Anna Gould Dodge, widow of Anson Dodge, who deeded it in the early 1900s to sons of Belle Stevens Taylor in exchange for land at Frederica. Lawrence later became the property of the Sea Island Company.

Oatlands

Oatlands, just south of Lawrence, was included in the holdings of colonist James Bruce. In 1788 the place was sold by Bruce's daughters, Rebecca and Elizabeth, to James Harrison. In the early 1800s Oatlands became the property and part-time home of Dr. Robert Grant of the river plantation, Elizafield, on the mainland. In later years it was owned by the Couper family. The old place passed through various hands until the 1940s when it was acquired by Captain Douglas Taylor, son of Belle Stevens Taylor, in exchange for property at Frederica, now included in Fort Frederica National Monument. At Captain Taylor's death in 1977 Oatlands was inherited by his stepson, Nathaniel I. Hasell. The tabby foundations of the old Grant house are still standing.

Sinclair

Sinclair, the property that was developed in Oglethorpe's time by Archibald Sinclair, was known in plantation days as St. Clair, evidently a corruption of the name Sinclair.

In 1745 this tract was named as one of the successful plantations on St. Simons Island. However, the property was not listed in the 1755 Entry of Claims, which indicates that the family had left the island and that the Sinclair grant was vacant.

In 1765 the land was granted to Donald Forbes. Forbes sold to Lachlan McIntosh, whose son, Major William McIntosh, lived in the old plantation house until his death in 1799. A headstone placed by the Daughters of the American Revolution marks Major McIntosh's grave, and nearby are the little brick tombs of his two children.

The property was bought from the McIntosh estate by Major Pierce Butler, who sold to Alexander Wylly; and Sinclair, known at that time as St. Clair, was included in Wylly's Village Plantation. When Mrs. Wylly's mother, Mrs. Ann Armstrong, came from the Bahamas to make her home on St. Simons, she lived in the old St. Clair house where she died in 1816. And when the Wyllys' daughter, Frances, was married to Dr. William Fraser, "late of the Royal Navy" and brother of John Fraser, the couple lived for a time at St. Clair before moving to Darien, where Dr. Fraser served as mayor.

The house was later used as a meeting place for the *bon vivant* St. Clair Club. It was also headquarters for the Agricultural and Sporting Club organized by island planters in 1832. The old plantation house burned in 1857.

Over the following years the place belonged to various owners, and in 1954 a bronze marker was erected on the Sinclair tract by the Georgia Historical Commission.

The Village

The Village, on the eastern side of the island, was the plantation home of the Alexander Wylly family.

Alexander Campbell Wylly, born in Savannah and educated at Oxford, remained loyal to England during the Revolutionary War, and served as an officer in the British Army. At the close of the war, the Wylly family went to live in the Bahamas, where young Captain Wylly was married to Margaret Armstrong, the daughter of another loyalist family.

In the early 1800s, when much of the bitter feeling against Britain had been forgotten, Captain Wylly, with his wife and four children, returned to Georgia. For several years they lived on Jekyll Island, where three more children were born to the family.

When Captain Wylly bought the Sinclair property on St. Simons Island, the family lived for a time in the old house described as a big, rambling bungalow overshadowed by a great live oak known locally as "Old England." It was here that the youngest Wylly daughter, Caroline, was born.

Captain Wylly added adjacent land to his original purchase until his holdings covered more than a thousand acres. Included in the property was the old Salzburger settlement, and it was from this tract, known as the German Village, that the Wylly plantation took its name.

Additions were built onto a cottage already on the land, and the result was a great sprawling house large enough for the Wylly family and their many friends and relatives who visited often from Savannah, England, and the Bahamas.

Although Alexander Wylly and his wife lived on St. Simons Island for the rest of their lives, their loyalty to England never changed. Three portraits dominated the walls of the Village drawing room—one of their eldest daughter Susan, painted by Gilbert Stuart; the other two of the Duke of Wellington and Admiral Nelson, in the opinion of Captain and Mrs. Wylly "the greatest men of the nineteenth century."

Perhaps because of their allegiance to England, no Village slaves were taken by force when the British occupied the island in the last days of the War of 1812. Every attempt was made, however, to get the Wylly Negroes to leave. All refused except Jim, who was inclined to believe the extravagant promises made by the British. His family and friends finally persuaded him to stay, but afterward they always called him "Jim-Gwine-Runaway."

When the youngest daughter, sixteen-year-old Caroline, was married to James Hamilton Couper in 1827, Captain Wylly wore his regimentals "for the first and only time since he left Nassau," and the marriage lines were read in front of the Wellington and Nelson portraits in the Village drawing room. From the letter of a relative of the Wyllys we have a description of the evening wedding, attended by all of the island families "which made it so crowded there could be no dancing."

"At eleven we went to supper in the dining room with an overflow table set in the piazza—cold roast and boiled turkey, stuffed hams, oyster pies, paté of shrimp and crab, syllabub by the hundred glasses, and the punch bowl twice filled. At twelve the health of the bride and groom was drunk in full glasses, and they bowed and curtsied goodnight and took leave for Cannon's Point, from where they will go tomorrow to Hopeton on the early flood tide, in Mr. Couper's big boat, the *Lady Love*."

Susan Wylly died in 1829. The next year the oldest son, Alexander William, married Sarah Spalding, daughter of Thomas

Spalding of Sapelo. Captain Wylly died in 1833, and in 1838 the younger son, John, was killed by Dr. Thomas Hazzard in a quarrel over the boundary line between the Village and the Hazzard property.

Mrs. Wylly and her unmarried daughters continued to live at the Village until her death in 1850. The daughters remained for a time on the plantation, and later moved to Savannah, where the Stuart portrait of lovely Susan Wylly hangs in the Owens-Thomas House Museum. On St. Simons Island a bronze historical marker points out the site of the old Salzburger settlement which is still known as the German Village.

Over the years the Wylly land was divided into different tracts and belonged to various owners. Part of the old Village grounds eventually came back into possession of descendants of the family, while part was included in the property known as Musgrove Plantation.

Musgrove

Musgrove, a twentieth-century plantation with an eighteenth-century name and grounds that were nineteenth-century cotton fields, lies along Village Creek on the east side of St. Simons Island. Named for the half-Indian "Princess" Mary Musgrove who played an important part in early Georgia history, the plantation was created in 1938 as a part-time home for the Reynolds-Bagley family.

With its five hundred acres of high ground and some seven hundred and fifty acres of protective marshland; with its pines, palms and ancient live oaks, its natural plantings of vines, shrubs and flowers, Musgrove was for almost four decades a secluded retreat for its owners, "the world forgetting by the world forgot."

Change came in 1976 when the plantation became renowned as the site of President-Elect Jimmy Carter's unprecedented pre-inaugural cabinet meeting. Mementos of the historic event, treasured along with eighteenth- and nineteenth-century relics found on the grounds, add another dimension to the heritage of Musgrove Plantation.

West Point and Pikes Bluff

West Point and Pikes Bluff, just north of Frederica, were the plantations of Colonel William Wigg Hazzard and his younger brother, Dr. Thomas Fuller Hazzard. The West Point property, which had belonged to Donald Mackay, then to James Spalding, and later to Lachlan McIntosh, was purchased by Colonel Hazzard in 1818.

Adjoining West Point to the north, the Pikes Bluff tract, which included Oglethorpe's old Pikes sentry station, was the property of Edmund Matthews, rector of Christ Church, Frederica. After Mr. Matthews's death in 1827, Pikes Bluff was bought from his estate by the Hazzards and became the home of the younger brother.

The brothers were communicants of Christ Church, where Colonel Hazzard served a number of terms as warden and Dr. Thomas served on the vestry. Both represented Glynn County in the state legislature. They were enthusiastic sportsmen, with their racing boats, *Shark* and *Comet*, and their famous pack of deer hounds. Both were writers of some prominence locally. The colonel wrote a short history of Glynn County in 1825, and the doctor published articles on agriculture, on the treatment of influenza, and on the culture of flowers "as conducive to health, pleasure and rational amusement."

Part of the Hazzard property joined the Village land, and in December 1838 a bitter dispute over boundary lines resulted in John Wylly of the Village being shot by Dr. Thomas Hazzard. He was tried for aggravated manslaughter but was not convicted.

Dr. Thomas Hazzard died in 1849 and his widow sold to Colonel Hazzard, who cultivated West Point and Pikes Bluff as one large plantation. After the colonel's death his family moved to South Carolina, and in 1882 his heirs sold the property to James C. Chapman "late of Kent, England," and a layreader for Christ Church, Frederica.

The property was unoccupied for years until twentieth-century owners, Dr. and Mrs. Maxwell Berry, restored part of the old plantation and built a gracious, columned house enjoyed by three generations of the family. In 1955 West Point passed from the Berry estate to other owners, and it was announced that the property would be divided into residential lots. In 1957 a small portion of the tract was purchased for addition to the adjoining Fort Frederica National Monument.

As for the Pikes Bluff part of the old Hazzard plantation, it passed through various hands before being acquired by the Sea Island Company. As with Cannons Point, a preliminary archaeological survey has pinpointed sites of historical significance to be preserved in case of future development.

Orange Grove

Orange Grove, located south of Frederica on Dunbar Creek, belonged for much of the twentieth century to descendants of colonial owners.

The tract was originally granted to John Terry, silversmith and recorder of Frederica, who "planted hundreds of orange trees and called his plantation Orange Grove." The Terry tract was later vacated and the property was granted to James Bruce, a Savannah merchant who also owned a lot in Frederica Town.

In 1790 James Bruce's daughter, Rebecca, was married to Major Samuel Wright of Savannah. Major Wright had come to Georgia before the Revolutionary War, had served as an officer with the American forces, and after the war had operated a "vendue store in Savannah on the Bay." After their marriage Samuel and Rebecca Bruce Wright made their home on St. Simons Island on the plantation known as Orange Grove.

From the first year of his residence on St. Simons Island, Major Wright was prominent in local affairs. He served as a commissioner of Glynn Academy in 1791 and 1792, represented Glynn County in the state legislature for five terms, was elected commissioner for the town of Frederica in 1803, and served as a justice of the Inferior Court from 1791 until his death in 1804.

On February 2, 1808, the Wrights' daughter, Mary, was married to George Abbott of Frederica in what must have been the first marriage ceremony solemnized by the Reverend Mr. William Best in the newly organized parish of Christ Church, Frederica.

George Abbott, a lineal descendant of John Abbott, Bishop of Sussex, had come from Ireland to St. Simons in the late 1700s and had settled at Frederica, where he operated a mercantile business. When regular mail service for the island was established in 1800 George Abbott was the first postmaster. He was one of the founders of Christ Church, Frederica, and laid the cornerstone for the church built in 1820.

George and Mary Wright Abbott's children and their orphaned cousin, Deborah Abbott, grew up on Orange Grove Plantation in the house known as Rose Hill. When the girls were grown the younger daughter, Ann, was married to James Gowen, son of William and Mary Harrison Gowen, early settlers of St. Simons Island.

The Orange Grove property passed out of Wright-Abbott possession shortly after the War Between the States and remained out of the family until 1929 when it was purchased by Albert Fendig, Sr., and his wife, Gladys Gowen Fendig, a direct descendant of Major Samuel Wright. The Fendig house on Dunbar Creek was only a few hundred feet from the old pile of bricks that marked the ruins of the Wright home, and the site of the Abbotts' Rose Hill could be seen nearer the road.

After Orange Grove had been in the Fendig family for four decades the historic tract became part of the property known as Sea Palms West. Some of the early inhabitants of Orange Grove are commemorated by the names of Terry Creek, Abbott Lane, and Major Wright Road.

St. Clair and Black Banks

St. Clair, sometimes known as New St. Clair, and Black Banks were the plantations of the Gould family.

James Gould, a native of Granville, Massachusetts, built the original St. Simons lighthouse. Descendants believe that he arrived in 1794 in connection with the shipping of timbers for the United States Navy. Later he operated a lumbering business on the St. Marys River, which separated south Georgia from Spanish east Florida. In the early 1800s he and his wife, the former Jane Harris of New Providence, with their children and slaves, narrowly escaped with their lives when their house was burned by marauding Indians.

While he and his family were staying in Savannah with Jane's relatives, Captain and Mrs. Samuel Bunch, James Gould learned that the government was taking bids for the erection of a lighthouse on St. Simons Island. He submitted a bid which was accepted on May 25, 1807. The lighthouse was to be constructed at the south end of the island on a four-acre plot of land that had been sold to the government for the sum of one dollar by John Couper of Cannons Point. Specifications called for an octagonal tower 75 feet high topped by a 10-foot iron lantern, or light chamber, equipped with a set of oil lamps suspended by chains. In addition to the light tower, the contract included a keeper's cottage with detached kitchen.

The lighthouse was completed in 1810 and was formally established in 1811. James Gould was appointed by President Madison to serve as the first keeper, a position that he was to fill for twenty-seven years. He lived with his family in the keeper's cottage at the foot of the tower, and leased adjacent land for cultivation. Since no assistant was appointed, James Gould trained some of his slaves to keep the lamps cleaned and filled with oil, and to take their turn at the nightwatch in the light chamber. One helper was so devoted to his work with the lamps that his fellows nicknamed him "Lamp Black."

Soon after the end of the War of 1812, James Gould bought

First St. Simons Lighthouse, commissioned in 1811. James Gould was the builder and the first keeper.

his first St. Simons property, a tract that included land purchased from the Commissioners of Confiscated Estates and acreage from the estate of Major Samuel Wright. The entire 900-acre plantation, known as St. Clair, or New St. Clair, lay across the center of the island from Black Banks River to Dunbar Creek.

Research has uncovered no record of any of this property ever having been claimed by Archibald Sinclair, tithingman at Frederica, whose Sinclair tract on the northeast side of the island was known in plantation days as St. Clair. It is possible, however, that part of the New St. Clair land had also been claimed by Archibald Sinclair and that it, too, had been called Sinclair in the early years.

On the New St. Clair Plantation, James Gould built a spacious two-storied tabby house with one-story wings at either side, and in the surrounding fields he planted sea island cotton. His two sons, James F. and Horace Bunch, were sent to preparatory school in New Haven and afterward to Yale, and his daughters, Mary and Jane, were educated at the Moravian Seminary in Bethlehem, Pennsylvania.

In 1820 James Gould's wife died, leaving Mary, as eldest daughter, to take charge of her father's home, with the help of her mother's sister, "Aunt Caroline." From an unpublished manuscript written by a member of the family, we have a word picture of the beauty brought to St. Clair by Mary's love of roses: "The house stood on a slight eminence, and Mary planted roses so successfully and in such abundance that the place took the name of 'Rosemount.' Cloth-of-gold and Marschal Neil roses covered the south side of the house, and multiflora bloomed on the garden fence. Blossoms were cut in the rose garden daily and sent by the basketful to the house."

The front approach to Rosemount, through a grove of live oaks, magnolias, and cedars, was a winding tabby walk bordered by century plants, crape myrtles, oleanders, and orange trees. In the orchard were figs, pomegranates, seedling peaches, plums, and bittersweet oranges.

In addition to the management of his plantation and his duties as lighthouse keeper, James Gould was active in the parish of Christ Church, Frederica, and was one of the first wardens when the church was built in 1820, an office to which he was elected time and again over the years. During one of his terms as warden, his two sons, James F. and Horace B., served as vestrymen.

Adjoining St. Clair to the south was a tract known as Black Banks, which before the Revolutionary War had belonged to loyalist John Graham. By purchase from the Commissioners of Confiscated Estates, James Gould added this tract to his holdings, making his entire property more than 1,500 acres.

Black Banks was later deeded to the eldest son, James F., or Jim, who had married in New Haven after his graduation from Yale. On his plantation Jim Gould built a two-and-a-half-storied tabby house surrounded at the second floor level by a broad columned piazza. His New England wife was not happy on the island, and eventually Jim sold Black Banks to his brother, Horace, who was married to Deborah Abbott, niece of George and Mary Abbott of Orange Grove.

As James Gould grew older, he suffered greatly from rheumatism, and in 1837 he was forced by ill health to give up his position as keeper of the St. Simons light. He died in 1852. The younger daughter, Janie, was married and living in Baltimore. The St. Clair Plantation was left mainly to Mary Gould, who proved to be as capable at managing the cotton fields as she was at growing roses and managing household affairs at Rosemount. She was so devoted to the plantation that it was difficult for Horace and Deborah to persuade her to leave when the island was evacuated in 1861.

Like other residents of St. Simons, the Goulds packed boats and flats with a few choice pieces of furniture, with boxes of clothing and foodstuffs, with a pen of hogs and coops of chickens. Then Mary, Aunt Caroline, Horace, and Deborah, with their children and a few house servants, set out for the safety of the mainland. Half way across the sound one of the flatboats capsized, sending hogs, chickens, and furniture overboard. Perhaps the hogs saved themselves by swimming to a nearby island, later given the name of Hog Island, and perhaps the timbers of a wreck, visible when the water of the sound is clear, are those of the Gould flatboat that overturned in 1861.

On the mainland Horace was not able to find quarters large enough for the whole family, but he found a dilapidated cottage in Burneyville for Deborah and the children, and a small furnished house in Blackshear for Mary and Aunt Caroline, who were later joined by Janie when her husband went into the Confederate Army. Although Horace Gould was almost fifty years old, after the women and children were safely housed he, too, joined the Confederate Army, where he served under General Joseph E. Johnston, and as captain of infantry under General Hood in the Battle of Atlanta.

When the war was over Horace Bunch Gould was one of the first planters to return to St. Simons Island. He found the St. Clair house, Rosemount, burned to the ground and Black Banks in the possession of a group of freedmen. He managed to buy back the Black Banks property, and with the help of some of the former Gould slaves part of the land was cleared and cultivated again. With her beloved Rosemount gone, Mary Gould lived with relatives in New York until 1870, when she returned to St. Simons two years before she died. A carved granite rose marks her tombstone in Christ Church cemetery.

During the postwar years, when the communicants of Christ Church parish had no house of worship, Horace Gould held services each Sunday at Black Banks. He died in 1881, a short time before his young friend, Anson Dodge, rebuilt Christ Church. In the following years, Horace's daughter, Anna, became Anson Dodge's devoted second wife.

Most of the St. Clair and Black Banks property passed, over the years, into other hands. The St. Clair residential development and the Sea Palms Golf and Country Club were located on the acres that were once St. Clair Plantation. Part of Horace Gould's land was eventually divided into building lots for the Black Banks subdivision, while part is still in the possession of members of the Gould family.

Mulberry Grove and Harrington Hall

Mulberry Grove Plantation, to the south of the Gould property, was developed after the Revolutionary War by Raymond Demere, Jr., son of Captain Raymond Demere, who owned Harrington Hall in the Frederica area in the early days of the colony. At Raymond Demere, Jr.'s, death in 1829, his grandsons, Joseph, Lewis, John, and Paul, inherited the Harrington property. John Fraser Demere, son of Paul and Annie Fraser Demere, and the fifth generation of the family, was born at Harrington Hall in 1841.

The Demeres did not return to St. Simons Island after the War Between the States, and their land was never cultivated again. No trace remains today of Harrington Hall and Mulberry Grove. The site of Harrington Hall has been marked by the Georgia Historical Commission as one of the earliest grants on St. Simons Island, and a residential section south of the old place has been known for years as Harrington.

When the airport was enlarged to include the family burial ground on the old Mulberry Grove property, the Demere tombstones were moved to the cemetery at Christ Church, Frederica.

Kelvin Grove

Kelvin Grove, which included most of the southeast part of the island, was the plantation of the Cater-Postell family. The property was made up of various tracts, the first one bought by Thomas Cater in the 1790s.

At Thomas Cater's death, the plantation was inherited by his young son, Benjamin Franklin Cater. The boy's guardian, Major William Page of Retreat, saw to the management of Kelvin Grove until young Cater was of age.

Benjamin F. Cater married Ann Armstrong, niece of Mrs. Alexander Wylly of the Village. Their daughter, Ann Armstrong

Cater, was married to James Postell of the well-known Huguenot family of South Carolina. James and Ann Cater Postell made their home at Kelvin Grove, and his record books, still in existence, give a description of the property as well as an idea of the operation of one of the large sea island cotton plantations.

Kelvin Grove contained more than 1,600 acres of cleared and cultivated land, timberland, meadow marsh, and beach property. The three-storied house of pink tabby, set in a grove of live oak, cedar, magnolia, and mulberry trees, was surrounded on three sides by a wide piazza and was surmounted by a balcony, or widow's walk, which gave a view of the ocean and of the island for miles around. On the grounds grew orange, lemon, and olive trees, and "figs in abundance." In the broad fields grew sea island cotton.

Records of the duties of the fieldhands in the cotton fields included ploughing, planting, chopping, picking, ginning, "fanning," cleaning, and packing the cotton into big tow bags to be sent to market. The work of the plantation also included raising corn, potatoes, peas, turnips, and other food crops, as well as clearing new ground, cleaning ditches, cutting hay, splitting clapboards, cutting posts, fencing, hauling shell for roads, fishing, gathering oysters, tending the boats, and "carrying the mail." Important work for the younger hands was "minding the fields" or "minding the birds," that is, driving off the flocks of birds until grain, peas, etc. could be harvested.

Listed separately from the fieldhands were the "jobbers"—carpenter, gardener, houseboy, nurse, cook, seamstress, and housemaid.

James Postell's hobby was gathering collections of seashells, butterflies, and birds' eggs. He corresponded and exchanged shells with other collectors, and his books on conchology, ornithology, and lepidoptera are still in the possession of his descendants.

The Postells were among the few St. Simons families who returned to the island soon after the War Between the States. They found their twelve-room house, which was occupied by twelve families of freedmen, in such uninhabitable condition that it had to be razed and replaced.

The extensive plantation, eventually divided among the children of James and Ann Cater Postell, included the site of the Battle of Bloody Marsh and the present residential area known by the old name, Kelvin Grove. This part of the property was sold in the early 1900s to Mrs. Maxwell Parrish, who spent each winter in a cottage near the battle site. Intensely interested in the history and antebellum customs of coastal Georgia, Lydia Parrish worked indefatigably to revive the old shouts and chanteys described in her *Slave Songs of the Georgia Sea Islands* (1942). In the years following Mrs. Parrish's death, the property passed to other ownership; the Kelvin Grove subdivision was developed, and the Bloody Marsh battle site was added to the National Parks System.

Also formerly part of the Cater-Postell plantation are the areas occupied today by the residential developments of the Meadows, Wesley Oaks, Oglethorpe Park, East Beach, and Highland Acres. The Malcolm McKinnon Airport is also on land that was once part of the Kelvin Grove Plantation.

In 1935, when the tract sold to the county by Clifford Postell was being cleared for the airport, laborers uncovered Indian relics of such importance that work was delayed until representatives from the Smithsonian Institution could examine the site. Excavations made in 1936 disclosed evidence of an ancient Indian village and burial ground that provided links in the knowledge of the prehistoric inhabitants of the coastal area. A number of the many artifacts unearthed in the excavations, as well as a large stone ax head found on the property previously by Mr. Postell, are in the Smithsonian. Others are in the museum at Fort Frederica National Monument.

IO Brunswick

The town of Brunswick, on the mainland opposite St. Simons Island, was founded in 1771 by the Council of the Royal Province of Georgia, meeting in Savannah.

The tract of land selected for the new town belonged to Mark Carr, the same Captain Carr who had received large grants in the Midway area and who had deeded land for the port of Sunbury in 1758. His plantation across from St. Simons lay near the Turtle River and was called Plug Point, perhaps because tobacco was one of the principal products.

Captain Carr was granted other acreage in exchange for his holdings at Plug Point, and the property was surveyed and laid out in lots, streets, squares, parks, and commons. The new town was named after Brunswick in northern Germany, the seat of the reigning house of Hanover. The names of George Street and Hanover Park honored King George III; Kings and Queens Squares and Prince Street honored the royal family. Other streets, squares, and parks were given the names of prominent Englishmen of the day.

Settlement had hardly begun in Brunswick when the coast was deserted during the Revolutionary War. Even in the years after the war, the town grew slowly, but in 1789 it was made a port of entry, and in 1797 the county seat of Glynn was moved from Frederica to Brunswick.

It was about this time that Georgia's Revolutionary War hero-ine, Nancy Hart, with her husband, Benjamin, and their family came to live for awhile in Brunswick. Red-haired, cross-eyed, six feet tall, Nancy won her place in Georgia history by capturing a group of Tories singlehandedly when they came to her house in north Georgia when her husband was away at war.

Although Brunswick's first school, Glynn Academy, had been created by the legislature in 1788, the first building, a "neat house for school purposes, at a cost in excess of $10,000," was not completed until 1819. During the next few years the growth of the town seemed to be at a standstill. Tracts of the surround-ing land were occupied and cultivated by substantial planters, but most of the town lots were "left to grow up in briars and weeds." In 1826 two residents of the area, Urbanus Dart and William Davis, obtained from the state a headright to all of the lots on which no taxes were being paid. When the former own-ers protested, Dart and Davis announced that they would not claim the property of bona fide owners. Efforts were made to stimulate interest in the town. The state granted a charter for the Brunswick Canal Company to construct a canal connecting the Turtle River with the Altamaha in order that shipping from the interior might have access to the port of Brunswick. Work on the canal was begun, but the project was abandoned because of mis-management and labor and financial troubles.

A courthouse and jail had been built, as well as a scattering of houses and a few stores, when between 1834 and 1839 the town experienced a remarkable period of prosperity. A new charter was secured for construction of the canal, this time for the "Brunswick Canal and Railroad Company." Through the efforts of Thomas Butler King of St. Simons Island, capitalists from Boston became interested in the projects and undertook to fur-nish financial support for both railroad and canal. Loammi Bal-dwin of Massachusetts, one of the country's most distinguished engineers, was engaged to survey the proposed site of the canal.

The town of Brunswick was incorporated in 1836; a land company was formed, and construction was begun on a fine four-storied hotel, the Oglethorpe House. The first newspaper, the *Brunswick Advocate*, began publication; the Bank of Brunswick opened, and work was underway on railroad and canal. The streets of the town were busy with merchants, traders, sawmill operators, railroad and canal projectors, and the inevitable land speculators.

In June 1837 the Oglethorpe House, a "new and elegant establishment, having been fitted and furnished in a superb style," was ready for the "reception of company." The hotel announced that its bar would be stocked with the "choicest wines and liquors, and the larder filled with the best the market affords," with a "commodious Stable attached to the establishment, well stocked with hay and grain."

Harrington's Variety Store also opened in June 1837 with a complete stock of everything from gloves, hosiery, shawls, hats, boots, and shoes to nutmeg, cloves, ginger, brandy, wines, and molasses.

In the panic of 1837, the Boston investors withdrew their support from the railroad and canal enterprises, but the work was carried on with local capital, and Brunswick continued to prosper.

One of the outstanding social events of this period of prosperity was the Regatta of the Aquatic Club of Georgia, held in Brunswick January 16, 1838, on an "extremely fine day which permitted the attendance of a large number of ladies."

In the first race, the *Goddess of Liberty*, owned by Henry duBignon of Jekyll Island, was defeated by the *Devil's Darning Needle*, "a blackamoor with a skin as dark as Othello's," owned by Richard Floyd of Camden County. Other boats from Glynn and Camden counties competed, and "Charles Floyd's green *Lizard* was on the ground but was thought too slippery a customer and was not allowed even to creep over the race course."

Following the races, the "Club with their guests to the number of 50 or 60 sat down to an elegant dinner at the Oglethorpe House and the evening was spent in the due observance of the rites of conviviality and good fellowship."

In 1838 another general store, Dart, Barrett & Co., opened with a "large and well-selected stock of Foreign and Domestic goods of every description." The Brunswick and Darien Stage announced that a two-horse coach would leave the Oglethorpe House at 7 A.M. weekdays for Grants Ferry near Darien, leaving for the return trip at 4 P.M. "Fare $2 each way, luggage extra." This made a convenient connection with the regular stagecoaches which came down the coast as far as Darien.

There was great excitement in the county when a deposit of fossil bones of extinct animals was uncovered by laborers working on the canal. James Hamilton Couper of Hopeton Plantation identified the fossils and sent specimens to museums in Charleston, Philadelphia, and Washington, D.C.

In 1839 business began to decline in Brunswick. Before the end of the year the bank and newspaper had "suspended operations" and the town's charter of incorporation had been returned to the state. Work on the railroad had come to a halt, and the canal project was abandoned, although it was almost finished.

A new building for Glynn Academy was completed in 1840, but there was no further construction in Brunswick for many years. The "boom" days were followed by a long depression. Newcomers moved away, and the bustling town dwindled to a quiet village of only four hundred people.

The town began to prosper again in the 1850s. According to a notice in Savannah's *Daily Morning News* of June 1, 1854, the Brunswick and Altamaha Canal was opened on that date. Construction was resumed on the railroad. The town was re-incorporated in 1856; a second newspaper, the *Brunswick Herald*, started publication; the Bank of Brunswick reopened. The town's first drugstore, Massey and Hillman, was opened in 1857. In that same year the economy of the area was stimulated by the purchase by the United States Government of Blythe Island, near Brunswick, as a proposed site for a Navy depot. In 1858 the First Methodist and First Baptist churches were built, and St. Marks Episcopal Church was organized. By 1860 Brunswick's population had more than doubled. The town was building on a solid foundation when its growth was interrupted by the War Between the States.

In October 1860 the young men of the area organized the Brunswick Riflemen. The following May they were mustered into the Confederate Army as part of a regiment of Georgia Volunteers stationed at Camp Semmes near the town. The Ladies Sewing Association was organized to make garments for the soldiers, and when an Army hospital was established in Brunswick the ladies lent sheets, blankets, and other necessary items from their own household supplies.

In December 1861, when the coast was blockaded by Federal gunboats, residents of Brunswick were ordered evacuated. Most of the families refugeed to Wayne and Ware counties. Two months later, when Confederate troops guarding Brunswick were ordered withdrawn, the railroad depot and the wharf were destroyed and the Oglethorpe House was burned by accident. On March 10 the town was occupied by Federal troops.

In the years following the war some of the coastal planters moved to Brunswick; former citizens returned; new families established residence, and the town began its permanent growth.

A temporary resident of the town in these postwar years was General John B. Gordon under whom some of the former Brunswick Riflemen had served in the Confederate Army. The general was especially interested in attempting to reorganize the First Baptist Church, but the people were too impoverished to undertake the expense of a church and the support of a minister. However, a Sunday School was organized with General Gordon as superintendant.

In 1874 Georgia's beloved Sidney Lanier visited with relatives in Brunswick as he sought to regain his health. The poet enjoyed long restful hours beneath a great live oak overlooking the sea marshes made immortal in his *Marshes of Glynn*.

In 1876 Brunswick suffered a yellow-fever epidemic that took the lives of a number of citizens, but by 1878 the town had recovered and had become a busy shipping center. A visitor at the time wrote that there were two railroads and a fine harbor and that the "ships, barks, brigs and schooners in port give a marine atmosphere to the town" which had a population of "upwards of 3,000 to which every day was adding."

In the decade of the 1880s Brunswick's population tripled, and a number of substantial business and residential buildings were erected. New stores were opened and there were drydocks, lumber mills, a barrel factory, a foundry, a plant to manufacture turpentine stills, and the beginning of a seafood industry. Shipping of lumber and naval stores increased enormously, and steamship companies operated out of Brunswick to New York, Boston, Havana, England, and Europe.

The pleasant climate and proximity to the sea drew visitors to the coast town as a year-round resort. The Oglethorpe Hotel, built on the site of the old Oglethorpe House, was the center of

The Oglethorpe Hotel, Brunswick, Georgia

social life for townspeople and vacationers, and the L'Arioso Opera House, seating eight hundred, added to the cultural life of the city. In 1889 a large brick building was completed to accommodate the growing student body of Glynn Academy and construction was begun on a handsome city hall.

Also in 1889, the Brunswick Harbor and Land Company was organized to develop nearby Colonels Island into a residential, industrial, and shipping community. Docks, wharves, warehouses, and a cotton compress were built, and lots were sold for a settlement to be called South Brunswick.

A second epidemic of yellow fever and the panic of 1893 not only halted business in Brunswick temporarily, but put an end to the Colonels Island development. Brunswick recovered, and the early 1900s were some of the port's busiest shipping years and a time of continued prosperity for the city. A fine brick Post Office, reminiscent of Independence Hall, was completed in 1902, and an impressive new Glynn County Court House was built in 1907.

In World War I shipyards along the Brunswick waterfront constructed ships and barges and attracted a number of newcomers to the region. With the increased population, a larger plant was necessary for Glynn Academy; therefore a new building was constructed in 1923, with an auditorium dedicated to Glynn County men who had lost their lives in the war.

As the long-leaf pines were cut out, lumbering and shipping declined, but the wealth of other forest products available in the region brought industrial plants and mills into the city and county. A growing seafood industry also added to the region's economy.

In 1924 Brunswick and St. Simons Island were connected by the Torras Causeway, named in honor of its engineer, Fernando Torras of Brunswick.

In the Second World War, shipbuilding again brought new residents to the port city, since many families who came for the duration of the war stayed or returned to live permanently. The Glynco Naval Air Station, commissioned in 1943, expanded in

Glynn County Courthouse, Brunswick, Georgia

the postwar years, and its personnel became part of the civic and social life of the area.

As the city's population continued to increase, Brunswick Junior College, a unit of the University System of Georgia, was opened in 1964, its enrollment growing steadily over the years.

As time passed, the Naval Air Station grew into a large complex known as the Naval Air Technical Training Center; to be followed in 1975 by the Federal Law Enforcement Training Center which meets the training requirements of thirty-four United States Government organizations.

In spite of its growth, Brunswick retains much of the charm of earlier days. Reluctant to part with its ancestral live oaks, the city has left many of the venerable trees to spread their shade over the streets with their English names. Its parks, squares, and gardens bloom with azalea, poinsettia and hibiscus, with camellia, dogwood and roses, with redbud, wisteria, clematis and coral vine. The Court House lawn, known for a beauty unsurpassed by any public grounds in the country, is a spacious garden of almost every tree, shrub, and flower indigenous to the region.

To the regret of older residents, the gabled, turreted and porticoed Oglethorpe Hotel, a landmark since the 1880s, was razed to make way for more modern structures, but still standing are the old City Hall and the columned Court House; a new Federal Building has replaced the 1902 Post Office, which serves as the "new" City Hall. A number of residences constructed around the turn of the century still grace the wide streets of "Old Town Brunswick," now listed on the National Register of Historic Places.

Brunswick celebrated its two-hundredth anniversary in 1971, a progressive modern city with an indefinable atmosphere of yesterday.

II Sea Island

The opening of the Torras Causeway between St. Simons Island and Brunswick in 1924 was a milestone in resort history, since it led to the development of Georgia's famed Sea Island. Eugene W. Lewis tells how this came about in his *Story of Sea Island.* He gives us a picture of a congenial houseparty spending an evening around the big fireplace of the Coffin home on Sapelo—"the usual gathering of hosts and guests in hunting breeches, riding togs, etc., mixing light conversation, shelling pecans, popping corn, reading." A newspaper article about the causeway between Brunswick and St. Simons caught Mr. Lewis's eye, and he and Howard Coffin fell to discussing the idea of buying property on the island. Howard Coffin, always interested in new ideas, proposed that they run down aboard the *Zapala* next day to look into the situation.

And so, more than a century and a quarter after those friends and partners, John Couper and James Hamilton, came to St. Simons, another pair of friends played their role in the drama of the coastland. After their first inspection of the island, the two friends returned day after day to tramp across the overgrown acres of the old cotton fields; and just as St. Simons had attracted Couper and Hamilton in the 1790s, so the beautiful island stirred the imaginations of Howard Coffin and Eugene Lewis. It was in 1925 that Coffin purchased his first property, a part of old Retreat Plantation. Like those other friends, the two from Detroit became owners of various tracts of land—tracts which included many of the same acres that had once belonged to John Couper and James Hamilton.

As he continued to explore, Howard Coffin became enthusiastic over a five-mile strip of beach and woodland along the outer edge of St. Simons, separated from the main island by a narrow creek. Soon he was centering all his interest in the little barrier beach that had been known as Fifth Creek Island, Isle of Palms, Long Island, and, more recently, Glynn Isle. In this long-neglected piece of land the master-pioneer saw an opportunity to open to the world the charm and beauty of the historic Georgia coast.

Glynn Isle was purchased and renamed Sea Island, and in the imagination of Howard Coffin it was transformed into a place of palm-bordered streets, grassy lawns and flower beds, comfortable houses, and a luxurious hotel.

The lonely beach with its background of sand dunes and tropical woodland gave little promise of becoming the resort and residence colony of Howard Coffin's dreams. There was no electricity on the island of St. Simons, no telephone system, and transportation of labor and supplies was difficult. But, Eugene Lewis says, Howard Coffin "was of that early school of automobile pioneers, a lusty, gusty group of self-reliant, visionary men who did not know the meaning of 'It can't be done.'" With the assistance of his cousin, Alfred W. Jones, who had helped with the development of Sapelo, Howard Coffin began work on his resort, and presently the quiet town of Brunswick and the sleepy island of St. Simons found themselves in a whirlwind of activity that wrought such changes that newspapers called Howard Coffin the "magician of Sapelo."

He formed the Sea Island Company, improved the causeway between St. Simons and the mainland, built a two-mile causeway to connect St. Simons and Sea Island, established a bus line from Brunswick, north to Savannah and south to Jacksonville, and put in an electric power plant and a telephone system. Construction was begun on a hotel for Sea Island and on a golf course on the old Retreat property. In Mr. Lewis's words, "Howard Coffin was boring with a big augur."

On the night of October 12, 1928, the Cloister Hotel was opened by a memorable ceremony in which a group of invited guests stormed the doors for admittance. The host, like the inn-keeper of old, clad in robe and slippers and tasseled nightcap and carrying a lighted candle, welcomed them into the hostelry and served them with food and drink. The Sea Island resort of Howard Coffin's dream had become a reality. After Mr. Coffin's death in 1937 the future of Sea Island was in the hands of Alfred W. Jones, and the hospitable resort, like the nineteenth-century cotton plantations, brought worldwide fame to the little coastal island of St. Simons.

A "brilliant gem in an Old World setting," Sea Island, with a charm all its own, delightfully combines natural and cultivated beauty, perfectly balances luxurious living and casual comfort. The Cloister Hotel is appropriately Spanish in architecture, a low, sprawling building of stucco and tile, of beamed ceilings, cloistered terraces, and sheltered patios. Set well back from the ocean, the hotel is surrounded by spacious lawns where vine and

The Cloister in the early days of the resort

shrub, hedge and border are in beautiful bloom all year. The cottage colony spreads along palm-lined Sea Island Drive and the cross streets with their names reminiscent of early coastal history.

Once a negligible part of Cannons Point Plantation, Sea Island enjoys a reputation for hospitality equal to the fabulous hospitality of the Coupers. From its very beginning, the charm and seclusion of the resort attracted newly married couples, and over the years the Cloister has entertained hundreds of newlyweds each year, some of them descendants of the honeymooners of the early days. After their enchanted stay at Sea Island, many young-marrieds find themselves almost as loath to leave the tropical shore as did that legendary couple who, invited to spend their honeymoon with the John Coupers at Cannons Point, lingered until after their second child was born.

Among Sea Island's greatest charms are the ancient live oaks, their branches overgrown with delicate green tracery of resurrection fern. State tree of Georgia, the live oak has come to be a symbol to commemorate notable people, places, and events. A favorite tree on the Cloister grounds, Constitution Oak, planted by President Calvin Coolidge in 1928, is of the same species that furnished timbers used in the building of *Old Ironsides*. Other named trees on the hotel grounds are the Oglethorpe Oak, grown from acorns from General Oglethorpe's English property; and Queen's Oak, planted by Juliana, Queen of the Netherlands, on her visit to the resort in 1952.

Through the years other Sea Island visitors of national and international prominence have included General and Mrs. Dwight D. Eisenhower; Vice-President and Mrs. Alben Barkley, who honeymooned on the island and returned often for vacations; Winston Churchill's daughter, Sarah, who was married on Sea Island; Governor Thomas E. Dewey, who was a frequent visitor; Vice-President Hubert Humphrey; Secretary of State Dean Rusk; and President Jimmy Carter.

Eugene O'Neill lived for some years on Sea Island, where he built a beach house called "Casa Genotta" for his name, Gene,

The Eisenhowers on Sea Island, May 1946

and his wife's, Carlotta. In a nautical workroom overlooking the Atlantic, O'Neill finished his grim *Days Without End* and wrote his only lighthearted play, *Ah, Wilderness!*

The Sea Island resort has grown steadily over the years with additional accommodations in guest houses; with the early Beach Club enlarged to twice its original size; with inconspicuous additions to the Cloister and improvements to nearby River House. New streets have been opened for an increasing cottage colony, and the River Club condominiums have been built overlooking the marshes. In February 1978 ground was broken for the luxurious Harrington House just south of the Sea Island Beach Club.

Rated among the world's finest hotels and resorts, the Cloister and Sea Island are often featured in leading publications in this country and abroad. Year after year the Georgia hotel and resort are the recipients of awards of excellence. As "one of the world's most interesting islands," Sea Island's international clientele increases each year.

In 1978 Sea Island and the Cloister celebrated their fiftieth anniversary. Taking part in the gala occasion were friends who were present that memorable evening of October 12, 1928, when the Cloister was first opened. Also participating were early cottage owners, the hotel's original guests, those who had visited repeatedly over the years, and local friends old and new. After days of celebration, the commemorative festivities concluded with a 1920s ball.

A highlight of the half-century anniversary was the publication of the book *This Happy Isle* by Harold Martin, who dedicated his story of Sea Island and the Cloister "to all those who for fifty years have come here to find Howard Coffin's 'place of peace and play and freedom' and to all those who have made them welcome."

12 Jekyll Island

Jekyll Island, little more than a stone's throw across the channel from St. Simons and smallest of the Golden Isles, has been perhaps one of the most widely known privately owned islands in the world. In its varied and romantic history Jekyll's ten-mile beach has been trod by Indian moccasin and friar's sandal, by boot of pirate and soldier and buckled pump of French aristocrat, by bare foot of slave and well-shod foot of millionaire. Called Ospo by the Indians, claimed by the Spaniards and settled by their missionaries, wrested from Spain by the English, legendary hiding place for a part of Blackbeard's loot, Jekyll was the island empire of a French family for a century, and within the span of little more than a quarter-century was a secret landing place for the last slave ship from Africa and vacation home for financiers of the nation. But time has obliterated traces of the island's inhabitants as relentlessly as the waves have washed their footprints from the sand. Buildings erected in the late eighteen and early nineteen hundreds by the Jekyl Island Club, a nineteenth-century graveyard, and some crumbling tabby ruins are the only signs remaining of all the lives that touched the island's shores in bygone years.

History records that General Oglethorpe named the island in honor of Sir Joseph Jekyll, who helped finance the Georgia colony; but coastal folk call it Jakyl, and word-of-mouth-history gives the name no such aristocratic origin. They say that a supply and receiving station for pirates and buccaneers located on the island in the 1600s was operated by a Frenchman named Jacques. The name Jacques' Island deteriorated into Jake's Isle, and finally Jakyl. Spelled Jekyl for many years, the extra "l" was added somewhere along the way, and Jekyll is now the accepted spelling.

In the early days of the colony a part of Jekyll was planted in fields of hops and grain and a brewery was built, for the British soldier must have his beer, and one of the first reports sent from the new colony states that they had already begun to malt and to brew. The plantation on Jekyll was in the charge of Oglethorpe's aide Captain Horton, who could be called to Frederica "by the firing of a Certain Number of Guns."

In June 1735 when Spanish emissaries from St. Augustine were sent to treat with Oglethorpe, he received them on Jekyll to prevent their seeing the fortifications on St. Simons. Colonial records describe the dinner at which the Spaniards were entertained on board the *Hawk*, with toasts to the kings of England and of Spain. Highlanders and British Regulars stood at attention on deck, and Tomochichi, with a band of Indians in war paint, came aboard. Presents were exchanged and "all differences adjusted." In August of the same year when Don Antonio de Arredondo came to confer with Oglethorpe, tents were pitched for him and his commission on the shores of Jekyll.

After the Spaniards were defeated in 1742, Jekyll was held as a military reservation for a number of years, until in 1765 the General Assembly passed an act which added it to the Parish of St. James. In the following year the island was granted to Clement Martin, and in 1784 it became the property of Richard Leake, whose daughter married Thomas Spalding. A prominent and successful planter, Richard Leake is said to have been raising sea island cotton on Jekyll as early as 1788. In the 1790s the island plantation was bought by Christopher Poulain duBignon, one of the group of Frenchmen who had formerly owned Sapelo.

Here upon their island domain, with much of the arable part

of Jekyll's eleven thousand acres planted in cotton, the duBignons lived the life of the French landowners from whom they were descended. The family residence was decorated with furnishings, pictures, and ornaments from the owners' native land, brought by their sailing vessel the *Commodore* on her annual voyage to France for supplies.

The life of Poulain duBignon would itself fill a book of adventure, for he had served with the French forces in India and had commanded a fighting vessel sailing under the *fleur-de-lis*. Confident that he was usually to be found in that part of the world where life was most exciting, some of his descendants wonder whether he first discovered the Golden Isles from the deck of one of the ships in the French fleet that came to the aid of the colonists in the Revolutionary War. Beautiful and serene as the isles appeared, they were nevertheless an adventurer's paradise, and life lost none of its savor for Poulain duBignon and his fellows after they cast their lot with the newly united states.

In spite of their velvet coats and satin breeches, their lace ruffles, silver buckles, and *savoir vivre*, these early settlers were a hardy race. They must always be prepared to protect their families and their possessions against possible invasion of their island estates. A sharp lookout was kept for strange sails; and when an unrecognized ship appeared along their shores the planters hurriedly buried their valuables, ordered the women and children upstairs, and called all hands to man the guns in case the visitor proved to be an enemy. A family tradition tells of a landing party fought off in the War of 1812, when the duBignons lost a number of slaves to the invaders. Told by the captives of valuables concealed on the island, a stronger force returned and made off with some of the family treasures. Stories are told of scar-faced strangers, landing from unknown ships, bearing charts of the island and digging for pirate gold. It is said that somewhere in the forest there is a tree with a copper hook in its trunk, and the tip of the hook points to the spot where the treasure chests are buried.

For nearly a century Jekyll Island was the home of Poulain

duBignon's descendants, and at the height of the plantation era the *vin d'honneur* of the French family made Jekyll a favorite gathering place for coastal society. Colonel Henry duBignon was an enthusiastic follower of the sport of boat racing, and his *Goddess of Liberty* was famous along the whole Atlantic seaboard. Painted white with a starred band of blue, the *Goddess* carried off the prize in many a coastal regatta.

The little island made world news when the slave ship *Wanderer* secretly landed its cargo upon the shores of Jekyll during a night of storm in 1858. As this was a number of years after the importing of slaves to the United States had been forbidden by law, the owners of the *Wanderer* were prosecuted and the case received wide publicity. The notoriety, together with the fact that this was the last ship to bring slaves directly from Africa to the United States, resulted in the *Wanderer* becoming legendary. Rumors of banquets at which planters were gathered, of wagers that such a cargo could not be landed, of bets covered—and collected—were never proved, but they still make good stories when dinner-table conversation turns to the days of the coastal planters when men lived for the high adventure of living and fortunes were made and lost overnight. The excitement over the *Wanderer* case was lost in the greater excitement of the prospect of war between the states. An iron soup pot used on the ship was left on the island, and some of the blacks who lived there all their lives proudly claimed descent from the Africans who escaped into the woods that dark and stormy night. When clouds hang low and the waves thunder upon the beach, they say that one may glimpse the flicker of flames in the shelter of the trees where fires were built that night to warm and dry the storm-battered crew and cargo of the *Wanderer*.

Like other coastal plantations Jekyll never regained its prosperity after the disastrous sixties, but the island remained in possession of the duBignon family until 1886 when it was bought by the famous Jekyl Island Club, a group of business leaders reputed at the time to represent a seventh of the wealth of the nation. The list of members included such names as Morgan,

The Clubhouse and Sans Souci Apartments on Jekyll Island

Vanderbilt, Astor, and Gould; Rockefeller, McCormick, Baker, and Biddle; Whitney, Armour, Allbright, Crane, Goodyear, Pulitzer, Macy, and Bliss. Membership in the club was by inheritance, and publicity of club activities was strictly avoided. Here in the most exclusive spot in the country the members and their families spent winter vacations in the months of January, February, and March of each year.

A clubhouse of Victorian architecture, an apartment house, and twelve-to-twenty-room "cottages" were clustered on the west side of the island along the inland waterway, convenient for members arriving by yacht. There was a private steamer to meet those who came by train to Brunswick. The forests furnished an abundance of deer, turkey, and quail, and were further stocked with English pheasant and with wild boar which had been presented to one of the members by the King of Italy. In addition to the sports of hunting and fishing there were swimming in sea and pool, golf on one of the finest dune courses in the world, tennis on outdoor and indoor courts, and croquet on the lawn of the clubhouse.

During the months when the members were in residence on their own "tight little island" the newspapers were apt to grow a trifle bitter over the complete lack of news, but it was a different story on one occasion in 1899 when a group of political leaders arranged to have a private conclave on Jekyll. They expected complete freedom from publicity for a behind-the-scenes playoff in the game of politics between President McKinley, who wanted a second term, and Speaker-of-the-House Reed, who never saw eye-to-eye with the administration. Referee was the famous Senator Mark Hanna, president-maker of the nineties and master manipulator, credited by some with being inventor of the national political machine. As the principals gathered, ostensibly seeking rest from the duties of political life, residents of Brunswick were agog with the arrival of the presidential party. A special train with "five of the most luxurious cars the railroad could furnish" brought President and Mrs. McKinley, the vice-president and his wife, and other notables to the little coastal city. Here they were met by their host, Assistant Secretary of the Interior Bliss, and the party proceeded by steamer to the island where the Club House was "tastily arranged for the occasion."

No newspapermen were allowed, and a "trocha" a hundred yards from the shores of Jekyll stopped all boats that attempted to approach. Joseph Pulitzer, in residence on the island at the time, no doubt would have liked to see his *New York World* headline the news of such an important event, but an alert reporter on the old *Brunswick Call* got wind of the goings-on, managed to get an exclusive wire, and flashed the news to an interested nation. For the cub reporter, L. J. Leavy, who later became editor of the *Brunswick News*, it was a never-to-be-forgotten day when he literally scooped the *World*. The meeting on Jekyll turned out to be a page of that chapter in the history of American politics, the machinations of which are described in detail by William Allen White in his autobiography. The upshot of the parley was that a bitter and thwarted Reed was ousted as speaker and retired from politics and McKinley returned for a second term.

Jekyll made national news once more for reporter Leavy around the turn of the century when he released an interview with a Lady-Somebody-or-Other who had arrived in Brunswick aboard a private car en route to the island. The story mentioned that her ladyship was smoking a cigarette, and the reporter was bombarded with telegrams from newspapers all over the country requesting confirmation of such an unbelievable statement. Upon receiving assurance that the reporter had actually seen the cigarette being smoked, the nation's papers felt free to print this sensational bit of news.

In 1947 Jekyll Island was purchased by the State of Georgia to be used as a state park; and the wide beaches, miles of roads through the forests, golf course, tennis courts, and swimming pool, and Jekyll's eleven thousand acres of tropical beauty were opened to the public.

It had been several years since members of the Jekyl Island Club had last visited the resort, and the first vacationers found some of the houses just as their owners had left them. Books and games still lay upon shelves and tables. There were old photographs of small boys in Buster Brown suits, and of decorous lawn parties with feminine guests wearing veil-festooned picture hats and seated under umbrellas, their trailing skirts protected by white cloth spread upon the grass. The inevitable tropical vines which had grown over many of the windows gave an eerie undersea color to the light filtering through the panes, and the empty houses seemed to have a hushed air of waiting and listening, glad to have their doors open again to visitors.

In those early days the park was accessible only by water, and visitors arrived aboard the old *Robert E. Lee* from Brunswick. Within the next few years extensive improvements were made on the island; a large part of the property was divided into building lots, and new roads and streets were given names appropriate to the history and location of the island. Some of the turn-of-the-century houses were leased to newcomers, and the Rockefeller Cottage became the Jekyll Museum. Public bathhouses, picnic grounds, and campgrounds were opened. A causeway and

Lawn party at Mistletoe Cottage, Jekyll Island

Cycling and horseback riding on the beach at Jekyll Island

·*The Rockefeller Cottage, Jekyll Island*

bridges connecting Jekyll Island State Park with the mainland were completed in 1954.

In the following years numbers of private homes were built in the residential areas, and Faith Chapel of Jekyl Club days was joined by other churches. Near the beach are motels and restaurants, a convention center, an aquarama with olympic-sized pool, and a shopping center. A modern fishing pier has been built, and an amphitheater for summer plays.

Historical markers identify points of special interest on different parts of the island. Reminiscent of plantation days is the family burial ground of the duBignons; and landmarks of colonial times are the site of "Georgia's First Brewery" and the remains of the Horton House marked with a bronze plaque erected by descendants of William Horton, first English resident of Jekyll.

13 Cumberland Island

Cumberland Island, south of Jekyll and last in the chain of Georgia's Golden Isles, shares the other islands' history of Indian legend and Spanish mission. Called Missoe (sassafras) by the Indians, the island was inhabited by the Timucuans, a Florida tribe whose customs and language differed from those of the Creeks of the upper islands. When the Spaniards settled along the coast they established a mission here, and both island and mission were called San Pedro. In the massacre of the missionaries San Pedro succeeded in fighting off the attack of the murderous pagans until help arrived from St. Augustine; but although it was the last of the island settlements to be relinquished, a few crumbling remains which may be those of the mission are the only evidence of more than a century of Spanish occupation.

The name of Cumberland was given the island soon after the colony of Georgia was settled. In 1734 when Chief Tomochichi and his family visited England, the old mico's nephew, young Toonahowie, met a lad near his own age, William Augustus, Duke of Cumberland, thirteen-year-old son of the king—two little princes of royalty, the dark-eyed, black-haired child of the wilderness and the fair-haired, blue-eyed child of generations of civilization. The *Gentleman's Magazine* tells us that the Indians particularly enjoyed watching His Highness take his riding lessons, and the two boys became such good friends that Prince William presented Toonahowie with a gold watch when the visit came to an end. And although colonial records show that the watch soon had to be returned to London for repairs, Toonahowie valued the gift and his friendship with the young duke so highly that it is said he requested the island of San Pedro to be named Cumberland in honor of William Augustus.

Fort William, or Prince Williams Fort, on the lower end of the island also honored the duke, and it is related that General Oglethorpe built a hunting lodge nearby which he called Dungeness after the royal county seat upon the "ness," or cape, in the County of Kent. On the upper part of the island was the "Star fort call'd St. Andrews," and old records say that Oglethorpe, "pressed by alarms of the Spaniards ordered Mr. Mackay to quit his Improvements in the Darien and to come down to take command at St. Andrews and fortify the same"—services for which Mackay was given a resolution of thanks by the Trustees and £100 sterling.

Garrisoned by British Regulars who had seen service at Gibraltar, Fort St. Andrews became the center of the little post town of Berrimacke, a village of several hundred people. For some years after the defeat of the Spaniards the frontier town remained inhabited. The *Report on New Georgia* of 1756 says that South Georgia contained two cities, Frederica and New Inverness, and one village, Berrimacke. During the following decade the garrison town disappeared; so the name of Berrimacke must be added to the list of dead towns of Georgia.

In the years from 1765 to 1768 royal grants on Cumberland were made to James Cuthbert, Jonathan and Josiah Bryan, John Smith, and James Habersham; and later most of the island was owned by Jonathan Bryan. In a newspaper of 1768 he advertised 7,500 acres for sale on Cumberland—"a great part fit for corn, rice, indigo, and cotton, and a quantity of liveoak and pine for ship building. Also extraordinary range for cattle, hogs, and horses." Large tracts of land on the island were later owned by Thomas Lynch and Alex Rose, but there seems to have been little homesteading or extensive cultivation of property in the years before the Revolution.

When William Bartram visited Cumberland on his journey along the coast in 1774, the pilot for the St. Marys River was living in old Fort William, but most of the large island was uninhabited. During this time when the lower part of Georgia was sparsely settled, Cumberland and the small islands near it were often used as a hideout for smugglers and others who were "none too anxious to be in the public eye." One of the small neighboring islands is still known by the descriptive name of Hush-Your-Mouth Island.

In the years succeeding the War for Independence, Cumberland was included in Camden County, which had been formed of St. Marys and St. Thomas parishes and named for the Earl of Camden, and some of the most prominent men of the state owned property on the island. Although there seems to be no indication that Lachlan McIntosh ever lived here we find in his will lands on Cumberland listed among his holdings, and McIntosh Field located on the island still bears his name. The Josiah Smiths lived for a time on Cumberland and it was the birthplace of their son Buckingham, who later lived in Florida, where he became one of the foremost antiquarians, diplomats, and scholars of his day. After several years spent in Mexico, where his father was United States consul, and where he himself served as secretary of the legation and as charge d'affairs, Buckingham Smith went to Madrid, where he made a study of the early Spanish history of our coast. His English translation of DeSoto's letters was considered one of the most valuable records of the great Spanish explorer's travels.

One of the largest plantations on Cumberland was the Stafford place, which covered about a third of the island. A unique system of operation made the Stafford Plantation one of the most prosperous and productive of the region. The owner divided his property into two distinct sections, each under its own management, and the rivalry which was encouraged between the two places resulted in the production of large and superior crops.

As a side line the plantation did a small business in the sale of horses. Old-timers used to remember when marsh tackies caught on the Stafford place could be bought for five dollars each.

Near the Stafford Plantation was one of the best known estates of coastal Georgia, Dungeness, the home of the family of General Nathanael Greene, commander of the American Revolutionary Army in the Southern Department. At the close of the war the grateful State of Georgia presented Mulberry Grove Plantation near Savannah to General Greene; and for years it was uncertain whether the property on Cumberland had also been a gift from the state. However, old records now in the Georgia Department of Archives show that the island property was bought by General Greene in a number of small parcels. It is said that he had selected the site and laid out gardens and designed plans for the mansion which he intended to build as a summer home, when he died suddenly of sunstroke in 1786.

Although the house was not built until years after Nathanael Greene's death, the plantation itself was given the name of Dungeness, as early papers of the Camden Land Court record a meeting there in February 1790. The property was undoubtedly under cultivation, and there was probably some sort of building already upon it where the Land Grant Court met—perhaps the original Dungeness hunting lodge built by Oglethorpe half a century before. General Greene's family was still living at Mulberry Grove Plantation at this time, and it was there that President Washington visited them in 1791, and it was in the nearby Savannah River that the oldest son, George Washington Greene, was drowned in 1793.

It was at Mulberry Grove that Eli Whitney invented the cotton gin. Young Whitney, recently graduated from Yale, was a member of the household as tutor to the Greene children. As a protégé of Mrs. Greene and of Phineas Miller, manager of the plantation, Whitney received encouragement and financial assistance from both. In fact, Whitney is said to have given Catherine Greene credit for adding the finishing touch to his invention. While watching the operation of the model, the often-told story has it, his hostess flicked the lint from the machine with her handkerchief remarking that it needed a brush. Whereupon the inventor exclaimed dramatically that she had completed the invention of the cotton gin.

In 1796, ten years after her husband's death, Catherine Littlefield Greene was married to Phineas Miller and the house of Dungeness was built, not as a summer home but as a permanent residence. The immense four-storied mansion was years in the building but it finally stood complete in all its massive dignity, "the most elegant residence on the coast." Built on an eminence formed by an ancient shell mound, its tabby walls, six feet thick at the base and four feet in the stories above, enclosed more than a score of rooms. Perfectly proportioned in spite of its size, the enormous house had four symmetrical chimneys to serve its sixteen fireplaces. Surrounded by twelve acres of gardens and olive-bordered terraces, with "an unsurpassed elegance of exterior and interior appointments," Dungeness appeared complete to the outside world but it was never entirely finished. A few of its many rooms must be left unceiled, since an old family superstition predicted dire misfortune for a completed house. But unfinished rooms on the fourth floor provided storage space for discarded toys and outgrown highchairs and cradles, for old humpbacked trunks full of ancestral finery. Dungeness was a house planned for the generations, built for families of children and children's children.

An account of the wedding of the one of the Greene daughters appeared in a newspaper dated April 27, 1802: "Married on Thursday evening last at Dungeness on Cumberland Island by the Honorable Phineas Miller, Peyton Skipworth, Jr., son of Sir Peyton Skipworth, Baronet, of Virginia, to Miss Cornelia Lott Greene, second daughter of the late Nathanael Greene"—the first occasion of note in the great house that for more than half a century was to see a pageant of eventful years.

The eldest Greene daughter, Martha Washington, was married to John Clark Nightingale; the younger, Louisa Catherine, to James Shaw. With their two families, the congenial household included the Millers, Nightingales, Shaws, and Mrs. Miller's son, young Nathanael Ray Greene.

"Caty" Littlefield Greene, favorite ballroom partner of General Greene's close friend, George Washington, and of the dashing Mad Anthony Wayne, had long been known as one of the most charming hostesses in the nation. Phineas Miller was prominent in state politics as senator from Camden County and justice of the Inferior Court; and the great mansion on Cumberland became the center of a social life equalled by few plantations in the country. In the famous house were entertained many of the distinguished military leaders and statesmen of the time as well as friends of the young people of the family.

The walled gardens where the seabreeze whispered through palms and rare clove and olive trees, with the soft scent of orange blossom, rose, and magnolia, must have seen many a flirtation, many a romance. Even the vicissitudes of war were not proof against the romance of the great house. When the enemy took possession of Cumberland Island in the last days of the War of 1812 and commandeered Dungeness for their headquarters, the British officers arrived in the midst of a Christmas holiday houseparty of young people from neighboring plantations. Members of the household were banished to the upper floors, and one can imagine the excitement of the girls and can almost hear their thrilled whispers and giggles as they tiptoed down to peep through the banisters at their captors. And the Englishmen in their gold-braided regimentals were not oblivious to the charms of their pretty captives. One young officer noticed especially dark-eyed little Ann Couper, daughter of the John Coupers of Cannons Point on St. Simons, for family legend has it that it was here that Captain Fraser first met his future bride.

During the weeks that followed, the young officer no doubt had occasion to make many important trips to the island of St. Simons. One of Ann Couper's letters, still in existence, written at Cannons Point on February 25, 1815, and addressed to John Fraser on Cumberland Island, says: "Ere this our President has ratified the peace, and I hope in a very short space of time we shall again see you on our little Island on terms of peace and goodwill not only to us but our whole country . . . the time is not perhaps very distant when if you are the amiable and noble being you appear to be, the sentiments of friendship which I now feel may be changed into reciprocal affection." Not many months later young Captain Fraser returned to St. Simons to win the hand of the pretty "prisoner of Dungeness."

But events at Dungeness did not always have a happy ending. In 1818 General Lighthorse Harry Lee spent his last days here with the family of his old friend Nathanael Greene. The general, who had been in failing health, was returning from the West Indies when he became ill and asked to be taken to the home of his friends on Cumberland Island. Young Phineas Nightingale was on the beach when the schooner approached and a dinghy put in to shore bringing General Lee, escorted by the captain and mate of the vessel. The lad ran to tell the family of the general's arrival, and to bring a carriage to the dock. In an account of the occasion we are given a picture of the boy and the old soldier in the carriage while the ship's officers walked alongside, with the family gathered on the terrace to welcome Nathanael Greene's old friend to Dungeness.

This was at the time when negotiations were under way in connection with the cession of Florida to the United States, and there were several government ships, with marine and army detachments on board, anchored in the sound. During the weeks that General Lee was at Dungeness he was under the care of surgeons from the fleet and was visited daily by the ships' officers. In spite of expert medical attention and the loving care with which he was surrounded, the general died on March 25, little more than a month after his arrival at Cumberland Island. The flags of the fleet flew at half-mast, and a newspaper of the day describes the military funeral with the cortege moving under crossed swords to the muted notes of a regimental band.

A volley of musketry was fired and a bugle sounded taps as the old soldier was laid to rest in the family burial ground of Dungeness. A tombstone was sent by his son, Robert E. Lee, who visited his father's grave more than once. Cumberland Island was proud to be the resting place of the statesman and soldier who served with such distinction under Washington and who, upon the death of his general, spoke those immortal words, "first in War, first in Peace, and first in the hearts of his countrymen." Although the body of Lighthorse Harry Lee was later moved to Lexington, Virginia, to rest by that of his famous son, the tombstone still marks the place of his grave in the Dungeness burying ground.

Dungeness was inherited by Louisa Greene Shaw, who willed it in turn to her nephew Phineas Miller Nightingale, and for many years the Shaws and the Nightingales and their families lived on the plantation which continued to be noted for its lavish hospitality. Stories are handed down of houseparties, of Christmas trees that touched the high old ceilings, of New Year's dances and Thanksgiving dinners, of groaning banquet boards when the men of the family entertained the famous Camden Hunt Club—riotous affairs, they say, of feasting, and imbibing, and conversing, which began in late afternoon and lasted far into the night.

When the winds of war blew over the coastland in the 1860s, the inhabitants of Cumberland hurriedly packed their belongings and fled to the mainland, hoping to return later to their island homes. But returning owners found nothing but wasteland of the fields whose cotton had only a few years before been the pride of the London Exposition; nothing but ruins of the houses where they had lived so graciously. The Stafford place was never extensively cultivated again although its owners returned to live out their lives on the island. The house of Dungeness had survived the war, but had failed to survive war's aftermath. Despoiled and burned during the days of Reconstruction, only blackened walls and chimneys remained of the palatial mansion; and the family of Dungeness never returned to live on Cumberland Island.

An article published in *Lippincott's Magazine* in 1880 describes a visit made to Cumberland by Frederick Ober. He found few people living on the island; erosion had claimed the southern point, and the site of old Fort William had disappeared into the channel. The site of Fort St. Andrews was marked by ruined walls, and nearby was a well believed to contain ten thousand pounds in silver which was said to have been concealed there by the English when the Spaniards came up the coast in 1742. The skeleton walls of Dungeness still stood amidst the overgrown gardens and terraces.

The plantations on Cumberland lay deserted until 1882 when the greater part of the island became the property of the Thomas Carnegies of Pittsburgh, Pennsylvania. Both the Dungeness and Stafford plantations were included in the estate, and a new Dungeness house was built—a huge gabled and turreted place that stood upon the same foundation as the mansion designed by General Greene. Like Catherine (Greene) Miller, Lucy Coleman Carnegie was one of the brilliant hostesses of the nation, and the great house was filled with a succession of visitors who shared the Carnegies' delight in the semitropical island.

Old pictures show deep shady verandas with comfortable rocking chairs and hammocks; there were mastiffs and Russian bear hounds and stables of carriage and saddle horses and fat little ponies for the children. Old newspaper clippings tell of hunting and fishing parties and golf on the course with its famous short hole of sixty yards "so beset with hazards that a three was welcome and a four not unusual." As in antebellum days, the hospitality of the island became a tradition in the social life of the nation, and the name Dungeness was known throughout the country. The yacht *Dungeness* was often in the news, since Mrs. Carnegie was a boating enthusiast, first woman member of the exclusive New York Yacht Club; and the "Waltz Dungeness" was composed in honor of the Carnegies' famous house.

The Dungeness mansion, like the one before it, was built for the generations, and for almost half a century members of the Carnegie family enjoyed it as a part-time home. As the years went by, the island property was divided into individual estates;

Dungeness, built by Thomas Carnegie on Cumberland Island in the 1880s

The ruins of Dungeness

within a radius of eight miles were Stafford Place, Grey Field, Plum Orchard, and the Cottage. Several times remodeled and modernized, the house of Dungeness was finally left uninhabited. Standing in aging, massive dignity in its walled gardens, the old place was a symbol of the centuries of Cumberland Island—built on the shell mound of a forgotten race; gnarled orange trees in its tangled gardens fragrant inheritance of Spanish days; its name a legacy of English defenders of the colony; its foundation a nostalgic reminder of plantation times; the old mansion itself typical of the elegance of the 1890s. The great house burned in 1959.

The north end of the island, called High Point, was a popular summer resort around the turn of the century. The Hotel Cumberland, built by W. P. Bunkley and operated by his nephew, L. A. Miller, with its well-appointed cottages had ample accommodations for five hundred guests. There were sailing, rowing, motoring, and fishing boats; bowling alleys, a shooting gallery, a livery stable with fine saddle horses, and an orchestra for entertainment and dancing. An "elegant fast steamer" made the twenty-two-mile trip from Brunswick daily, with a second special boat on Saturday. A horse-drawn trolley was provided to transport visitors from the dock to the hotel.

As the popularity of St. Simons as a resort increased, that of less accessible Cumberland decreased. Part of High Point remained in the Bunkley-Miller family, and the hotel property at the north end of the island eventually became the private property of the Candler family of Atlanta. A few ruins and contours of breastworks mark the site of old Fort St. Andrews, but the ancient well has never been discovered with its secret horde of silver hidden by the British two centuries ago.

As the sea encroaches upon different parts of the coastland it sometimes destroys historic landmarks and sometimes discloses evidence of inhabitants of former centuries. In the Smithsonian Institution in Washington a fragment of an old dugout canoe is labeled "one of the few known examples showing the prehistoric method of manufacture, was unearthed in Feb. 1932 on Cumberland Island, Georgia. It may be a relic of the Timucuan Indians who inhabited the coast of Georgia and north Florida in the 16th century. Lacking metal the coastal Indians made dugouts by alternately burning and scraping with shell instruments."

With the island in private ownership for so many years and accessible only by boat or plane, Cumberland's natural beauty lay undisturbed. Woods roads wound through semitropical forests, and the beach often showed the hoof prints of diminutive donkeys imported from Sicily and of wild horses said to have descended from those brought by the Spaniards.

In 1972 Cumberland Island was established as a National Seashore Park administered by the National Park Service, Department of the Interior. In 1975 the south end of the island was opened to visitors, with transportation provided by boat from the town of St. Marys across the sound.

The primary objective of the National Seashore program is "to preserve and interpret the natural and historic aspects of the site" and "to encourage active participation in outdoor recreation in a pleasing environment." To achieve the first objective, Cumberland offers informational and interpretive tours. To achieve the second, campsites and hiking trails are provided, and a program of limited deer hunting was introduced in 1980. There are also opportunities for bird watching, shell hunting and beach combing, and for photographing, painting, sketching, or just enjoying the ancient windblown trees, the magnificent towering dunes, and the miles of unspoiled beach.

14 St. Marys

No story of Georgia's Golden Isles would be complete without including St. Marys, the river town across the sound from Cumberland. Like other sections of the coastal mainland St. Marys has always been closely associated with the history of the islands. The old town stands upon a bluff that was once the site of an Indian village inhabited by a Timucuan tribe and ruled, according to legend, by a queen who was the most beautiful woman in all the Indian nations.

A few miles from St. Marys in the forest near Crooked River State Park stands the mysterious ruin called locally the old sugar house, which is believed by many people to have been the sixteenth-century mission of Santa Maria de Guadalupe. The walls, a hundred and fifty feet long and half as wide, outline a once spacious two-storied building whose arched doorways, pillared porticoes, and both wide and lancet windows might well have been those of an ancient cloister.

People who think that the ruins are indeed those of the Santa Maria mission like to imagine what a beautiful church it must have been, standing in the midst of the wilderness, surrounded by its gardens of fruits and flowers. And what a beautiful place it is today, even with all trace of the timbers of rafter and roof, of floor and beam, of door and sill lost in the decay of the years. Twisted vines and tall trees grow within the walls of ancient tabby, the rough gray shell softened by moss and fern and by dull red lichen which the superstitious say has splotched the walls ever since the bloody massacre on that dark night of horror when the tomahawk of the pagan was raised against the cross of the priest. And they say that the tread of a moccasined foot may be heard in the depths of Dark Entry Swamp, and that a traveler who drinks from enchanted Sweetwater Branch will surely return.

Part of the Debatable Land in the early days of the colony, this lower coastal territory remained unsettled until after the defeat of the Spaniards, and few farms were developed during those years while Florida was still in Spanish possession. Among the early settlers of the region were French people from the Evangeline country. When the Acadians were driven from their homes in Grand Pré in the middle of the eighteenth century, some of the exiles found refuge in this section of Georgia, and while many wandered on in search of family and friends, some spent the rest of their lives in this newly settled coastal country.

When Florida was ceded to England in 1763 the population of southeast Georgia increased, and although there were no towns in the region there were numerous plantations and farms. Large grants were made to planters from South Carolina and to many prominent citizens of the Georgia colony. A tract of land near the St. Marys River, known as the Pagan Plantation, was owned by Charles and Jermyn Wright, brothers of Sir James Wright, Georgia's last royal governor; and it was on this property that the infamous Fort Tonyn was built at the beginning of the Revolutionary War. The southern coast was harassed by privateers commissioned by East Florida's Governor Tonyn, and the fort named for him was the rendezvous of the Florida Rangers, a lawless band who preyed upon the settlers. After the fort had withstood all attacks by the patriots it was destroyed by the Rangers themselves when they withdrew into Florida. It was near the Pagan Plantation, the site of Fort Tonyn, that the town of St. Marys was built nearly a decade later.

Although Florida had passed back into Spanish possession in

1783 and the border region was troubled by depredations of Indians who were encouraged by the Spaniards, the population of south Georgia increased steadily after the close of the war. Camden County was generous with land to new settlers, and old records show one Jacob Weed to have received extensive grants in the region. In 1787 a group of public-spirited citizens of the county bought 1,620 acres from Jacob Weed for the purpose of founding a town as the county seat of Camden and as a shipping point for the rich agricultural and lumbering country. It was upon this land, on the bank of the St. Marys River at a point called Buttermilk Bluff, that the town of St. Marys was built.

Timbers cut in the inland forests were floated down river, and caravans of creaking ox-drawn wagons made their way to the port town as the settlers hauled cotton from the plantations, and peltries and naval stores from the woodlands. New businesses were established, and refugees from the uprising in Santo Domingo increased the town's French population.

For several years after the founding of the river port there continued to be troubles with the Indians. A letter written in 1794 complained of a large body of Indians in Spanish pay; and Colonel Jacob Weed, commandant of militia for the county, reported raids by bands of Indians in which settlers were killed, women and children taken prisoner, livestock stolen, and houses burned. By the turn of the century more towns had been built, and in 1801 the county seat was moved from St. Marys to more centrally located Jeffersonton. In the following year St. Marys was incorporated, and the river town became increasingly important as a shipping and lumber center and as a point of supply for plantations of the region.

It was in this year of 1802 that Major Archibald Clark came to live in St. Marys. Born in Savannah, educated in New England, young Clark opened a law office and brought his bride to the port town. It was in the Clarks' house that Aaron Burr was entertained when he visited St. Marys in 1804. Described as energetic, wealthy, and progressive, Archibald Clark owned extensive properties in the county as well as a large sawmill on the river. Since St. Marys was the southernmost port of the Atlantic seaboard, an office was established by the government to collect customs and to prevent smuggling from the Spanish-owned province of Florida. In 1807 Major Clark was appointed collector of the port.

St. Marys' first church was built in 1808, a Union Church to serve all denominations. We are told that its bell had an unusually clear and silvery tone, caused, they say, by a large number of silver dollars that went into the melting pot when the bell was cast. Just as the belfry of Christ Church, Frederica, and its bees figure in island tales, so the belfry of this church has its place in the legends of St. Marys. It once played an involuntary part, according to local tradition, in the landing of a schooner-load of contraband rum and cigars smuggled in from Florida. One midnight when a smugglers' ship had secretly entered the harbor, their accomplices ashore managed to hoist the minister's horse up into the church belfry, along with an ingenious arrangement of hay tied to the bell rope to attract the townspeople's attention away from the waterfront so the cargo could be landed unmolested.

At the beginning of the War of 1812 when Spain refused to permit United States forces to occupy east Florida, there was a general feeling of uneasiness along the southern coast. Troops were stationed at the port town and a fort was built at Point Peter upon the St. Marys River, but the British did not attack until 1815. The war was actually over at this time, but news traveled slowly in those days. The fort was captured, the town of St. Marys was occupied by the enemy, and the Clark house was commandeered as headquarters for Admiral Cockburn. Major Clark as collector of the port had a hundred thousand dollars of government money in his possession, and upon his refusal to disclose its hiding place he was taken prisoner, but when news came that the Treaty of Ghent had been signed Major Clark was released and the British forces were withdrawn.

Even with the end of the War of 1812 St. Marys' and Camden County's troubles were not over. Constant vigilance was necessary against smuggling from Florida, and unfriendly relations between the settlers and the Indians led to hostilities sometimes called a "petty civil war." A letter written in 1817 reports the "situation of our frontier truly distressing," adding that it was "uncertain whether the Indians or our frontier citizens were the first offenders." In 1818 the disbanded militia was drafted for frontier duty. After the "Floridas" were ceded to the United States, border disturbances subsided and St. Marys and Camden County enjoyed the peace and prosperity of plantation days.

Among the large plantations mentioned in old papers are Antrim, Mariana, Fairfield, Refuge, John Houston McIntosh's New Canaan Plantation, and General Floyd's Bellevue Plantation with its famous house built in the shape of an anchor. The land around St. Marys was suitable for a wide variety of crops. A plantation offered for sale listed its products as cotton, rice, cane, corn, peaches, sweet and sour oranges, lemons, cherries, figs, and quince. Mulberry trees were set out in an effort to revive the silk industry, and old letters mention pecan groves which were probably some of the first in Georgia.

In addition to its importance as a shipping, trading, and lumber town, St. Marys became one of the leading shipbuilding centers of the southern coast. Ocean-going vessels built in the shipyards were launched with elaborate ceremonies and festivities. The port town was the social and cultural center of the region and residents frequently entertained visiting government officials with brilliant banquets and receptions. Important social events were dress parades of the "Camden Chasseurs of Horse," dinners of the celebrated Camden Hunt Club, and regattas held by the Aquatic Club and the St. Marys Boat Club. Some of the finest racing boats on the coast were built in the river town—dugout canoes "fashioned of cypress, artistically finished with mahogany and copper trimming."

In 1828 the Union Church became the Independent Presbyterian Church, and its basement was occupied by a private academy. Attended by young people of St. Marys and by children of wealthy planters of the county, the school outgrew its quarters and moved into the New Academy building. About 1829 a beautiful house was built near the church for the residence of the minister. It was of classic Greek Revival architecture with spacious grounds featuring plantings of orange trees, which gave the place its name, Orange Hall. The Reverend Horace Pratt and his family lived here while he was pastor of the Presbyterian Church, and the hospitality of their home was expressed by the words carved in the over-mantels of two fireplaces— "Happy is the home that shelters a friend" and "O turn thy rudder thitherward awhile, Here may the storme-beat vessel safely ryde! This is the port of rest from troublous toyle, The World's sweet Inn from pain and wearisome turmoyle."

In his memoirs an old-time resident, James S. Silva, reminisces of the St. Marys of antebellum days. Born there in 1832, he spent his boyhood in the river town, and his recollections at the age of eighty-two present a picture of St. Marys in the years of her prosperity. He tells of regular passenger boats which stopped at the port and of a weekly mail coach. There were cotton warehouses and stores along the waterfront, a bank, an inn, and a tobacco warehouse where cigars were made. The city market, which was built upon pillars, also housed the fire department whose equipment consisted of "two ladders and a number of leather fire-buckets hung upon pegs." The market was surmounted by a belfry whose bell announced fresh meats and vegetables for sale and also clanged out the fire alarm. The residential part of the town, which stood back from the waterfront, had wide streets with central greens shaded by arching trees and bright with flowering shrubs. There were picnic excursions and shad-fishing expeditions on the river, and opossum and coon hunts in the "bay-gall swamps" at night by the flare of "light'ud knots"; and there was sport for riflemen along the river banks when alligators floated down from the Okefenokee Swamp.

In the late 1840s there was a decline in the fortunes of St. Marys. More of the products of the county were being taken to inland markets, and less of the trade of the plantations came to the river town. There were fewer visitors at the inn, and the bank failed. A generous citizen bought the bank building and gave it to the Catholics to be used as a church; there were at this time also a Methodist and an Episcopal church in St. Marys.

It was in the year 1848 that the town's distinguished citizen, Archibald Clark, died. Major Clark had served in the state legislature, had been mayor of St. Marys for many years, and he died while still holding the office of collector of the port, which he had held through the administrations of nine presidents. Appointed by Thomas Jefferson, he died just a few months before the inauguration of Zachary Taylor in 1849.

When St. Marys, like the rest of the country, found itself caught up in the maelstrom of war most of the inhabitants refugeed to the inland safety of the little village of Traders Hill. Shelled from the waterfront, many of St. Marys' buildings were destroyed, but much of the residential part of the town escaped serious damage. Returning citizens found that Orange Hall, the Clark House, the Presbyterian Church, and many other beloved landmarks were still standing. Since the New Academy had been demolished, the basement of the Presbyterian Church was again used as the "Old Academy."

Planters and businessmen made every attempt to rebuild the prosperity of their region, but although St. Marys again became the county seat in 1871, the old-time importance of the town was never regained. There was no longer the great plantation trade; most of the inland lumber was shipped by rail and St. Marys had no railroad. Visitors to the town in the late 1800s described it as a quiet little fishing village of grass-grown shady streets.

Efforts were made to revive St. Marys in the first decade of the twentieth century. It was during this time that a newspaper, the *Southeast Georgian* (established in 1894 in the nearby town of Kingsland), moved to the river port and advertised itself as the "Official Paper of the City of St. Mary's and the County of Camden—Dollar a Year—No Pay, No Paper." In 1926 the *Southeast Georgian* moved back to Kingsland; two years later the county seat was moved to Woodbine; and old St. Marys fell into a somnolence from which it seemed the town would never recover. Ten miles from the main highways of the state, the river port's principal contact with the outside world was an old motor bus with train wheels which operated on rails laid down to Kingsland.

In the 1930s when the popular comic-strip artist Roy Crane and his wife were vacationing at Sea Island they visited historic points of interest along the coast. His imagination captured by St. Marys' old motor bus, the artist made sketches of it and before long the quaint conveyance found itself as the Toonerville Trolley sharing the adventures of Wash Tubbs and Captain Easy.

After the county seat was moved to Woodbine, St. Marys' courthouse was used as a public school. Since the building was of wooden construction, valuable records had always been stored in a small concrete room adjoining the courthouse. When the county records were moved a number of out-of-date papers and ledgers were left sealed in the strong-room. Almost forgotten for a quarter-century, the existence of the old papers was brought to the attention of officials in 1951 when curious schoolboys found a way into the storeroom. These records, letters, etc., contain much valuable data on the early days of the county, and they are now preserved in the courthouse at Woodbine with copies at the State Department of Archives.

After dozing for three quarters of a century, St. Marys roused herself in the 1940s when the Gilman Paper Company, St. Marys Kraft Corporation, brought the town back to life. New buildings were constructed, and the *Camden County Tribune* began publication in 1950. Modern houses appeared on the shady old streets whose names honor the founders of the town, streets that converged at the wharves where the shrimp boats docked, masts tall against the sky, nets drying in the sun. New life had come to St. Marys but treasured landmarks still remained.

In the center green of the principal street a bronze historical marker calls attention to the Washington Oak and Pump. According to tradition, the old tree was planted in 1799 to commemorate George Washington's death. And the wooden pump is said to be the only remaining example of the pumps that supplied water to the town in the early days.

Nearby is the Presbyterian Church that was built in 1808, a

St. Marys Presbyterian Church

charming white-painted meetinghouse with the legendary belfry which generations of small boys have wanted to climb to prove that the story of the smugglers and the horse *could* be true. A 1980 renovation left the historic building looking as it must have looked when it was completed in the early nineteenth century.

The Archibald Clark house still stands, as does Orange Hall, which was purchased in 1951 by the Gilman Paper Company in order to preserve it as a historic site. In 1960 the fine old house was presented to the town of St. Marys and now serves as headquarters for the Chamber of Commerce. It is listed in the National Register of Historic Places.

In 1958, a century and a half after the United States Customs Office was established in St. Marys, the little town again came

Orange Hall, St. Marys

into national prominence when nearby Kings Bay was made an ammunition loading terminal for the United States Army. But before the military terminal was fully activated, its purpose was made obsolete by newer weapons and nuclear explosives. The wharf built by the Army was later leased to a shipping company, and the property was sometimes utilized for summer training of U.S. Army Reserve units.

In 1978 it was announced that Kings Bay was considered the best site for redeployment of the Poseidon Fleet Ballistic Missile Submarine Squadron from Rota, Spain. Plans were developed for the inactive military terminal to be converted to a refit base known as Naval Submarine Support Base, King's Bay. As activity increased on the 16,000-acre government property the population of St. Marys increased and, as time goes on, even greater growth is expected. As St. Marys continues to expand, the unique character of the early part of the old Camden County port town is protected against undesirable change by historic district zoning.

Few places have played such widely divergent roles as this coast town of Georgia. In the eighteenth century it shared the tragedy of the exiled Acadians; in the nineteenth century it was part of the plantation era; and in the twentieth century it was host to the quaint motor bus of the comics and to the United States Navy's most sophisticated submarines.

15 Always the Golden Isles

"This other Eden, demi-paradise—these precious stones set in a golden sea . . . this blessed plot, this earth, this realm, these Golden Isles of Georgia." So might Shakespeare's famous lincs have been penned had the bard ever visited the islands that have been called the Golden Isles of Guale, the Golden Isles of the Spanish Main, and the Golden Isles of Georgia—but always the Golden Isles.

The traveler along the coast today sees little evidence of that truly golden age in the history of coastal Georgia, the half-century when the Land of the Golden Isles was one of the most productive agricultural regions in the world. The highway runs mile after mile through swampland where great cypress trees stand knee-deep in the dark water, through marshlands where acres of rice once produced their golden harvest, between roadside ditches crowded with lavender-blue water hyacinths and brown velvet cattails, and by shadowed pools starred with water lilies.

The bare dooryards of unpainted cabins are swept clean with brooms made of bundles of leafy branches as were the avenues of the antebellum mansions, and an occasional slow-moving ox-cart recalls the olden days when oxen worked the fields of the great plantations. Here and there a cane patch is a reminder of the crop that once shared the supremacy of cotton and rice along the coastland; and the simple cane mills turned by plodding mules suggest the cattle-impelled mills of earlier days. At harvest time those initiated into the delights of syrup-cane like to peel the outside from the green stalks and chew the succulent inside heart, or to drink the cups of cold cane juice offered at roadside stands.

The lumbering of early days remains a leading industry of the region, and the scarred "working trees" of the piney woods still produce the rosin that has been a marketable product of Georgia from the earliest days of commerce. The pine barrens, once considered worthless, have proved valuable sources of material for the pulp and paper industries. In a reforestation program designed to prevent depletion of the trees and to insure an endless supply of pulpwood for the mills, the cones of the slash pines are gathered each September and the seeds are removed, dried, and planted. Reminiscent of the early trading of the region are the small markets for skins and for swamp products such as roots, herbs, sweetgum (the liquid-amber of colonial days), and deer-tongue, the colloquial name for a wild plant that is sometimes mixed with tobacco.

Various uses have been found for the Spanish moss that hangs from the coastal live oaks. First used to fashion skirts for the Indian women, it later found a market as an inexpensive stuffing for furniture, mattresses, and cushions. Gardeners and nurserymen find the moss a useful sun-screen when spread on wire netting over delicate plants. It has been noted that it will live indefinitely if a few tendrils touch the wood of posts or framework from which it draws the moisture necessary for its existence. With characteristics of both parasite and airplant the gray-green moss is said to be injurious to some species of trees such as water oak or cherry laurel, but the great deep-rooted live oaks seem to be impervious to its presence.

One feature of the coastland that has remained unchanged from time immemorial is the fishing which was enjoyed by the Indians and colonists and which is the delight of the sportsmen of today. Almost unchanged, too, is the sport of hunting. Although no trace remains of the buffalo, which the colonists found abundant on the coastland, deer, wild turkey, quail, marsh hen, and wild duck still make the region a favorite spot for hunters. *El lagarto* of the Spaniard, the "crocodile" of the colonist, and the twenty-foot alligators reported by William Bartram are no longer plentiful in the tidal creeks and rivers, but an occasional two- or three-foot specimen may still be found in the marshes, to the consternation of the houseparty hostess who may have one of the scaly little monsters added to her problems when her youthful visitors return from a successful 'gator hunt.

The Golden Isles, with their forests, marshes, creeks, rivers, and flowing artesian wells, attract birds of every description. Gulls, terns, and pelicans swoop over the waves; sandpipers and willets run along the beaches; skimmers, osprey, and water turkeys frequent the coastal waters; cranes, blue and white heron, and rare egret fish in the inlets; and the early riser may sometimes see the ungainly hunched walk of the wood ibis break into the grace of flight. Hundreds of species call the islands home, and great numbers of migratory birds are seasonal visitors: wading birds, swimming birds, diving birds; singing birds, warbling birds, cooing birds. Bird lovers come to write, to classify, to photograph, to sketch, to paint, or just to look and listen.

The intracoastal or inland waterway, which passes to the leeward of the Golden Isles, offers high adventure for the landlubber around the docks where fishermen and boatmen foregather with their salty talk and tall tales. All sorts of craft ply the waters of this busy passage that stretches from Maine to Miami— smelly fishing craft, trim speedboats riding the waves in the wake of palatial yachts, barges loaded with cargoes of every description, schooners with masts etched against the sky and sails filled with Old World romance. A favorite landmark is the little rock quarantine island near Brunswick, where ships used to stop for inspection; it is said to have been built entirely of ballast.

The inhabitants of an island have an existence different from that of people who have always lived in the shelter and protection of the mainland. The open sea and the wide stretch of salt marshes offer a feeling of seclusion and relaxation, found nowhere else; but island people live more hazardously than do their inland neighbors. Extravagant as is her sunshine, nature is equally authentic in her less pleasant moods; and in time of war an island must be an armed fortress or without defense. Life on the Golden Isles has been gracious but hazardous; down through the years the islands have had many a grim battle with man and with nature. Here in their kingdom-by-the-sea live a charming people; from gallant ancestors they have inherited that serenity of spirit so often mistaken for apathy. Like their sturdy coastal cedars they meet the buffetings of the world with a sort of stubborn acquiescence, sure that the winds will die down and the clouds will break away, and the sun will still be shining and the fish will still be biting.

The ageless charm of the Land of the Golden Isles is a subtle mingling of past and present. Hers is not lost romance, but rather, like wine of rare vintage, romance to which the years have given added bouquet. The oleanders planted a hundred years ago have their roots deep in the past, and yet they blossom beautifully in the present. The faint fragrance of yesterday mingles with the salty smell of the sea and its invitation to fun and fishing. Looking over the golf courses on the acres that were once fields of sea island cotton, one feels a sort of vague nostalgia— but the pulse quickens to the beckoning green of the fairways. Sighs for the gracious days of the past are lost in the laughter of the present.

And the Golden Isles, drowsy with age, dream of their yesterdays, their todays, and their tomorrows, secure in the belief that theirs is a treasure that "rust does not corrupt nor thieves break through and steal."

Bibliography

Books

Andrews, E. W., and C. M. Andrews, eds. *Jonathan Dickinson's Journal, 1697*. New Haven: Yale University Press, 1945.

Andrews, Edward Deming. *The People Called Shakers*. New York: Oxford University Press, 1953.

Armes, William D., ed. *The Autobiography of Joseph LeConte*. New York: D. Appleton and Company, 1903.

Armstrong, Margaret. *Fanny Kemble, A Passionate Victorian*. New York: Macmillan Company, 1938.

Bartram, John. *Diary of a Journey Through the Carolinas, Georgia, and Florida, 1765–66*. Philadelphia: The American Philosophical Society, 1942.

Bartram, William. *The Travels of William Bartram*. Philadelphia: James and Johnson, 1791.

———. *Travels in Georgia and Florida, 1773–74*. Annotated by Francis Harper. Philadelphia: The American Philosophical Society, 1942.

Bolton, Herbert E., and Mary Ross, eds. *Arredondo's Historical Proof of Spain's Title to Georgia, the Debatable Land*. Berkeley: University of California Press, 1925.

Bourne, Edward G., ed. *Narratives of the Career of Hernando DeSoto*. Translated by Buckingham Smith. 2 vols. New York: A. S. Barnes and Company, 1904.

Boyer, Samuel P. *Naval Surgeon*. Edited by Elinor and James A. Barnes. 2 vols. Bloomington: Indiana University Press, 1963.

Bremer, Frederika. *Homes of the New World and Impressions of America*. Translated by M. Howitt. New York: Harper and Brothers, 1853.

Cate, Margaret Davis. *Our Todays and Yesterdays*. Brunswick, Ga.: Glover Brothers, Inc., 1930.

Cate, Margaret Davis, and Orrin S. Wightman. *Early Days of Coastal Georgia*. St. Simons Island, Ga. Fort Frederica Association, 1955.

Clarke, William Bordley, ed. *Early and Historic Freemasonry of Georgia*. Savannah: Braid and Hutton, Inc., Printers, 1924.

Cooney, Loraine M., and H. Rainwater, comps. and eds. *Garden History of Georgia*, including Florence Marye's *Georgia's Early Gardens*. Atlanta: Peachtree Garden Club, 1933.

Coulter, E. Merton. *Georgia: A Short History*. Chapel Hill: University of North Carolina Press, 1933.

Coulter, E. Merton, ed. *Georgia's Disputed Ruins*. Chapel Hill: University of North Carolina Press, 1937.

Coulter, E. Merton. *Thomas Spalding of Sapelo*. Baton Rouge: Louisiana State University Press, 1940.

Dau, Frederick W. *Florida Old and New*. New York: G. P. Putnam's Sons, 1934.

Ferrier, William W. *Origin and Development of the University of California*. Berkeley: University of California Press, 1930.

Fitzpatrick, John Clement, ed. *The Diaries of George Washington*. 4 vols. Boston: Houghton Mifflin Company, 1925.

Goulding, Francis R. *Sapelo or Child-Life on the Tide-Water*. Philadelphia: Claxton, Remsen, and Hoffelfinger, 1880.

Graff, Mary B. *Mandarin on the St. John*. Gainesville: University of Florida Press, 1953.

Hall, Basil. *Travels in North America in the Years 1827 and 1828*. London: Simpkin and Marshall, 1829.

Harris, Joel Chandler. *The Story of Aaron the Son of Ben Ali*. Boston: Houghton Mifflin Company, 1897.

Henderson, Archibald. *Washington's Southern Tour, 1791*. Boston: Houghton Mifflin Company, 1923.

Jenkins, Charles Francis. *Button Gwinnett, Signer of the Declaration of Independence*. Garden City: Doubleday, Page and Company, 1926.

Johnson, Amanda. *Georgia as Colony and State.* Atlanta: Walter W. Brown Publishing Company, 1938.

Johnson, G. G. *A Social History of the Sea Islands.* Chapel Hill: University of North Carolina Press, 1930.

Jones, Charles C. *The History of Georgia.* 2 vols. Boston: Houghton Mifflin Company, 1883.

Jones, William C. *Illustrated History of the University of California.* Berkeley: University of California Student Co-op. Society, 1901.

Kemble, Frances Anne. *Journal of a Residence on a Georgian Plantation, 1838–1839.* New York: Harper and Brothers, 1863.

Knight, Lucian Lamar. *Georgia's Landmarks, Memorials, and Legends.* 2 vols. Atlanta: Byrd Printing Company, 1913.

LeConte, Joseph. *'Ware Sherman* (with introductory reminiscences by daughter Caroline LeConte). Berkeley: University of California Press, 1937.

Leigh, Frances Butler. *Ten Years on a Georgia Plantation.* London: R. Bentley and Son, 1883.

Lovell, Caroline Couper. *Golden Isles of Georgia.* Boston: Little, Brown and Company, 1932.

Lyell, Sir Charles. *Second Visit to the United States, 1846.* 2 vols. New York: Harper, 1849.

McCall, Hugh. *History of Georgia.* 2 vols. Savannah: Seymour and Williams, 1811; rpt., Atlanta: A. B. Caldwell, 1909.

McCrady, Edward. *History of South Carolina.* 4 vols. New York: Macmillan Company, 1897.

Martin, Harold H. *This Happy Isle.* Sea Island, Ga.: Sea Island Company, 1978.

Morris, Richard B., ed. *Encyclopedia of American History.* New York: Harper and Brothers, 1953.

Murray, Amelia. *Letters from the United States, Cuba, and Canada.* New York: Putnam, 1856.

Northen, William J. *Men of Mark in Georgia.* 6 vols. Atlanta: A. B. Caldwell, 1907.

Osterweis, Rollin G. *Rebecca Gratz.* New York: G. P. Putnam's Sons, 1935.

Parrish, Lydia. *Slave Songs of the Georgia Sea Islands.* New York: Creative Age Press, Inc., 1942.

Perkerson, Medora Field. *White Columns in Georgia.* New York: Rinehart, 1952.

Pope-Hennessy, Una, ed. *The Aristocratic Journey* (letters of Mrs. Basil Hall during sojourn in America 1827–1828). New York: G. P. Putnam's Sons, 1931.

Reese, Trevor R. *Frederica, Its Place in History.* Sea Island, Ga.: Fort Frederica Association with the National Park Service, 1969.

Smith, George G. *The Story of Georgia and the Georgia People, 1732 to 1860.* Macon, Ga.: George G. Smith Publishing Company, 1900.

Smith, Joseph W. *Visits to Brunswick, Georgia, and Travels South.* Boston: Addison C. Getchell and Son, Printers, 1907.

Stacy, James. *History of the Midway Congregational Church.* Newnan, Ga.: S. W. Murray, Printer, 1903. Revised and reprinted in 1951 as *History and Records of Midway Church* with addenda by Elizabeth Walker Quarterman.

Stevens, William B. *A History of Georgia.* 2 vols. New York: D. Appleton and Company, 1847.

Suddeth, Osterhout, and Hutcheson. *Empire Builders of Georgia.* Austin, Texas: The Steck Company, 1951.

Swanton, John R. *The Indian Tribes of North America.* Bureau of American Ethnology, Smithsonian Institution. Washington, D.C.: Government Printing Office, 1950.

Van Doren, Mark, ed. *Correspondence of Aaron Burr and His Daughter Theodosia.* New York: Covici-Friede, Inc., 1929.

White, George. *Historical Collections of Georgia.* New York: Pudney and Russell, 1854.

White, George. *Statistics of the State of Georgia.* Savannah: W. Thorne Williams, 1849.

White, W. A. *Autobiography of William Allen White.* New York: Macmillan Company, 1946.

Williams, George W. *St. Michael's, Charleston, 1751–1951.* Columbia: University of South Carolina Press, 1951.

Wister, Fanny Kemble., ed. *Fanny, the American Kemble.* Tallahassee, Fla., 1972.

Articles

Bryan, Mary Givens, and Beatrice F. Lang. "Burial of Light Horse Harry Lee on Cumberland Recalled," in *Camden County Tribune*, St. Marys, Ga. (January 27, 1956).

Burns, Olive Ann. "Getting Off the World on Ossabaw Island," in *Atlanta Weekly* (May 11, 1980).

"Captain Dunlop's Voyage to the Southward, 1687," in *South Carolina Historical and Genealogical Magazine*, vol. 30, no. 3 (July 1929).

Cobb, Norman J., and Don McWaters. "Historical Report on Evelyn Plantation," in *Georgia Historical Quarterly*, vol. 55, no. 3 (Fall 1971).

Govan, Thomas P. "Report on Georgia Banking, 1810–1861," in *Journal of Southern History*, vol. 4, no. 2 (May 1938).

Hawes, Lilla M., ed. "The Papers of Lachlan McIntosh, 1774–1799," in *Georgia Historical Quarterly*, vol. 38, no. 3 (September 1954).

Justus, Lucy. "Mrs. West Finds a Landlord," in *Atlanta Journal and Constitution Magazine*, June 12, 1977.

Lewis, Bessie. "Old Fort King George, Located near Darien," in the *Savannah Morning News*, October 25, 1932.

Nightingale, B. N. "Dungeness," in *Georgia Historical Quarterly*, vol. 20, no. 4 (December 1938).

Ober, Frederick. "Dungeness, General Greene's Sea Island Plantation," in *Lippincott's Magazine*, vol. 26 (August 1880).

Scruggs, C. P. "Sapelo Joins the Fold," in *Georgia Magazine*, February–March 1970.

Thornton, Ella May. "Bilali—His Book," in *Law Library Journal*, vol. 48 (1955).

Government Documents

American State Papers, Finance Series: Containing the report from Sec. of Treasury to House of Representatives concerning transfer of Gov't. funds to Bank of Darien. Washington, D.C.: Gales and Seaton, 1834.

County records and papers in Georgia Department of Archives and History, Georgia State Library, Georgia Historical Society, and Glynn County Records Vault.

Fort Frederica Site Report, MS. in office Fort Frederica National Monument, 1945.

Georgia Colonial, Revolutionary, and Civil War records, published and unpublished, in Georgia Department of Archives and History, Georgia State Library, and Georgia Historical Society.

Soil Survey of Glynn County, Georgia. Containing information on rice plantations. United States Department of Agriculture. Washington, D.C.: Government Printing Office, 1912.

South Carolina Colonial records, University of South Carolina Library, Columbia.

United States Census, 1790, of Charleston, South Carolina.

United States Government Light List re establishment of lighthouses on Georgia Coast. Washington, D.C., 1882.

Newspapers and Periodicals

Atlanta Constitution

Atlanta Journal

Brunswick News

Camden County Tribune (St. Marys, Georgia)

Darien Gazette

Darien Telegraph

Gentleman's Magazine and Monthly Intelligencer (London, England)

Georgia Gazette (Savannah)

Savannah Morning News

Southeast Georgian (Kingsland)

Southern Agriculturist and Register of Rural Affairs (Charleston, S.C., 1800s)

Manuscript Collections

Butler, Pierce, clippings in scrapbook (vol. 2, part 2), collected by Thompson Wescott, Pennsylvania Historical Society, Philadelphia.

Butler, Pierce, letters in British Museum (copies privately owned).

Carnegie scrapbooks (copies in Georgia Department of Archives and History, Atlanta).

Childs, C. W., "History of Brunswick," Brunswick Library.

Couper papers and account books in Southern History Department, University of North Carolina Library, Chapel Hill.

Couper papers in Sanger Collection, Georgia Historical Society, Savannah.

Graham scrapbook, St. Simons Library.

Hartridge, Agnes, "The Goulds of St. Clair and Black Banks," privately owned.

Midway records, copies in Georgia Department of Archives and History, Atlanta.

Parker, W. H., "History of Christ Church, Frederica," Cate Library, Georgia Historical Society, Savannah. "North End Plantations of St. Simons Island," privately owned.

Shaker clippings from Shaker scrapbook in Western Reserve Historical Society, Cleveland, Ohio.

Silva papers, copies in Georgia Department of Archives and History, Atlanta.

Taylor, Josephine Burroughs, "Johnston-McNish Family," privately owned.

Washington papers in Manuscripts Division, Library of Congress. Contain letters from the Reverend Mr. William McWhir to George Washington.

Privately owned grants, deeds, letters, ledgers, journals, and scrapbooks.

Pamphlets and Booklets

Bicentennial Midway Church and Society. Privately printed. 30 pp.

Boys Estate, Glynn County, Brunswick, Georgia. Publication by the Estate. 14 pp.

Cain, Charles C., Jr. *The G.A.R. Dining Club.* Privately printed. 34 pp.

Coulter, E. Merton. *Boating as a Sport in the Old South.* Reprinted from *Georgia Historical Quarterly*, vol. 27, no. 3 (September 1943). Savannah: Georgia Historical Society. 17 pp.

Flags of Five Nations (a collection of historical sketches, legends, and stories of the Golden Isles of Guale). Privately printed. 94 pp.

Gilbert, Harriet B. *Hundred Years of First Baptist Church, Brunswick.* Brunswick: Knight Printing House, 1955. 28 pp.

Godley, Margaret, and Lillian Bragg. *Stories of Old Savannah.* Privately printed. 35 pp.

Lewis, Bessie. *The Story of Old Fort King George.* Privately printed. 12 pp.

Lewis, Eugene W. *The Story of Sea Island.* Privately printed. 26 pp.

Lewis, Eugene W. *Yesterday on Hamilton and St. Simons Island, Georgia.* Privately printed. 20 pp.

Martin, Josephine Bacon. *Midway Georgia in History and Legend.* Savannah: Southern Publishing Co. 25 pp.

Torrey, H. N. *The Story of Ossabaw.* Privately printed. 20 pp.

Winn, D. Watson. *Christ Church, Frederica.* Savannah, Ga.: Byck Co., 1910. 46 pp.

Wylly, Charles Spalding. *Annals and Memoirs.* Brunswick, 1920.

Photo Credits

Page 45
Midway Church. Photograph by Robert Orchard.

Page 53
Midway Colonial Museum. Photograph by Robert Orchard.

Page 58
Ruins of the slave cottages at "Chocolate." Courtesy of the Sea Island Company.

Page 59
Architect's drawing of the Old South-End House on Sapelo built by Thomas Spalding circa 1800. Reprinted from *Golden Isles of Georgia* by Caroline Couper Lovell (Boston: Little, Brown and Co., 1932).

Page 64
South End House, Sapelo, as rebuilt by Howard Coffin. Courtesy of the Sea Island Company.

Page 65
The indoor pool at South End House. Courtesy of the Sea Island Company.

Page 66
Charles Lindbergh on the Georgia coast. Courtesy of the Sea Island Company.

Page 67
Mr. and Mrs. Howard Coffin and President and Mrs. Calvin Coolidge at Sapelo, Christmas 1928. Courtesy of the Sea Island Company.

Page 68
Calvin Coolidge posing for a portrait by Frank Salisbury. Courtesy of the Sea Island Company.

Page 91
Bartram's "Lost Gordonia." Courtesy of the University of Georgia Libraries.

Page 96
Rice preparation on the Georgia coast in the early years of the twentieth century. Courtesy of the Sea Island Company.

Page 107
Frances Anne Kemble. Portrait by Thomas Sully, Pennsylvania Academy of the Fine Arts, Philadelphia.

Page 131
Charles Wesley preaching to the Indians. An engraving by F. Bromley from the painting by R. R. McIan. Courtesy of the University of Georgia Libraries.

Page 142
Ruins of the barracks, Fort Frederica National Monument. Photograph by Robert Orchard.

Page 143
Fort Frederica. Photograph by Robert Orchard.

Page 147
Anson Dodge. Courtesy of Anna Marie Gould.

Page 147
Ellen Dodge. Courtesy of the Coastal Georgia Historical Society.

Page 148
Christ Church, Frederica. Photograph by Robert Orchard.

Page 153
Lighthouse and Keeper's Cottage, now the Museum of Coastal History, St. Simons Island. Photograph by Robert Orchard.

Page 178
The Warwick Vase. Courtesy of the Sea Island Company.

Page 181
Neptune Small recounting his adventures in the Civil War. Courtesy of the Sea Island Company.

Page 183
Ceremony held upon the return of the clock to Retreat Plantation. Courtesy of the Sea Island Company.

Page 195
First St. Simons Lighthouse. Reprinted from *Our Todays and Yesterdays* by Margaret Davis Cate (Brunswick, Ga.: Glover Brothers, Inc., 1930).

Page 207
The Oglethorpe Hotel, Brunswick, Georgia. Courtesy of the Georgia Historical Society.

Page 209
Glynn County Courthouse, Brunswick, Georgia. Photograph by Gil Tharp.

Page 213
The Cloister in the early days of the resort. Courtesy of the University of Georgia Libraries.

Page 215
The Eisenhowers on Sea Island, May 1946. Courtesy of the Sea Island Company.

Page 221
The Clubhouse and Sans Souci Apartments on Jekyll Island. Reprinted from *The Jekyl Island Club* (New York: Photogravure and Color Co., 1916).

Page 224
Lawn Party at Mistletoe Cottage, Jekyll Island. Reprinted from *The Jekyl Island Club* (New York: Photogravure and Color Co., 1916).

Page 224
Cycling and horseback riding on the beach at Jekyll Island. Reprinted from *The Jekyl Island Club* (New York: Photogravure and Color Co., 1916).

Page 225
The Rockefeller Cottage, Jekyll Island. Reprinted from *The Jekyl Island Club* (New York: Photogravure and Color Co., 1916).

Page 235
Dungeness, built by Thomas Carnegie on Cumberland Island in the 1880s. Courtesy of Burnette Vanstory.

Page 235
The ruins of Dungeness. Courtesy of Burnette Vanstory.

Page 246
St. Marys Presbyterian Church. Photograph by Caroline Carter.

Page 247
Orange Hall, St. Marys. Photograph by Dorsey Harris.

Index

Stephens, Alexander, 48
Stevens, Annie, 139
Stevens, Belle, 140
Stevens, Capt. Charles, 138, 139, 140
Stevens, Sarah Dorothy Hay, 138, 140
Stevens, William B., 115
Stewart, Daniel, 41, 42, 47, 52
Sunbury, Ga., 36, 39, 40, 42, 46, 47, 50, 51, 161, 202
Sunbury Historical Site, 50

Taylor, Belle Stevens, 140, 187
Taylor, Capt. Douglas, 187
Taylor, President Zachary, 178, 244
Teach, Edward (Blackbeard), 72, 217
Tebeauville, 99, 120, 121, 122, 125
Tegelaar, Jan Gabriel, 169
Terry, John, 132, 192
Timucuan Indians, 226, 237, 238
Tomochichi, 5, 7, 8, 13, 218, 226
Toonahowie, 7, 8, 226, 227
Torras, Fernando, 208
Torrey, Dr. H. N., 20, 21, 23
Torrey, William, 23
Tranquil Plantation, 43
Troup, Camilla Brailsford, 124
Troup, Clelia, 81
Troup, Gov. George M., 88
Troup, Dr. James McGillivray, 81, 124
Troup, Matilda, 125, 126, 128
Troup, Ophelia, 125
Turner, Joseph, 144

Union Agricultural Society, 60, 87, 162
Union Church, St. Marys, 241
United States Fish and Wildlife Services, 71
University of California, 49
University of Florida,

Department of Anthropology and Archaeology, 174
University of Georgia, 35, 49, 69
University of Georgia Marine Institute, 69, 70
University of South Carolina, 49
University of the South, 116

Village Plantation, 187, 188–90

Waldburg, Jacob, 32
Walton, George, 43
Wanamaker family, 20
Wanderer, slave ship, 220
Ward, John E., 97
Washington, President George, 46, 84, 104, 229, 231, 245
Weed, Jacob, 240
Wesley, Charles, 130, 131, 144, 160
Wesley, John, 27, 28, 130, 160
West, Eleanor Torrey, 23, 24
West Point Plantation, 191, 192
White, George, 115
Whitney, Eli, 229
Willson, James, 33
Wilson, President Woodrow, 48, 73
Winn, Rev. D. Watson, 146
Wister, Owen, 173
Wister, Sally Butler, 173
Woodbine, Ga., 244, 245
Woodmanston Plantation, 40, 43, 48
Woolford, Cator, 117, 118
Wright, Charles, 239
Wright, Sir James, 239
Wright, Jermyn, 239
Wright, Mary, 193
Wright, Rebecca Bruce, 192
Wright, Maj. Samuel, 192, 193, 196
Wylly, Alexander Campbell, 113, 187, 188, 189
Wylly, Alexander William, 189
Wylly, Caroline, 113, 188, 189